OBAMANOMICS

OBAMANOMICS

*How Barack Obama Is Bankrupting You
and Enriching His Wall Street Friends,
Corporate Lobbyists, and Union Bosses*

TIMOTHY P. CARNEY

Since 1947
**REGNERY
PUBLISHING, INC.**
An Eagle Publishing Company • Washington, DC

Cataloging-in-Publication data on file with the Library of Congress

ISBN 978-1-59698-612-1

Published in the United States by
Regnery Publishing, Inc.
One Massachusetts Avenue, NW
Washington, DC 20001
www.regnery.com
Manufactured in the United States of America

10 9 8 7 6 5 4 3 2 1

Books are available in quantity for promotional or premium use. Write to Director of Special Sales, Regnery Publishing, Inc., One Massachusetts Avenue NW, Washington, DC 20001, for information on discounts and terms or call (202) 216-0600.

Distributed to the trade by:
Perseus Distribution
387 Park Avenue South
New York, NY 10016

To my old boss Bob Novak—
his country's good servant,
and God's first.

CONTENTS

FOREWORD

If one asked the average American to describe how big business affects the major policy battles occurring in Washington, D.C., he would probably say that the business community funds armies of well-heeled lobbyists who regularly descend on the Capitol to thwart the "progressive" agenda of national health care, cap-and-trade climate schemes, and expanded regulations for Wall Street and other industries. This is, after all, the popular perception of the political position of the business community. It is also mistaken.

In reality, the typical corporate lobbyist opposes free markets and champions *corporatism*—an economic system where the government intervenes in the economy for the benefit of certain politically connected business interests. These lobbyists often claim their client's cause is an exception to their staunch free-market principles. My staff refers to these lobbyists as "libertarian, buts" because they often begin their pitch to us with, "I'm a libertarian, but in this case government intervention is necessary because . . ."

Of course, the politicians who champion this corporatism never admit they are acting to advance business interests. Instead, they wrap their schemes in the language of charity and compassion for the least among us—even though it is precisely the least among us who will suffer most from the economic damage that will inevitably result from the expansion of the welfare-regulatory state.

Big-spending, big-regulating politicians will often denounce the very corporate interests that stand to benefit from the latest government intrusion into the private sphere. The recently passed tobacco legislation provides an excellent example. Lobbyists for the largest tobacco company helped draft the bill and supported it because it largely protected the interests of the industry giant while harming the small tobacco companies that can't afford to spend thousands of dollars on lobbyists. However, anyone who listened to the debate on the bill would have thought this legislation was a legislative death sentence for "Big Tobacco."

The myth that big business is a friend of freedom confuses the liberty movement as to just what is the major threat to economic liberty. This confusion reveals itself in the very language used by pro-liberty activists, journalists, and even some scholars. How many times do we hear defenders of the market describe their enemy as "socialism?" Yet, there is no substantial political constituency for socialism—a system where government directly owns and operates business. Instead, the real threat to the free market is corporatism.

Exposing the ways big business has worked to undermine liberty and explaining how the anti-market policies enrich large corporate interests at the expense of average Americans is a vital task

for the freedom movement. My friend and teacher Murray Roth-
bard, the founder of the modern libertarian movement, always
encouraged libertarians to concern themselves not only with learning and promoting libertarian theory, but also with discovering
and exposing the powerful interests that use the welfare state to
enrich themselves at the expense of our liberty and prosperity.

I have no doubt that Murray would appreciate Tim Carney's
work. Tim's book, *Obamanomics: How Barack Obama Is Bankrupting You and Enriching His Wall Street Friends, Corporate
Lobbyists, and Union Bosses*, picks up where his first book, *The
Big Ripoff,* left off. Tim looks past the progressives' anti-business
rhetoric to expose how big business benefited from the stimulus
bill, and how the current administration has adopted its predecessor's policy of funneling taxpayer money to failed Wall Street
firms. Continuing Wall Street bailouts—and even installing one of
the key architects of the bailouts as treasury secretary—is a
strange definition of "change you can believe in."

Perhaps the most useful section of the book is the chapters
detailing how the insurance and pharmaceutical industries are
lending their clout to the push for nationalized health care.
Despite the sound bites from the pro-ObamaCare politicians and
their cheerleaders in the media about the evil insurance companies, the insurers are actually on Obama's side in promoting a
giant expansion of the government's role in health care. And why
not? A major plank of the health care plan is to force every American to have health insurance—in other words, to make every
American a customer of the insurance industry. Yet, if one believes
the media, it is the *opponents* of nationalized health care who are
doing the bidding of the large insurance companies!

It is true, as Tim points out, that the insurance industry opposes
the "public option." However, for all the sound and fury the public option has generated on both sides of the debate, the proposal

to force all Americans to obtain a government-approved health insurance policy represents as great a, if not a greater, threat to health freedom as the government-funded public option. This is because the so-called "individual mandate" is a back door to national health insurance. After all, if Congress requires individuals to purchase insurance, Congress must define what insurance policies satisfy the government mandate. Thus, Congress will decide what is and is not covered in the mandatory insurance policy.

Yet, as I write this, it appears unlikely that the final bill will create a system resembling the socialized medicine model of Canada or Great Britain. Instead, it appears likely that any health care "reform" plan that actually passes Congress will reject both the free market and socialism in favor of corporatism—which, in its current incarnation, Tim aptly calls "Obamanomics."

Every libertarian and free-market conservative who still believes that large corporations are trusted allies in the battle for economic liberty needs to read this book, as does every well-meaning liberal who believes that expansions of the welfare-regulatory state are done to benefit the common people.

Congressman Ron Paul (TX)

CHAPTER 1

OBAMANOMICS 101

THE PARTNERSHIP OF BIG BUSINESS AND BIG GOVERNMENT

President Barack Obama, if he gets his way, will increase government control over the U.S. economy in ways previously thought impossible. In itself, this is no surprise, because he is a liberal Democrat who repeatedly promised during his campaign to defend the little guy against the evils of corporate America. According to candidate Obama,

> The reason that we're not getting things done is not because we don't have good plans or good policy prescriptions. The reason is because it's not our agenda that's being moved forward in Washington—it's the agenda of the oil companies, the insurance companies, the drug companies, the special interests who dominate on a day-to-day basis in terms of legislative activity.[1]

But this anti-corporate rhetoric is precisely the opposite of the reality. In truth, President Obama's policy prescriptions spell profits for the biggest and most well-connected businesses. Just as President George W. Bush, with his bailouts, spending sprees, and new entitlements, abandoned the free market at the behest of Wall Street and drug makers, Barack Obama's vision of bigger government is also the dream of corporate lobbyists.

A close study of lobbying records, campaign contributions, and legislative language paints a different picture from the Obama-vs.-Big Business narrative that Obama projects and the media believes. Instead, Obama and Big Business are partners in advancing an agenda of borrowing, spending, taxing, regulating, and subsidizing.

Obama's healthcare reform, stimulus spending, global warming legislation, and auto industry bailouts are ambitious packages of regulations, taxes, mandates, and spending that benefit Big Business—what corporation wouldn't welcome more taxpayer-funded subsidies, regulation that crowds out competition, and government mandates that drive more business to them? There are other big beneficiaries as well: politicians, who gain more power; and lobbyists, who gain more influence.

The victims are small businesses crushed by regulations and taxes; taxpayers—especially future taxpayers who will be burdened by the debt financing today's spending sprees; and consumers, who face higher prices and fewer choices.

What should we call this Big Business–Big Government agenda pursued by President Obama? Although robust corporate-government collusion was hardly invented by the current administration, the United States has not seen such a consistent practitioner of corporatism in more than half a century. Moreover, crucial elements of Obama's program, such as his crusade against global warming, were lacking from the New Deal and other similar precedents, undermining direct analogies to them. It's fitting then to name this Big Business–Big Government practice *Obamanomics*.

Make no mistake—President Bush's Wall Street bailout was probably America's biggest dose of corporate socialism since World War II. But President Obama has seen Bush's $700 billion and raised him another couple trillion—and counting.

WHAT IS OBAMANOMICS?

Obamanomics is the political strategy of partnering government with the biggest businesses in order to create new regulations, taxes, and subsidies. Most famously, Obama forged a deal with the same drug industry he had demonized during his presidential campaign, and the industry then put up $150 million in advertising to advance healthcare "reform."[2] Obama's allies have also included health insurers, a tobacco giant, energy companies, automakers, Wall Street banks, and the U.S. Chamber of Commerce.

The economic law underlying Obamanomics—opaque to most journalists and contrary to conventional wisdom—is this: increased government control centralizes industries and favors the biggest businesses.

The great irony of Obamanomics is that Obama campaigned so hard against "special interests" and lobbyists. But his agenda of increasing government control in every corner of the economy requires partnering with those very special interests.

Indeed, even as Obama touts his Big Business–Big Government policies, he often attacks corporate America. He boasted about battling Big Tobacco during a Rose Garden signing ceremony for a bill Philip Morris reportedly helped draft.[3] As he rolled out a healthcare plan that would profit drug makers, insurers, and hospitals, Obama denounced his opponents as agents of the "special interests."[4] And his climate change regulations, backed by the most entrenched special interests, are supposedly a broadside against captains of industry.

Obama has ushered in a new kind of corporatism in a populist disguise. This book aims to expose it.

NOT IMPUGNING MOTIVES

Let me clarify what this book is *not* arguing.

I do not think Obama is "rewarding his donors" in any sort of quid pro quo. He is not trying to butter up corporations in order to land a cushy job in 2017. And I won't trot out the ridiculous attack used against Bush that Obama simply loves corporate America more than he loves Main Street America.

I trust Obama's intentions. His aim, I assume throughout this book, is simply to make this country better. He is also clear that he thinks what is best for this country, at least for now, is more federal government control—of Wall Street, of Detroit, of health-care, of energy, of our money.

His policies favor Big Business not out of nepotism or corruption, but out of tactical necessity—he needs powerful allies—and out of economic reality: expanding the government tends to boost Big Business.

But when the media actually notice that Big Business supports an Obama policy, or that an Obama regulation helps Big Business, they write it up as an anomaly. They are shocked at the "strange bedfellows."[5] But after a while, it should no longer seem strange. Obama and Big Business work together so closely and so frequently, they have formed—to adapt a phrase from President Dwight Eisenhower—the Obama–Industrial Complex.

THE BIG MYTH

Obama, however, paints his push for bigger government as a crusade against the excesses of Big Business. The president gets away with this thanks to the persistence of what I call *The Big Myth*. The Big Myth is the fable that Big Business and Big Government are rivals—that regulation curbs Big Business, and that above all Big Business wants a laissez-faire economy.

The myth seems logical. For one thing, the prevailing rhetoric supports it. Businessmen often extol the virtues of the free market, and those politicians most interested in increasing government are the same ones who most vociferously attack the evils of corporate America.

For example, in June 2009, the U.S. Chamber of Commerce—the nation's largest lobbying group representing the broad business community—launched its "Campaign for Free Enterprise." The Chamber proclaimed, "It's time to remind all Americans that it was a free enterprise system based on the values of individual initiative, hard work, risk, innovation, and profit that built our great country. We must take immediate action to reaffirm the spirit of enterprise in America."[6]

Meanwhile, Democratic populists took the opposite side in this alleged battle. During the 2008 Democratic presidential primary season, former North Carolina senator John Edwards was the pro-government, anti-business bomb-thrower. When asked during a debate in Iowa about the environment, Edwards answered, "I think first of all we need to recognize what the obstacles are to the change that everyone believes is necessary. And the obstacles are oil companies, power companies—all those entrenched interests that stand between America and the change that it needs."[7]

At a campaign rally outside Des Moines, Edwards sounded the same note on healthcare: "Corporate power and greed have literally taken over the government, and we need a president who's willing to take these powers on. It is the only way we're going to . . . have universal health care."[8]

Edwards's rhetoric—like the U.S. Chamber's—painted the battle lines: Big Government liberals on one side, Big Business on the other. This, of course, was false. Enron, General Electric, and Duke Energy all have lobbied for restrictions on greenhouse gas emissions, as chapter six will show. Pfizer, Aetna, and Wal-Mart all lobby for some sort of "universal healthcare," as related in chapters four and five.

And the Chamber's Campaign for Free Enterprise? In the middle of that, the Chamber endorsed the multi-billion-dollar Cash-for-Clunkers corporate welfare scheme.[9]

The political angle of the Big Myth is the assertion that Republicans are the Party of Big Business. Now, Republicans certainly aren't the anti-Big Business Party, but neither are the Democrats. Campaign finance and lobbying records show that both major parties, in truth, are the parties of Big Business—the Democrats just get away with hiding it. More on that in chapter two.

But the Big Myth is an important tool for Obama. It allows Democrats to paint their opponents as profiteers or corporate shills. During the healthcare debate, Obama repeatedly denounced those who oppose "reform" because they "profit financially or politically from the status quo." Liberal journalists—especially those at GE-owned MSNBC—parroted this line of attack.

The Big Myth also allows Big Business to win its favors under the radar. Newspapers regularly report when corporations lobby against stricter regulations, but when corporations join the "reform" side, there is less media attention.

And so, the Obama–Industrial Complex hides behind the Big Myth.

BUSH BAILOUTS AND BARACK PIERCE THE BIG MYTH

Events at the end of the Bush administration and in the first year of Obama's presidency should have put the Big Myth to rest.

Bush ended his term in office by creating a $700 billion tax-payer-funded slush fund for Wall Street, and then he opened the bailout doors to Detroit automakers before handing the slush fund keys over to President Obama.

Obama had won the White House with the help of Big Business, out-raising the Republican nominee from nine of the ten most politically active industries, according to the Center for Responsive Politics.[10] He quickly gave the world a hint of Obamanomics by entrusting command of his White House to Rahm Emanuel, a Goldman Sachs alumnus and Bill Clinton fundraiser with proven experience in marshalling Big Business behind Big Government while playing both for his own profit.

Then Obama picked Bill Richardson and Tom Daschle for his cabinet—both men with track records of Big Business–Big Government collusion.

President Obama's first major act was passing a pork-laden, $787 billion stimulus bill aggressively backed by the U.S. Chamber of Commerce and every major business group—not to mention the corporate lobbyists who thought they had died and gone to heaven. He followed that with a push for healthcare reform in which he allied with pharmaceutical companies and, to a large extent, with HMOs. His other major 2009 effort was for a global warming bill that had the robust backing of some of the biggest players in all corners of industry.

Along the way, Obama signed a tobacco regulation bill drafted in part by Philip Morris, a children's health insurance subsidy championed by insurers and drug makers, and a Cash-for-Clunkers program that funneled billions of dollars to automakers.

Needless to say, if George W. Bush and Ben Bernanke didn't kill the Big Myth, Barack Obama should have. The myth's endurance is testament to Obama's rhetoric, most reporters' economic prejudices, and the short memory of political journalists, who find themselves repeatedly noting, "*In an odd alliance, Big Business is supporting Obama's Big Government program.*"

THE LAWS OF OBAMANOMICS

Underlying Obamanomics are some basic economic facts and political realities. These are the Four Laws of Obamanomics, paired below with some of the lobbying strategies that exploit these laws.

1) During a legislative debate, whichever business has the best lobbyists is most likely to win the most favorable small print. Similarly, once a bill has passed, the business with the best lawyers and lobbyists will best be able to craft the regulations and learn how to game them. A big business, counting on this fact while lobbying for more government spending or control, is employing *The Inside Game*.

2) Regulation adds to overhead, and higher overhead crowds out smaller competitors and prevents startups from entering the industry. When corporations, knowing this, lobby for more regulation of their industry, I call this the *Overhead Smash*.

3) Bigger companies are often saddled by inertia, meaning robust competition is a threat. Adopting regulations that stultify the economy is the equivalent of raising the basketball hoop to twenty feet at half-time: it protects the lead of whichever team is ahead. When Big Business seeks to stultify the economy to hold back smaller competitors, I call it *Gumming Up the Works*.

4) Government regulation grants an air of legitimacy to businesses, boosting consumer confidence, often beyond what is warranted. This is *The Confidence Game*.

Of course, these laws of Obamanomics are related, and the tactics almost always overlap. Rarely is one tactic at play without some trace of another. I use the term *Regulatory Robbery* to encompass all these tactics—and there are other common forms of Regulatory Robbery aside from the four listed above.

For Obama's first year in office, a key corporate tactic has been *Making an Offer You Can't Refuse*—when government requires customers to buy certain products. One more practice that often appears in Obamanomics is *Subsidy Suckling*—coming to the teat of government for some taxpayer-provided sustenance.

An important note: there are, on the Left, often Big Government proposals that would be devastating to Big Business. In healthcare, for instance, there's the single-payer idea—that government should be the HMO for all. This would drive private insurers out of business and possibly reduce profits for providers. Proposals like this get lip service from liberal politicians, but once those politicians get in the room with the staffers, lobbyists, and consultants, there's inevitably a tack "toward the center"—really, a tack toward Big Business.

Understanding the laws of Obamanomics is critical to understanding today's confusing political landscape. Without knowing these laws, one is left wondering why Big Business wants to be regulated. Ignorant of these laws, most reporters think industry support of Big Government is a sign of consensus rather than a form of favor-seeking.

In brief, Obamanomics boils down to this: every time government gets bigger, somebody's getting rich.

This book names the names.

CHAPTER 2

ELECTION 2008

THE TRIUMPH OF BIG BUSINESS

"**A**nd as people have looked away in disillusionment and frustration," counseled Barack Obama, a freshman senator with only two years in Washington, "we know what's filled the void: The cynics, and the lobbyists, and the special interests who've turned our government into a game only they can afford to play."[1]

Obama, evoking Abraham Lincoln by announcing his candidacy in Springfield, Illinois, painted a bleak but accurate picture of the situation in Washington and the power of corporate lobbyists. "They write the checks and you get stuck with the bills. They get the access while you get to write a letter."

But Obama promised Hope. And Change. "They think they own this government, but we're here today to take it back. The time for that politics is over. It's time to turn the page."

Obama sounded this theme for the next twenty-one months. Largely, the media and the public bought it: John McCain's campaign was dominated by lobbyists, we were told, while Obama led a grassroots effort reflecting spontaneous enthusiasm for change. McCain raised funds from corporate fat cats, but Obama gathered small donations from regular Americans. McCain would deliver tax cuts for Big Business, while Obama would curb the excesses of corporate America.

But the fine details of the 2008 campaign reveal a much different picture. Obama's campaign received far more money from the most entrenched special interests than did McCain's. Even the biggest oil companies gave more to Obama. And those vaunted small donors? Obama's proportion of small donations to large ones was just about the same as McCain's.

In fact, as this chapter shows, Obama fiercely attacked McCain's proposals that would have slashed corporate welfare, while Obama's plans would keep Big Business's spigot of subsidies flowing freely. And once Obama won the election, he assembled a governing team peppered with masters of the "revolving door" between corporate America and government.

Obama's election, in other words, was a triumph for Big Business.

THE MONEY TRAIL

Goldman Sachs, Exxon Mobil, Microsoft, Boeing, Pfizer, and General Electric—these companies are the poster-children for "special interests." They are huge and well-connected corporations in key industries. And they have something else in common: employees and executives of these companies all gave more— much more—to Barack Obama than to John McCain in the 2008 election.[2] Of course, Obama raised far more money *overall* than McCain, so it's not surprising he took more from these industry giants—unless, of course, you believed Obama's rhetoric that his campaign depended on the regular people and small donors while McCain's was a servant of special interests.

But some of these industrial titans gave so much more cash to Obama that it's hard not to conclude the businesses saw profit in his presidency—not because they "owned" him, but because Obama's penchant for Big Government was good for their business.

Take, for example, the most notorious "special interest": Goldman Sachs. Goldman is arguably more intimately tied up with government than is any other company. The firm regularly swaps executives with the White House, regardless of which party controls it, and profits from subsidies and bailouts in all corners of the economy—from Wall Street to ethanol plants. Fittingly, Goldman was the source of more campaign contributions in 2008 than any other company. It also provided Obama with *four times* as much money as it did McCain—$997,095 to $230,095.[3] Microsoft employees were even more one-sided, giving Obama more than *ten times* more money than McCain.

But the Obama campaign pitched the idea, and the mainstream media swallowed it, that small donors were Obama's bread and butter, freeing him "from the tug of big-money corporations and special interests," as the Associated Press put it.[4]

The AP should have checked the numbers. According to the nonpartisan Center for Responsive Politics (CRP), employees and executives at AT&T, which the center lists as the number one "heavy hitter" of campaign finance since 1989, gave more money to Obama than they had to any candidate in history, exceeding their donations to McCain by 30 percent. The rest of the top ten heavy hitters of the last two decades include labor unions and Goldman Sachs, each of which, if they donated money for the 2008 election, gave more to Obama than to McCain.

CRP also reports that lawyers comprised the top-spending industry in 2008, followed by the "securities/investment" industry, which includes Wall Street and hedge funds. The real estate industry ranked third. These industries all gave more to Barack Obama than to any other candidate. In fact, Obama was the favorite candidate of the seven most politically prolific industries. Of the top ten industries, only insurance placed Obama as low as second place, with McCain slightly outraising him $2.4 million to $2.3 million.

Now, we should note that Obama's and McCain's fundraising cannot truly be compared directly. First, McCain's primary season was much briefer than Obama's; McCain effectively won the contest by February, when Mitt Romney withdrew, while Obama had to fight until June before Hillary Clinton conceded. As a result, Obama was forced to raise much more primary election money than was McCain. Second, Obama outpolled McCain for most of the campaign, so some businesses may have simply supported the frontrunner.

Additionally, Obama eschewed federal matching funds in the general election—the first candidate to do so since the program's creation in 1974. So McCain was prohibited by law from raising private funds in the general election, while Obama had unlimited license to raise and spend money—which he did with unprecedented skill.

Thus, you can't conclude that an industry "preferred" Obama just because it gave him more money. But the impressive numbers Obama garnered from leading industries point to some equally important conclusions. First, the storyline is false that Obama's fundraising advantage over McCain was due to small donors. His advantage over McCain was largely due to industry donations. And second, Obama clearly didn't consider industry leaders to be his opponents.

In other words, Big Business may or may not have "preferred" Obama, but it sure didn't fear him.

HEALTHY DONATIONS

A favorite "special interest" Obama picked on during the campaign was the healthcare sector. He ran ads assailing the drug industry's influence in Washington, and he threatened to battle intransigent insurance companies in order to reform healthcare. But that didn't seem to dent that sector's generous support of Obama and his party.

Donations from the health sector went to Democrats by 54–46 percent in 2008. Obama pulled in $19.4 million from the sector, more than two-and-a-half times McCain's tally of $7.4 million.[5] In fact, Obama received more money from the healthcare sector than did the top ten Republican recipients combined.

HMO donations favored Democrats by 60–40 percent. Receiving over three times the amount of HMO money than McCain, Obama's $1.4 million take was more than the combined HMO haul by the Republican nominees for president in the last five elections.[6] Notably, even Hillary Clinton significantly outraised McCain from this industry in 2008.

Drug makers behaved the same way, giving Obama $3.57 for every dollar they gave McCain.[7] The industry's largest donor, Pfizer, gave more than four times as much cash to Obama as to McCain. Likewise, hospital and nursing home contributions favored Obama 4 to 1 over McCain.

Star-struck by a new liberal icon, the media turned a blind eye toward the obvious coziness between Obama and the HMOs, drug makers, and hospitals. Reporters just weren't interested in asking why these industries were overwhelmingly favoring the candidate who was vilifying them, and what they expected to get from him. The fact that all these industries stand to benefit hand-somely from Obama's proposed healthcare reform, as shown in chapters four and five, mysteriously escaped the media's attention.

BIG BAD OIL

"He's willing to spend nearly $4 billion on more tax breaks for big oil companies—including $1.2 billion for Exxon alone." This attack on McCain, pronounced by Obama while campaigning in Nevada, became a staple of Obama's campaign.[8] Obama repeatedly accused McCain of seeking a giant tax cut for Big Oil as these com-panies were raking in record profits and the rest of the economy was limping. "Every time you fill your tank, the oil companies fill their pockets," intoned one Obama campaign ad. "Now Big Oil's filling John McCain's campaign with $2 million in contributions."[9]

But the two claims—that McCain was handing Big Oil a spe-cial tax break and that Big Oil was bankrolling McCain—were both misleading. The tax cut claim originated in a report by the Center for American Progress (CAP), a George Soros-funded non-profit closely allied with the Obama campaign and the Demo-cratic Party.[10] The assertion was deliberately deceptive because it implied McCain was singling out oil companies for tax breaks, without noting that McCain was proposing to reduce the income tax rate on *all* corporations from 35 percent to 25 percent. For that reason, the nonpartisan PolitiFact, operated by the *St. Peters-burg Times*, rated the tax-cut claim as "barely true."[11]

The allegation that Big Oil was fueling McCain's campaign was also disingenuous. Although McCain did receive much more money from the oil and gas industry than did Obama, this over-looks an inconvenient fact: the five largest oil companies—the ones Obama grouped as "Big Oil" and the CAP report listed by name—gave more combined to Obama than to McCain. And the one oil company Obama called out by name, Exxon, funded Obama ($117,946) much more than it funded McCain ($73,326). Obama's Exxon take was just about equal to George W. Bush's—*in 2000 and 2004, combined.*[12]

Obama also raised more money from No. 2 Chevron than did McCain—or any politician in history, for that matter.[13]

OBAMA AND THE CORPORATE MOONSHINERS ON THE DOLE

Barack Obama was certainly good at staying on message, hammering McCain with a few repeated attacks. In the first debate of the general election, Obama went after McCain on energy:

> And I have to say, Senator McCain and I—I think—agree on the importance of energy, but Senator McCain mentioned earlier the importance of looking at a record.
>
> Over 26 years, Senator McCain voted 23 times against alternative energy, like solar, and wind, and biodiesel.
>
> And so we've got to walk the walk and not just talk the talk when it comes to energy independence.[14]

Obama's campaign website listed those twenty-three anti-"alternative energy" votes.[15] Notwithstanding Obama's reference to "solar, and wind, and biodiesel," most of these votes were actually against subsidies for corn ethanol—one of the most flagrant corporate-welfare boondoggles of the last half-century and a program few outside the industry defend today.

But Obama continually cited McCain's votes against ethanol subsidies to impugn his environmental record. He dinged McCain for voting against the 2002 energy bill, a vote which placed

McCain in a tiny minority of eleven senators. A *St. Petersburg Times* editorial explained the bipartisan support for the measure and its ethanol mandate:

> [Majority Leader Tom] Daschle and the Democrats will find little opposition from Republicans, who are in a bidding war to see who can give the most subsidies to agribusiness. And that is what this is all about, corporate welfare. Agribusinesses propped up by price supports already produce a surplus crop, so they are looking for ways to sell more corn. One way is to force gasoline refiners to use more ethanol.[16]

Even Democratic senators Hillary Clinton, Chuck Schumer, Dianne Feinstein, and Barbara Boxer voted with McCain against the bill, assailing the ethanol mandate as "corporate welfare."[17] Obama also attacked McCain for voting against the 2005 energy bill, and against the amendment mandating ethanol.

Schumer, while debating that 2005 bill, concisely explained the harm of an ethanol mandate: "It hurts drivers and it hurts the free market. It is a boondoggle because it takes money out of the pockets of drivers and puts it into the pockets of the big ethanol producers."[18] Ethanol, in other words, is a sop to Big Business at the expense of the average consumer. Yet Obama not only attacked McCain for standing up for consumers, he promised during his 2008 campaign effectively to outlaw all cars that couldn't run on a blend of 85 percent ethanol.[19]

McCain consistently opposed the ethanol ripoff, including another vote against the 2007 energy bill. And he suffered for it. After the Republican platform reversed itself and adopted McCain's position against ethanol handouts, a Minnesota news website reported on the political fallout:

There's anxious buzz sweeping across corn country about an abrupt change in the Republican platform on corn ethanol that was adopted at the party's convention in St. Paul.

... "It's a little alarming that we as a Republican Party are taking that stance," said Brad Finstad of Comfry, Minn. "In corn country there will be some independence from the GOP on the issue," said the three-term Republican who is ranking minority member on the Minnesota House Agriculture Finance Division.[20]

Sure enough, Obama ended up sweeping corn country, thanks in part to his firm commitment—and McCain's opposition—to corn ethanol subsidies.

OBAMA PROTECTS THE HMOS

McCain's healthcare reform proposal was the target of some of the sharpest attacks by the Obama campaign. And here, once again, Obama supported Big Business while McCain defended consumers.

McCain proposed to begin taxing employer-provided healthcare benefits while offering an offsetting $5,000 tax credit toward buying health insurance. The goal was to inject more competition into the healthcare market by removing government disincentives to finding your health insurance outside of your employer.

Unsurprisingly, health insurers have lobbied hard to preserve the employer-based system and to torpedo proposals like McCain's. And Obama took the insurers' side, warning that McCain's plan would cause the "unraveling of the employer-based health care system."[21] This was a line Obama borrowed from the biggest corporate lobby in town, the Chamber of Commerce,[22]

whose members found McCain's proposal "very discomforting."[23]
Obama ran campaign ads warning that McCain "would tax your
healthcare benefits for the first time ever"—without mentioning
the offsetting $5,000 tax credit.[24] Meanwhile, Obama was collect-
ing more money from HMOs than any other candidate in history.

Throughout 2008 Obama enthusiastically flailed the "special
interests," but his Big Business-friendly proposals and prolific corporate fundraising told a different story. Once he got elected, the
picture became even clearer.

RAHM EMANUEL: "THE INTERSECTION OF MONEY AND POWER"

If a Hollywood screenwriter were to invent the prototypical
ruthless political operative, he would create Rahm Emanuel—and
the producers would probably reject the character as over-the-top.
Any notion that an Obama White House would spell the end of
Big Business influence in Washington should have been dispelled
three days after the election, when Obama named this consum-
mate corporate-political insider as White House chief of staff.

"A portrait of the often murky, below-the-surface intersection
of money and power and politics."[25] That's how the *Chicago Tribune* described Emanuel in 2003, and it's a good overall description of Obamanomics. The Obama–Emanuel White House has
governed by standing at this intersection, collecting tolls, and paying out favors—and it's building more entrance ramps into this
intersection and multiplying its own power, all of which yields
rewards for the most connected businesses.

Emanuel's record, to say the least, does not smell of good government. A Chicago political operative, he got his start in 1989 by
raising funds for Richard M. Daley's first mayoral campaign. This
was the beginning of a close, long-lasting relationship between the
two men. A decade later, when Emanuel ran for Congress, he got

another helping hand from the Daley Machine. Federal investigators in 2005 found that the chief of Daley's water department had deployed city workers to campaign for Emanuel in his hotly contested 2002 Democratic primary for an open House seat. The *Chicago Sun-Times*, in a piece titled "Daley Machine Corruption Helps Emanuel Win First House Race," reported on the sleaze: "City Hall officials ordered the city's top water boss, Donald Tomczak, to marshal his political army of city workers for Mayor Daley, Congressman Rahm Emanuel and other politicians, according to a federal court document released Monday and other sources."[26]

Emanuel's stint with the Clintons also fails to impress good-government types. In November 1991, the Arkansas governor hired Emanuel to be his top fundraiser. Clinton's campaign was cash-poor when Emanuel arrived, but Rahm became its rain-maker, reaching out to Wall Street, Hollywood, and other "fat cats," as he called them. In July 1992, the *New York Times* reported the campaign "has received most of its checks from large law firms, investment houses and real estate companies."[27] The top source of Clinton campaign cash was Goldman Sachs, a company that sixteen years later would also become Barack Obama's top corporate source of funds.

Interestingly, while Emanuel was pumping Goldman for campaign cash back in 1992, he also earned $35,000 ($53,000 in 2008 dollars) directly from the company.[28] A Goldman spokesman said Emanuel "analyzed local political races" for the firm.[29] That's a hefty retainer for a guy who's also working full time as a campaign fundraiser for a presidential campaign—and it was an important stream of income, considering the Clinton campaign only paid him $60,000.[30] (Emanuel also received some support that year from his old friend Daley, who paid him $15,000 in consulting fees.)[31]

The money connection between Goldman, Emanuel, and the Clinton campaign reeked of influence peddling. Corporations are prohibited from contributing to federal elections, but by taking care of about a quarter of Emanuel's 1992 compensation, Goldman could have been making a backdoor contribution to the Clinton campaign. In another sign suggesting Goldman–Clinton rules-bending, federal auditors later found that Goldman had improperly given discounts for work it performed for the Clinton campaign.[32]

Emanuel embodied the Clinton campaign's blending of policy and fundraising, a feature that would later characterize the Clinton White House. A 1992 *New York Times* piece reported:

> Associates say Mr. Emanuel has played an unusual role for a finance director, getting involved in strategy sessions that transcend money. He had a leading role in advising Mr. Clinton to select Senator Al Gore as his running mate, they said, a decision that not only enhanced the ticket in the polls, but also brought on a whole new network of fund-raisers.[33]

Under Emanuel's direction, the campaign's fundraising played fast and loose with the rules. According to federal auditors, the campaign improperly took $4.1 million in taxpayer money.[34] For instance, at the end of the primary, rather than retiring its debt, the campaign paid some legal fees with leftover cash—a way to keep its debt high in order to qualify for more public financing, the auditors charged.[35] The *Washington Post* reported, "The audit also disallowed nearly $338,000 in primary campaign expenses that couldn't be documented. . . . Among the payments disallowed were $52,000 to Rahm Emanuel, the campaign's chief fund-raiser."[36] Auditors also flagged the discounts from Goldman and other companies.

After Clinton was elected, Emanuel took charge of organizing the inaugural, presenting another opportunity for White House coziness with big donors. Despite the populist imagery of arriving in D.C. by bus, Clinton's inauguration was opulent—Emanuel raised and spent $25 million from big donors such as AT&T, Enron, Pfizer, and Anheuser Busch.[37]

In light of Emanuel's corporate ties, his appointment by Clinton as a senior White House advisor raised some eyebrows. Fred Wertheimer, a campaign-finance watchdog with the liberal group Common Cause, told the *Washington Post* at the time that Emanuel's West Wing job was "a very dangerous appointment for the Clinton administration because it places in the White House an individual whose principal responsibility has been to raise huge sums of money from special interests seeking influence over government decisions."[38]

Emanuel's actual work in the White House is not a matter of public record. But in light of his prior record, it's hard not to assume a connection between his presence in the West Wing and the endless parade of fundraising scandals that beset the Clinton administration.

EMANUEL MASTERS THE REVOLVING DOOR

When Emanuel left the Clinton White House for the private sector in 1998, he leveraged his political clout for personal profit with startling efficiency, making $1.6 million in two-and-a-half years. Combing through Emanuel's financial records, the *Chicago Tribune*'s Mike Dorning found a "tale of money and power, of leverage and connections, of a stunningly successful conversion of moxie and a network of political contacts into cold, hard cash."[39]

Emanuel left the White House in 1998 for a job handling politically sensitive deals for Bruce Wasserstein, "a high-rolling Wall Street dealmaker who was one of Clinton's most active fundraisers in the financial community," according to the *Tribune*.

At Wasserstein's firm, Emanuel quickly called Bernard Schwartz, CEO of Loral Space and Communications. Emanuel

knew Schwartz well—a defense contractor, Schwartz had contributed $1.5 million to Clinton's 1996 campaign.[40] (Loral later
received special permission from Clinton to launch a satellite
aboard a Chinese rocket—even though Loral at the time was the
subject of a federal investigation for possibly transferring
weapons-capable satellite technology to the Chinese military.[41]
The company paid a $14 million fine in 2002, and the federal gov-
ernment declined to prosecute.) Schwartz took Emanuel's call and
hired him to explore possible acquisitions. Remarkably, Emanuel
was also hired by another man who had donated generously to re-
elect Clinton: S. Daniel Abraham, CEO of Slim-Fast.

The Clinton administration directly intervened in private sector
deals in ways that enriched Emanuel. For example, in one deal, telecom giant SBC bought fellow telecom company Ameritech, intend-
ing to hold onto Ameritech's home-security company, SecurityLink.
But Clinton's Federal Communications Commission disallowed the
acquisition, and ordered SBC to sell SecurityLink. Emanuel happened to be representing a willing buyer—venture capital firm
GTCR Golder Rauner. The *Tribune* explained, "Under a regulatory deadline to divest itself of SecurityLink, SBC financed all but
$100 million of GTCR's $479 million purchase of the firm. Less
than six months later, GTCR resold the company for $1 billion,
earning a quick $500 million on its investment."

After two-and-a-half years getting rich at the intersection of Big
Business and Big Government, Emanuel took his new wealth, his
corporate connections, and his old government ties and ran for
Congress from Chicago. GTCR partners and employees generously chipped in more than $12,000 to his campaign.

GREED IS GOOD

In his successful congressional race of 2002, Rahm Emanuel
raised a stunning $667,000 from the financial sector, according to

the Center for Responsive Politics.[42] Only two House candidates had a bigger haul: Michael Oxley, chairman of the Financial Services Committee, and House minority leader Richard Gephardt, who was also running for president. Emanuel was the only non-incumbent in the top-15 list.

The "securities and investment" industry—which consists of investment banks like Goldman Sachs and Merrill Lynch as well as brokerages like Morgan Stanley—gave more money to Emanuel than to any candidate, including sitting congressmen.[43] Emanuel even outraised senators Chris Dodd and Max Baucus, the chairmen, respectively, of the Senate's Banking Committee and its Finance Committee. It was an extraordinary performance for a first-time, non-incumbent candidate from outside New York.

By 2006 Emanuel was the Chairman of the Democratic Congressional Campaign Committee (DCCC), where he boosted the committee's fundraising from $93 million in 2004 to a record $140 million[44] while more than doubling the DCCC's haul from Wall Street. Then, in 2008, Emanuel became the first congressman to take in more than $100,000 from the hedge fund industry, pulling in more than the next three congressmen combined.

Rahm Emanuel is indisputably a Wall Street favorite. There is, and always has been, a symbiotic relationship between them. Unsurprisingly, Emanuel was a driving force behind the $700 billion Wall Street bailout, and a tireless advocate of more housing bailouts.

Emanuel reeled in so much cash from Wall Street because he had so many friends there dating back to his days dialing for Clinton's dollars. Those friends of Rahm would become friends of the Obama White House.

BILL RICHARDSON'S "PUBLIC-PRIVATE PARTNERSHIPS"

"As governor of New Mexico," the president-elect said on December 3, 2008, as he introduced his nominee for secretary of commerce, "Bill showed how government can act as a partner to support our businesses."[45]

Those words took on a new meaning a month later when news emerged that one of Governor Bill Richardson's donors—who had won $1.5 million in state contracts—was under criminal investigation.

Richardson was forced to withdraw his nomination, but he still embodies Obamanomics: a politician who increases government influence in the economy with the assistance of Big Business. That his actions and policies would lead to scandal is to be expected— the business–government coziness he and Obama both favor is a breeding ground for corruption.

The root of Richardson's scandal was his much-touted "public-private partnerships," which were pitched as a kind of "third-way" compromise where government calls the play but private industry carries the ball. And Richardson saw that his partnerships fit well into Obamanomics. "The catchphrases of your economic plan," he said to Obama on stage while accepting the nomination, "investment, public-private partnership—that is the Department of Commerce."[46]

But putting money and power that close together is asking for trouble. Richardson's record as governor—a record Obama had presumably vetted before naming him to run Commerce—turns up a string of dubious dealings.

The deal that sunk Richardson centers on a man named David Rubin. Rubin ran an investment firm called Chambers, Dunhill, and Rubin. He later changed the name to CDR, in part because Chambers and Dunhill didn't exist. Rubin just "liked the sound of them together," according to Bloomberg News.[47]

Los Angeles mayor James Hahn, a few years back, had named Rubin as a commissioner of the city's housing authority, which hands out hundreds of millions of dollars in housing subsidies.

CDR had teamed up with Freddie Mac to create a program to advance homeownership among low-income families.

In Pennsylvania, Rubin served on the gubernatorial transition team of Democrat Ed Rendell in early 2003. But Rubin was tight with other Philly pols, too. A Bloomberg article tells the story:

> In April 2001, [CDR] hired Ron White, a bond lawyer and chief fund-raiser for Mayor John Street, as a consultant, paying him a $5,000 retainer to help CDR win work with the city, according to court documents from a federal corruption trial.
>
> Rubin donated $15,000 to Street's election committee from December 2000 to June 2003, the records show. In addition, CDR gave White three tickets to the 2003 Super Bowl game in San Diego and also provided a limousine ride to the stadium. White brought Philadelphia Treasurer Corey Kemp to the event.
>
> White also asked Rubin to donate money to the 2004 presidential campaign of Reverend Al Sharpton. Public disclosure of a contribution to Sharpton "would destroy me personally," Rubin said, according to telephone transcripts from the Philadelphia trial. White suggested sending the money to White's federal political action committee. On April 4, 2003, Rubin donated $5,000 to the PAC. The same day, the PAC wrote a $1,000 check to Sharpton.
>
> Philadelphia paid CDR $150,000 for advice on derivatives, while banks paid CDR at least $515,000 from profits they earned on transactions with the city, documents show.[48]

In Florida, CDR began dealing municipal bonds. The Securities and Exchange Commission found in 2007 that CDR had failed to disclose its fee structure to clients.[49]

And of course, there's a Chicago connection. Bloomberg explains, "Milan Petrovic, who raised $1.96 million for [impeached former Illinois governor Rod] Blagojevich, introduced CDR to Illinois budget and debt officials, according to e-mails obtained under a public records request."[50]

In September 2008, Rubin shelled out $28,500 to the Obama Victory Fund,[51] earning him admission to an exclusive Obama Victory Fund dinner at Hollywood's Greystone Mansion.[52] By that time, Rubin had become well-known in Democratic circles, both as a donor and as a man who did intimate—and at times unsavory—business with government at many levels.

Municipal bonds, subsidized housing, government contracts—Rubin epitomized the "private" half of public-private partnerships, which made it appropriate he would be intimately tied to Bill Richardson. Rubin donated at least $110,000 to various campaigns and committees controlled by Richardson. Soon afterward, Rubin received $1.5 million in contracts from the state government.[53] These contracts became the focus of the ongoing federal investigation that ultimately forced Richardson's withdrawal from his nomination to head the Commerce Department. As of this writing, however, no authority has accused Richardson of anything illegal or unethical.

Many of Richardson's "private partners" have reaped enormous profit from their associations with him. Take Bruce Ratner, a developer whose firm, Forest City, is one of the nation's largest builders and a prominent player in public-private partnerships. According to *Governing* magazine:

> [I]n the early 1970s, [Forest City] won a HUD contract to build subsidized housing around the country. That, in turn, put the company in close touch with state housing agencies and city governments. "By virtue of that business, we learned how to deal with government," says Jim Ratner, who runs Forest City's commercial group. "We understood better than we ever

had before how a partnership is created with government that gives them what they want, and gives the company what it wants."[54]

More accurately, Forest City gave *politicians* what they wanted—the firm was the top source of funds for Richardson's presidential campaign. In addition to the $53,700 employees and executives there gave Richardson's campaign,[55] the company gave $220,000 in contributions to New Mexico politicians.[56] Richardson also enjoyed a free trip in Forest City's corporate jet. What did Forest City get? A slew of subsidies, including special tax carve-outs for developers lobbied for and signed by Richardson. Called "tax-increment financing," one subsidy effectively gave the developer a cut of the future property tax revenues that would go up because of the development.

Bruce Ratner also gave the maximum contribution to Obama's campaign.[57]

Then there's the New Mexico public-private partnership in horse-racing and slot machines. Santa Fe gives out only a few licenses to run these tracks. A recent licensee was Horse Racing at Raton, a partnership that includes, as a 30 percent stakeholder, a man named Marc Correra. Correra's father Anthony was a big donor to Richardson's first campaign for governor. Anthony, who assisted in Richardson's transition to office, directed a nonprofit established by Richardson, and later helped organize a Richardson fundraiser for Obama.[58]

And as if foreshadowing Obama's push for healthcare reform, when Richardson was pushing for universal health insurance in 2007, his backers included Blue Cross/Blue Shield of New Mexico and Presbyterian Healthcare Services. Presbyterian's CEO James Hinton praised Richardson's focus on "the need for a partnership between the public sector and the private sector."[59]

Richardson was pushing for mandates that everyone purchase health insurance, paired with subsidies for private health insurance. Hinton and his wife both gave the maximum to Richardson's presidential bid, among their nearly $30,000 in reported campaign contributions. (They also gave $1,000 to Richardson's 2006 Governor campaign.)

So the real partnership here seems to entail Richardson promising to require all New Mexicans to buy a product that Hinton happens to provide, while Hinton gives a cut of his profits to Richardson's campaign for president. Unsurprisingly, Richardson became quite popular with health insurers; the second largest corporate source of funds for his presidential bid was insurer Torchmark Corporation.[60]

Richardson's career should have been a cautionary tale for Obama about intimate connections between Big Business and Big Government, and the corruption and conflicts of interest they inevitably create. Instead, it was enough of an inspiration that Obama picked Richardson to run the Commerce Department.

TOM DASCHLE: THE NON-LOBBYIST LOBBYIST

In picking Daschle—who as an adviser to the K Street law firm Alston and Bird has spent the last four years burning up the sheets with the nation's fattest insurance and pharmaceutical interests—Obama is essentially announcing that he has no intention of seriously reforming the health care industry.

... Regarding Daschle, remember, we're talking about a guy who not only was a consultant for one of the top health-care law firms in the country, but a board member of the Mayo Clinic (a major recipient of NIH grants) and the husband of one of America's biggest defense lobbyists—wife Linda Hall lobbies for Lockheed-Martin and Boeing. Does anyone really think that this person is going to come up with a health care proposal that in any way cuts into the profits of the major health care companies?[61]

That was the re-printable portion of liberal *Rolling Stone* writer Matt Taibbi's reaction when Obama named former senator Tom Daschle as secretary of health and human services. The liberal media capably documented just how Daschle turned political clout and big government into big money. So let's allow the other journalists to make the case against Daschle, before we go into healthcare in more depth in chapter four.

Liberal *Salon* writer Glenn Greenwald:

[Daschle] embodies everything that is sleazy, sickly, and soul-less about Washington. It's probably impossible for Obama to fill his cabinet with individuals entirely free of Beltway filth—it's extremely rare to get anywhere near that system without being infected by it—but Daschle oozes Beltway slime from every pore.[62]

And the *Washington Post*:

The release of the financial statement [Daschle] submitted to the Office of Government Ethics details for the first time exactly how, without becoming a registered lobbyist, he made millions of dollars giving public speeches and private counsel to insurers, hospitals, realtors, farmers, energy firms and telecommunications companies with complex regulatory and legislative interests in Washington.

Daschle's expertise and insights, gleaned over 26 years in Congress, earned him more than $5 million over the past two years, including $220,000 from the health-care industry, and perks such as a chauffeured Cadillac, according to the documents.[63]

Daschle's failure to pay taxes on his company limousine helped derail his nomination, and Greenwald's column might have been the nail in the coffin. And this is the man Obama chose as his healthcare reform czar. This is the man Obama wanted as his health and human services secretary.

Why would Obama, who promised a new era of transparent, clean government, want to give top positions to Daschle, Richardson, and Emanuel—three guys whose records blurred the line between politics and corporate America? Because Obama's goal of increasing government control over the economy counted Big Business as an indispensible ally.

CHAPTER 3

STIMULATING
K STREET

WHY LOBBYISTS LOVE OBAMA

Thirteen CEOs stood in the Roosevelt Room in the West Wing of the White House, invited there by the president to drum up support for his stimulus.[1] The chiefs of Xerox, Motorola, IBM, and Google were there.[2] Nearby, White House economic advisor Jason Furman conducted a private briefing for corporate lobbyists whose clients stood to profit handsomely from the bill.

If you had listened to Barack Obama on the campaign trail, you'd think this was a scene from the dark days of the Bush administration. Obama had railed against just this sort of thing. "In the last six years," he declared, "our leaders have thrown open the door of Congress and the White House to an army of Washington lobbyists who have turned government into a game only they can play."[3]

But this double-dose of corporate access—CEOs in the Roosevelt Room and corporate lobbyists down the hall—occurred in the Era of Change. *Obama* was the president entertaining the corporate executives. *His* White House was the one overrun by lobbyists. And it was *his* stimulus that promised billions in rewards to Big Business.

Three weeks into Obama's presidency, the *New York Times* reported that the corporations that benefited most from the stimulus had helped shape it during discussions with Obama's advisors before his election.[4] Thus, the stimulus became the signpost for the Obama administration. The largest spending bill in history, tailored to the likings of Big Business, triggering a swarm of lobbying—this was one of Obama's first acts. It would be prophetic.

A pure representation of Big Government, Obama's stimulus was a dream come true for K Street lobbyists. And there's no need to assign bad motives; Obama didn't aim to enrich lobbyists and fulfill Big Business's wish list. He simply set out on a path of Big Government injecting itself deeply into the economy. The inevitable result was a lobbyist feeding frenzy and a Big Business feast.

THE STIMULUS: LET THE GOOD TIMES ROLL (FOR LOBBYISTS)

Barack Obama's Big Government agenda is, whether Obama likes it or not, good news for lobbyists. You don't have to take my word for it. Check out this *New York Times* piece from August 2009:

> Mr. Obama's jampacked domestic agenda, from new rules for Wall Street to limits on carbon emissions, has set off a full-scale lobbying brawl involving the "narrow interests" he derided in

his Inaugural Address. The health care fight represents the biggest brawl of all.

The $133 million in lobbying expenditures by health industry interests in the second quarter of 2009 alone—the most of any sector by far, according to the Center for Responsive Politics—hardly sounds like the change Mr. Obama or his supporters had in mind. And in fact the strategic course the White House has chosen may have had the unintended effect of increasing the breadth and complexity of the battle involving those interests.[5]

Howard Paster, a Bill Clinton-aide-turned-lobbyist, commented, "In general, the view of lobbying is that it's just as effective on the Hill as ever."[6] That, in fact, turned out to be an understatement.

Early on, lobbyists recognized the grand possibilities of an Obama presidency. *The Hill*, a Capitol Hill newspaper, reported that lobbyists were thrilled with Obama's election:

K Street lobbyists expect a bonanza this year because of the aggressive agenda of President Obama and congressional Democrats.

"Big government is back," said Mark Ruge, who heads the policy group at K&L Gates. "It's going to be a very, very active Congress."

A day after the Inauguration of Obama, lobbying firms were releasing weak 2008 money numbers, but realized that big government was going to mean big demand from corporate America for lobbyists to play offense and defense on their behalf.[7]

And indeed, despite its anti-corporate rhetoric, Obama's young administration has brought boom times for lobbyists. This is because increasing government control over the economy increases the demand for lobbyists. The more subsidies and regulations there are, the more a business's success depends on government. And the more a business depends on government, the more it needs lobbyists.

Obama's biggest gift to K Street was the stimulus, which enriched lobbyists from nearly every industry. With more than 800 lobbyists working on it,[8] the stimulus particularly benefited the tech industry and its representatives. A trade publication for "green technology" reported:

> President Barack Obama's $787 billion stimulus package has put clean-tech companies in "a feeding frenzy," says Jesse Berst, managing director of research firm Global Smart Energy. He recently told us that lobbying has become "intense" as utilities and technology vendors form partnerships and coalitions to better position themselves to get a bite of the funds.[9]

Some grittier industries also got in the game. The Portland Cement Association, for example, added to its $1.4 million annual lobbying effort by hiring Edmund Graber as its stimulus advocate.[10] A prolific political donor, Graber gave to more than a dozen politicians, both Democrats and Republicans, in the 2008 election.[11]

It's easy to see why concrete makers would invest in the well-connected: the stimulus allocates an estimated $48.1 billion to the Department of Transportation.[12] The bill also gave another $144 billion to state and local governments[13]—which account for nearly half of the concrete industry's business.[14]

You can't blame the cement makers or the tech companies for lobbying up for the stimulus—Obama was holding out a $787 billion bucket of other people's money, and any business would have been foolish not to take a run at the goodies. But you also have to wonder whether Obama really thought he could dramatically boost government spending and still keep his campaign promise to show the special interests the door.

Obama did propose ambitious controls on lobbying associated with the stimulus and the bailouts, but these ran into First Amendment problems—infringing on the right to petition the government. This highlights the impossible contradiction of maintaining an activist government that's not overrun by lobbyists.

Obama's later attempts at transparency had problems as well. *Pro Publica* reported:

[T]hough more than 800 lobbyists had registered to lobby on stimulus issues, only a handful actually appeared in lobbying disclosures on agency Web sites. Instead, lobbying firms were sending junior employees who were not registered lobbyists, or arranging direct meetings between government officials and clients.[15]

The stimulus proved to be a great preface to the Obama presidency, demonstrating that Big Government and open government don't mix, but Big Government and K Street get along just fine.

HOW THE STIMULUS BANKRUPTS YOU

Before looking closer at the beneficiaries of Obama's big spending, it's important to remember who's paying for all this. The $787 billion stimulus was an appropriations bill with no tax revenues to back it up. So the government borrowed all that money by selling bonds, treasury bills, and the like.

Government debt hurts regular Americans. It places us increasingly in hock to the Chinese government, which is buying the lion's share of our debt. Furthermore, someone eventually has to repay these loans. Most likely, that means higher taxes on future generations. In other words, your children are paying today's green-tech lobbyists. But, realistically, when today's loans come due, politicians will surely have some other bold, urgent priority to fund, meaning the current debt will be repaid by borrowing yet again.

In addition to hiking taxes on future taxpayers, government borrowing stokes inflation. It also sucks up capital that others could borrow, which typically drives up interest rates. So the stimulus, by borrowing so much, promises to raise prices in the future while boosting taxes and interest rates, making it harder for people to buy or sell a house or a car. Of course, by then Barack Obama will be retired in Hawaii—or maybe he'll be secretary general of the UN.

But these are not the only costs to regular Americans. The spending itself is destructive. Obama likes to call stimulus spending "investment," but government investment is much more politicized than private investment, creating a lot of wasteful projects of little value. As economist Veronique de Rugy notes:

> When Obama says, "We'll invest in what works," he means, "unlike you bozos." The president's faith in Washington is sweet, but politics rather than sound economics guide government spending. Politicians rely on lobbyists from unions, corporations, pressure groups, and state and local governments when they decide how to spend other people's money. By contrast, entrepreneurs' decisions to spend their own cash are guided by monetary profit and loss.[16]

And among its wide array of politically determined projects, the stimulus had one venture whose political machinations and enormous expense made it stand out even in the age of Obama: FutureGen.

THE LARGEST EARMARK IN HISTORY

"I know that there are a lot of folks out there who've been saying, 'Oh, this is pork, and this is money that's going to be wasted,' and et cetera, et cetera," Obama said while advocating the stimulus—the largest spending bill in history. "Understand, this bill does not have a single earmark in it, which is unprecedented for a bill of this size. . . . There aren't individual pork projects that members of Congress are putting into this bill."[17]

The truth of Obama's statement, however, depends on how you define *earmark*. If you judge by the intent of lawmakers—as opposed to the carefully crafted wording they wrote into the stimulus bill—the stimulus, in fact, contained the largest earmark in history.

When the House of Representatives first passed the stimulus, amid the many billions for renewable energy was a $2.4 billion appropriation "for necessary expenses to demonstrate carbon capture and sequestration technologies."[18] In the Senate's version of the bill, this was rendered as a $2 billion allocation for "one or more near zero emissions powerplant(s)."[19]

Now, Democrats argued this wasn't technically an earmark because it didn't specify which "near zero emissions powerplant" would be funded. But, as it turns out, there were no such powerplants in operation and only one in development—and it happened to be situated in the president's home state.

The plant, located in rural Mattoon, Illinois, was owned by a platoon of large coal and power companies. Called FutureGen, it was pitched as an experiment in "clean coal" technology. But

Illinois politicians saw it as something else: a tool for bringing ten-figure federal subsidies into downstate Illinois.

FutureGen's acquisition of the largest earmark in history demonstrates how increased government spending sets off lobbying feeding frenzies. It also aptly shows that favoritism toward Big Business is a bipartisan affair—while nearly all the advocates of the FutureGen earmark were Democrats, the project was the off-spring of former vice president Dick Cheney.

A brief flashback for some context:

For eight years, Democrats attacked the Bush administration for allegedly being in bed with Big Oil and Big Coal. One of their main targets was an energy task force Vice President Cheney had assembled in 2001. When the administration refused to disclose the details of the task force's meetings, a new liberal meme was born: "Cheney's secretive energy task force." It was at these meetings, liberals argued, where the administration sold out America to its biggest polluters. Or in the words of Sierra Club lawyer Alex Levinson, the task force "laid out the red carpet for Big Oil, Big Energy and Big Coal to formulate energy policy."[20]

Throughout the 2008 Democratic presidential primary, Obama often used a similar line. In New Hampshire in June 2007, he said, "The oil companies were allowed to craft energy policy with Dick Cheney in secret while every other voice was silenced.... The industry got everything it wanted."[21] Similarly, in Montana in May 2008 he declared, "Dick Cheney had an energy task force that came up with an energy policy that just served the interests of Big Oil and Big Gas."[22] And on another occasion, he proclaimed, "Take a look at how Dick Cheney did his energy policy. He met with environmental groups once, he met with renewable energy folks once, and then he met with oil and gas companies forty times, and that's how they put together our energy policy."[23]

The discerning reader will notice an important difference between the Sierra Club's rhetoric and Obama's: Obama never mentioned "Big Coal" as one of the bad guys. That's because as a senator, Obama championed FutureGen, declaring in mid-2006, "The FutureGen project is the future of coal in the United States."[24] Since the FutureGen project was originally proposed *in those Cheney task force meetings*, Obama refrained from criticizing Big Coal's role in those talks.

The project was groundbreaking: get ten or so of the biggest oil and power companies together in a joint venture, provide a billion dollars of federal aid, and charge the companies—known as the FutureGen Alliance—with creating a coal-fired power plant that gives off almost no pollution or greenhouse gasses. This would involve developing "carbon capture" technology: trapping carbon dioxide emissions underground so they don't contribute to the greenhouse effect.

Carbon capture is controversial. Advocates argue it's a breakthrough technology that would allow the use of coal—America's most plentiful natural resource and by far our cheapest source of electricity on a large scale—without the attendant pollution and carbon dioxide emissions. But its detractors believe the technology is "at best uncertain and at worst unworkable," as the *Economist* argued.[25]

The Bush White House announced the FutureGen initiative in 2003. The following year, Energy Secretary Spence Abraham sent his aide, former lobbyist Mark Maddox, out to pump up congressional support and to elicit a minority investment from corporate partners.

The Energy Department also had to decide among potential sites for the plant: two in Texas and two in Illinois. Obama was part of a congressional team advocating for Illinois. The team also included Illinois senator Dick Durbin (D), Illinois congressmen

Rahm Emanuel (D) and Ray LaHood (R), and Illinois governor Rod Blagojevich (D).

In December 2007, the Bush administration announced Future-Gen would be located in Mattoon, Illinois.[26] But a month later, the Energy Department scrapped the project, citing projected cost overruns. Critics accused Bush of pulling the plug once his home state lost out.

FutureGen's cancellation—and earlier, the fear of cancellation—triggered a massive lobbying effort. On June 22, 2007, Governor Blagojevich hired legendary K Street lobbying firm Cassidy & Associates to lobby for preserving FutureGen funding.[27] Cassidy lobbyists on this account included Kai Anderson, who had recently stepped down as chief of staff to Senate majority leader Harry Reid, and Marty Russo, a former Democratic congressman from Chicago. That fall, the FutureGen Alliance hired two lobbying firms,[28] including the Gephardt Group, headed by former Democratic House minority leader Dick Gephardt.

The individual companies in the FutureGen Alliance lobbied up, too. Peabody, the world's largest coal company, added to its lobbying army in February 2008, hiring the firm Bryan Cave LLP.[29] American Electric Power, another FutureGen Alliance company, in May 2008 hired a former congressional staffer, Alexander J. Beckles, to lobby on "carbon capture."[30]

FutureGen Alliance member Anglo American, a UK-based coal giant, also invested in K Street. Just after the 2008 election, the firm hired the Livingston Group along with its founding partner, former congressman Bob Livingston,[31] a Louisiana Republican who served as chairman of the House Appropriations Committee and briefly as Speaker of the House before news of his extramarital affair forced his resignation. To get FutureGen funds restored, Livingston subcontracted the lobbyist Mark Maddox[32]—

the same Mark Maddox who had previously helped to organize FutureGen when he worked in the Energy Department. This was a clear example of Washington's revolving door: the government hires you to manage a program, then a private company hires you to help it profit from that same program.

The lobbyists in 2008 pulled out all the stops to resurrect FutureGen. They tried to attach FutureGen funding to the Fiscal Year 2009 Energy & Water appropriations bill, and some attempted to stick it into the massive Wall Street bailout of October 2008. But they were unsuccessful—that is, until they found Hope and Change in the new Obama administration. Longtime FutureGen advocate Dick Durbin, a member of the Senate Appropriations Committee, got the FutureGen earmark into the Senate version of Obama's stimulus bill—a $2 billion line item for "one or more near zero emissions powerplant(s)."

Senator Tom Coburn, a tireless budget hawk, blew the whistle on the earmark and tried to strip it out.[33] "We all know what this is about," said Coburn, an Oklahoma Republican. "It's an earmark for a single plant."[34] In light of the unwelcome attention, the conference committee—the small group of lawmakers that reconciles the two chambers' bills—made the language more vague. The final bill simply provided $3.4 billion for "fossil energy research and development."

It was widely known in Washington that $1 billion of this would go to FutureGen. A *Washington Post* article in March 2009 explained the situation:

> Deep inside the economic stimulus package is a $1 billion prize that, in five short words, shows the benefits of being in power in Washington.
>
> The funding, for "fossil energy research and development," is likely to go to a power plant in a small Illinois town, a project

whose longtime backers include a group of powerful lawmakers from the state, among them President Obama.

    ...But now those same Illinois legislators—including Rahm
Emanuel, now White House chief of staff, and Ray LaHood,
now transportation secretary—control the White House and
hold key leadership positions in Washington, and FutureGen is
on the verge of resurrection.[35]

Sure enough, in June, Energy Secretary Steven Chu, who previously had called coal energy "my worst nightmare,"[36] declared he
would direct $1 billion of stimulus cash to FutureGen.[37] The lob-
byists had worked hard for their victory, and they were rewarded:
the *Post* reported lobbyists were paid more than $20 million for
work on FutureGen and other clean coal issues. FutureGen
Alliance employees did their part too, donating $3 million to con-
gressional and presidential candidates.[38] The losers in this story
were the taxpayers and their children, who someday will have to
repay another $1 billion in debt.

    Another big loser was the naïve voters who believed Obama's
campaign promises to increase government transparency.
Newsweek reported:

As a senator, Barack Obama denounced the Bush administration for holding "secret energy meetings" with oil executives at
the White House. But last week public-interest groups were dis-
mayed when his own administration rejected a Freedom of
Information Act request for Secret Service logs showing the
identities of coal executives who had visited the White House
to discuss Obama's "clean coal" policies.[39]

Secrecy and lobbying swarms, it turns out, were not caused by
some unique perfidy of the Bush administration, but by the draw
of billions of dollars of other people's money.

STIMULATING WHOM?

In the first debate of the 2008 general election, Obama assailed "the failed economic policies promoted by George Bush [and] supported by Senator McCain." These policies, Obama said, decreed we can "give more and more to the most, and somehow prosperity will trickle down."[40]

Then, as soon as he was elected, Obama's stimulus did exactly that, giving nearly a trillion dollars of our children's money to high-tech companies, road builders, and coal companies in the hope somehow prosperity will trickle down. But it won't; when politicians are handing out money, it's those with the best lobbyists who get their hands on it—and that's never Mom 'n' Pop.

As small business was left to cope with the recession on its own, Big Business reaped a bonanza from the stimulus. In September 2009, the *Wall Street Journal* reported, "The biggest recipients so far of the federal contracts awarded with stimulus money are large companies that faced little competition for the funds." Of the 22,000 such contracts signed with companies, only a fifth had gone to small vendors, the *Journal* found.[41]

The stimulus operates according to a pretty simple rule: the biggest companies with the most lobbyists get the most money. Take General Electric. The fifth-largest company in America, GE leads corporate America in lobbying-related spending. Unsurprisingly, GE profited enormously from the stimulus, as described in chapter ten. Moreover, GE revealed in an annual report that it influenced various governments' stimulus projects to emphasize "green" projects—projects that just happen to benefit GE's Ecomagination initiative for green business ventures:

As governments around the world structure their economic stimulus programs, virtually all of them include a "green" component designed to support and create jobs that will develop and advance tomorrow's competitive skills. Given our experience with ecomagination, we have had the opportunity to share our insights into the creation of "green collar" jobs with these governments. By some estimates, the total green component of all global stimulus programs now exceeds $400 billion. We are encouraged by this prioritization.[42]

And relying on Big Business is no guarantee that stimulus funds will be spent honestly and efficiently. In September 2009, the *New York Times* reported that $6 million in stimulus money went to a giant construction management company, Bovis Lend Lease LMB, that has been targeted in two criminal investigations in the last two years: one for a fire that killed two firemen at a Deutsche Bank building, and a second, ongoing investigation for over-billing, bribery, and other alleged misdeeds in big New York construction contracts.[43]

The stimulus was emblematic of the Obama administration's first few months: after winning election on promises to take on Big Business lobbyists, Obama ushered in a program of governmental shock and awe, bringing unprecedented prizes for both Big Business and their lobbyists.

OBAMA AND THE DEMOCRATS' ULTIMATE K STREET INSIDER

"He's leading by example," a voiceover said in one of Obama's campaign ads, "refusing contributions from PACs and Washington lobbyists who have too much power today."[44]

Obama waved this "no-lobbyist-money" flag high throughout both the primary and general election campaigns, signaling to voters and small donors that he was the candidate of change, that he represented the grassroots and not the elites, and that he would take on the "narrow interests" that currently run things in Washington. Six months before the Iowa caucuses, he sent out an email asserting:

> Candidates typically spend a week like this—right before the critical June 30th financial reporting deadline—on the phone day and night, begging Washington lobbyists and special interest PACs to write huge checks. Not me. Our campaign has rejected the money-for-influence game and refused to accept funds from registered federal lobbyists and political action committees.[45]

Fifteen months after denouncing appeals for big donations just before reporting deadlines, the Obama Victory Fund reeled in a $25,000 donation at the end of September 2008—just before the third quarter financial reporting deadline. That money was split between the Obama campaign and the DNC.

The donor, Fran Eizenstat, listed her occupation as "retired."[46] Two months earlier, her husband Stuart had maxed out to Obama for America, giving $2,300 to his primary election campaign.[47] The Obama for America filing also listed Mr. Eizenstat as "retired" and described him as "not employed."

But Mr. Eizenstat was neither retired nor unemployed. He was a federally registered lobbyist with clients including oil giant Shell International and private equity titan Kolberg, Kravitz and Roberts.[48] Interestingly, his previous political donation (a July 16 gift to Congressman Gary Ackerman)[49] and his succeeding one (a September 15 donation to a political action committee run by Congressman Charlie Rangel)[50] both listed Eizenstat as a partner at lobbying firm Covington & Burling. In fact, just a week after his donation to Obama, he began work for a brand new client in Ukraine.[51]

There is no record of Obama or the DNC returning Mr. or Mrs. Eizenstat's money, although a $200 donation Stuart had made to Obama in 2007 was returned.[52] Thus, a federally registered lobbyist and his wife gave more than $27,000 to Obama's election— as Obama claimed to reject all lobbyist money.

Obama has his defenses, though. Mrs. Eizenstat is not a lobbyist and never has been. Although she is personally enriched by her husband's lobbying and all of their belongings are jointly held, her donations are not technically lobbyist donations. And Stuart's donation—well, if he described himself as retired, how was the campaign supposed to know?

Here's how: Stuart Eizenstat is very well-known in Democratic circles. He was a staffer for President Johnson,[53] ran Hubert Humphrey's presidential campaign, and served four years as President Carter's chief domestic policy advisor. In 1993, President Clinton appointed him as U.S. Ambassador to the European Union, and Eizenstat later served senior roles in Clinton's Commerce and State departments before becoming the number two man at the Treasury Department. He has received high civilian awards from Secretary of State Warren Christopher, Secretary of State Madeleine Albright, and Secretary of the Treasury Lawrence Summers.[54]

So it's a safe bet the Democrats knew who Ambassador Eizenstat was, and knew that he had become a lobbyist, when they took the Eizenstats' donations. He is a textbook example of a high-powered lobbyist profiting from his government connections by influencing policy on behalf of corporate interests. In other words, he's the ultimate personification of the Big Business–lobbying nexus that Obama vowed to smash.

A week after Obama's election, when General Motors was looking to hire a lobbyist to help it secure a bailout, it hired Stu Eizenstat to prevail upon the president he and his wife had supported so generously.[55] Obama could already claim his first success at job creation.

THE LOBBYIST LOOPHOLE[56]

To signal his supposed seriousness in ending lobbying influence, President Obama's first executive act was to issue an ethics order curbing the actions of lobbyists in his administration and slowing the revolving door between government and lobbying.[57]

The order required all appointees to swear:

I will not for a period of two years from the date of my appointment participate in any particular matter involving specific parties that is directly and substantially related to my former employer or former clients, including regulations and contracts.

Additionally, it exacted this oath from incoming former lobbyists:

I will not for a period of two years after the date of my appointment: (a) participate in any particular matter on which I lobbied within the two years before the date of my appointment; (b) participate in the specific issue area in which that particular matter falls.

This means if you were recently a lobbyist and now you're in the Obama administration, you have to avoid the issues on which you lobbied and matters directly affecting companies for which you worked.

While Obama's supporters touted this as a "lobbyist ban," it is no such thing. For instance, Tom Vilsack, Obama's agriculture secretary, was a lobbyist until March 31, 2008.[58] But because he lobbied for the National Education Association and didn't lobby on food or agriculture issues, he could take charge of the Agriculture Department without crossing Obama's new ethical barriers. In fact, at least sixteen former lobbyists are serving in the Obama administration,[59] and most of them are exempt from the "lobbyist ban"—for instance, if it's been more than two years since they last were registered as lobbyists.

A few appointees couldn't find any loopholes, however, so President Obama utilized a flexible clause allowing him to waive the new rules if it's "in the public interest" or if "the literal application of the restriction is inconsistent with the purposes of the restriction." One waiver recipient is Deputy Secretary of Defense William J. Lynn, a former lobbyist for Raytheon, a military contractor that makes the Patriot and Tomahawk missiles.[60]

And at least one man has navigated around the "lobbyist ban" without even having a waiver: Mark Patterson, the chief of staff for Treasury Department head Timothy Geithner. A former top staffer for then-Senator Tom Daschle,[61] Patterson cashed out after Daschle's 2004 defeat and worked as a lobbyist at Goldman Sachs until April 11, 2008, after which he moved to Treasury.[62]

Lacking a presidential waiver, Patterson is obliged to recuse himself from "personally and substantially" participating in any matter involving Goldman. That would be a tall order for a top Treasury Department official, since Goldman is involved in nearly every corner of the financial sector—and many other sectors, too.

What's more, Patterson should be ineligible to participate in any issues related to his former lobbying activities. This could be a problem, because federal records show Patterson's lobbying activities involved banking regulations, insurance policy, monetary policy, executive compensation, commodities trading, foreign investment, real estate, pension issues, renewable energy subsidies, immigration, tax policy, mortgage lending, copyright, derivatives trading, tribal gaming, and regulation of credit rating agencies, among others.

Is there anything left for Patterson to do at Treasury? Maybe he just collects time sheets and changes coffee filters.

OBAMA AND THE LOBBYISTS

It's not that Obama has some secret fondness for lobbyists—it's that Obamanomics is inherently beneficial to lobbyists. Increasing government power always increases lobbyist influence. As government has more control over businesses and as subsidies and bailouts become a larger part of the economy, businesses are increasingly compelled to hire a lobbyist.

In short, Obamanomics shifts economic power from consumers, workers, and investors to politicians and bureaucrats. And that's good news for lobbyists.

CHAPTER 4

OBAMACARE IS CORPORATE WELFARE

REFORM THE HMOS CAN BELIEVE IN

Trying to follow Barack Obama's rhetoric can be dizzying. One minute he's rolling up his sleeves, promising to battle the evil corporate interests. The next minute he's vowing to get those same corporations on board for "Change."

The latter narrative is more correct, even if it leaves out some key details. On healthcare, the Obama line—and the industry line—is that the need for reform is *just so overwhelming* that even industry is coming to the table. Rahm Emanuel expressed this clearly in July 2009, declaring, "The very groups we have been talking to have been the most vocal opponents of health care reform; they are now becoming the vocal proponents for health care reform."[1]

But the truth is less flattering. Industry is not embracing ObamaCare because companies recognize the need for reform;

instead, the biggest businesses have come to understand that
Obama's healthcare reform will increase industry profits far
beyond anything the free market ever would allow—with those
added profits coming at the expense of patients and taxpayers.

The "reform" is really a raft of subsidies and special favors for
all the health sector businesses in the Obama–Industrial Complex—
the drug makers, insurers, and hospitals. The reform proposals,
in effect, will transfer wealth from ordinary Americans to these
well-connected businesses. Obama campaign proposals that
would have hurt these entrenched interests were quickly shuffled
aside when Obama took office.

Healthcare legislation was still taking form as this book went
to press, but the various proposals had enough in common that
we can make some general statements about the leading bills:

- Every reform proposal with significant congressional
  backing represented corporate welfare for the drug
  makers. This is why the drug makers ran advertisements supporting "reform."
- Health insurers objected strongly to only one major
  proposal: the introduction of a government-run
  insurer, known as the "public option." The other
  measures were all welcomed by the insurers, who also
  engaged in a million-dollar media campaign to support "reform."
- None of the proposals would have abolished the government's biggest favor for HMOs: the tax break for
  employer-sponsored health insurance.
- The reform proposals liberals have long championed—a single-payer plan in which the government is
  the sole health insurer in the country—never saw the

light of day. In fact, Obama repeatedly denied that he ever favored such a policy.

In effect, the debate within the pro-reform camp was this: should we: (A) increase subsidies for drug makers, HMOs, and hospitals, and *also* create a government competitor to the HMOs; or should we (B) just increase subsidies to drug makers, HMOs, and hospitals?

Meanwhile, healthcare companies provided unprecedented amounts of money to Obama's election. And in 2009, their favorite politicians included the congressional Democrats in charge of crafting the legislation Obama was championing. Nevertheless, it was the anti-reform side that Democrats and many media outlets accused of being health sector lackeys.

It's not that Obama's goal was to enrich Big Pharma and the HMOs. No, his past statements indicate he would drive the HMOs out of business if he could.[2] But Obama's real aim—increasing regulation and subsidies in the industry—was bound to end up as a sop to the big businesses in that same industry.

Barack Obama understands Obamanomics, so he knows Big Business will benefit from his Big Government plans. That's why he partnered with the drug makers—and in some ways with the HMOs—in order to "reform" the industry.

PREACHING TO THE CHOIR

Billed as a "townhall" in Portsmouth, New Hampshire, the president promised an honest and fair discussion of the healthcare bills on Capitol Hill at the time. But the meeting, held in August 2009, looked more like a pep rally.

The beginning of the transcript sets the tone:

THE PRESIDENT: Hello, Portsmouth! Thank you. (Applause.) Thank you so much. Everybody have a seat. Oh, thank you so—

AUDIENCE MEMBER: We love you!

THE PRESIDENT: I love you back. Thank you. (Laughter.)[3]

After laying out some policy proposals, Obama gave his account of the battlefield: "Despite all the hand-wringing pundits and the best efforts of those who are profiting from the status quo, we are closer to achieving health insurance reform than we have ever been."[4] He listed his allies in the battle: the American Nurses Association, the American Medical Association, and the AARP. Then he addressed his alleged opponents:

But let's face it, now is the hard part—because the history is clear—every time we come close to passing health insurance reform, the special interests fight back with everything they've got. They use their influence. They use their political allies to scare and mislead the American people. They start running ads. This is what they always do.

We can't let them do it again. Not this time.

This was the refrain of the 2009 push for healthcare reform: *the special interests killed reform in 1993, and they're trying to do it again.* But, if the nurses, doctors, and lobbying giant AARP were all on board, just who were these "special interests" that "are profiting from the status quo"?

They were presumably not the drug makers—a few weeks earlier, Obama had told the press that "we have made so much progress where we've got doctors, nurses, hospitals, even the pharmaceutical industry, AARP, saying that this makes sense to do."[5] So we're already running out of potential bad guys, here.

But there was one enemy left; Obama declared the whole healthcare crisis was "the story of hardworking Americans who are held hostage by health insurance companies." His Democratic colleagues echoed the charge. "It's almost immoral what they are doing," Nancy Pelosi said about health insurers. "Of course they've been immoral all along in how they have treated the people that they insure. . . . They are the villains. They have been part of the problem in a major way."[6] Democrats later wrote in an email to supporters, "[Obama is] under attack by Washington insiders, insurance companies, and well-financed special interests who don't go a day without spreading lies and stirring up fear."

It was a smart line of attack for Democrats—one dictated, the White House admitted, by poll numbers. In a speech given in Canada, Obama's then-chief pollster Joel Benenson revealed, "Initial reaction to [the public plan] wasn't as positive as it is now. . . . But we figured out that people like the idea of competition versus the insurance company, and that's why you get a number like 72 percent supporting it."[7]

In other words, the Democrats decided to sell their reform by attacking HMOs. But at the same time, the insurers were running advertisements calling—albeit, vaguely—for the passage of "reform." The insurance industry's lobby, America's Health Insurance Plans, spent more than $1 million running cable television ads touting their support for "bipartisan reforms that Congress can build on."[8]

Were insurers just lying about their position? No. At the heart of the conflicting messages was a bit of nuance: health insurers supported all the major provisions in the congressional reform bills except one—the government option. HMOs did not want to compete against a government insurer. Nobody wants new competitors, especially not one with the full might of the U.S. government behind it.

Aside from that, the insurers mostly jumped aboard the reform bandwagon.

CHRISTMAS COMES EARLY FOR THE INSURERS

"Unless everybody does their part," Obama told a joint session of Congress in September, "many of the insurance reforms we seek, especially requiring insurance companies to cover preexisting conditions, just can't be achieved. That's why under my plan, individuals will be required to carry basic health insurance."[9]

Champagne corks must have popped at health insurers' offices all over the country.

Obama was endorsing a policy present in both the House and the Senate legislation at the time: the individual mandate, which may be the most favorable policy proposal any business could ever hope to see. The federal government would *require* every American to hold health insurance. If you don't have health insurance, the government will fine you. This is, in the lingo of Obamanomics, *Making an Offer You Can't Refuse*.

You can imagine the envy of other industry lobbyists. Maybe the automakers could get a bill requiring everyone to own a car. Or the computer lobby could get its own "individual mandate." Why not Boeing? Or Smith & Wesson?

Obama hadn't supported the individual mandate on the campaign trail, but after a handful of meetings with insurance lobbyists and executives, and months of back-and-forth with Congress, Obama called on Americans to "do their part" by giving their money to Blue Cross.

This was how he would "cover everyone." It's like delivering the proverbial "chicken in every pot" by fining everyone who doesn't buy a chicken. And what about people who can't afford health insurance? Government subsidies—in other words, other taxpayers—will pay for them, of course.

Obama and the Democrats also proposed to expand Medicaid, a federal entitlement subsidizing insurance for the poor. This was another boon for insurers—James Carlson, CEO of Amerigroup Corp., predicted this measure could bring 10 million new customers for Medicaid administrators.[10] Marveling about the reform proposals in general, Carlson affirmed, "Most of what we're reading would grow our business dramatically."

And there was one more big treat for insurers—the House bill and one of the two Senate bills included an "employer mandate" requiring all employers to offer health insurance to their employees. While these bills exempt some smaller employers, the employer mandate, too, is a precious gift to insurers, in part because employer-based health insurance reduces competition among them. More on this below.

When you consider these "reform" provisions—amounting to *Subsidy Suckling* and *Regulatory Robbery*—it's hard to see how Democrats got away with claiming they were sticking it to the insurers. In fact, these gifts to insurers were so generous that as long as they got them, the firms agreed to major new regulations.

The two big regulation proposals are called "community rating" and "guaranteed issue." Community rating, in brief, is the idea that every insurance customer should pay the same rates, regardless of age, pre-existing condition, and so on. This regulation, on its own, would drive insurers to refuse coverage to old and sick people. So it was paired with guaranteed issue, which would require insurers to accept all paying customers.

Obama campaigned on these regulations and in November 2008, AHIP, the health insurers' lobby, endorsed them, too—as long as it got the individual mandate. "Health plans today proposed guaranteed coverage for people with pre-existing medical conditions in conjunction with an enforceable individual coverage mandate," AHIP wrote in a press release. [11] The statement also called for subsidies, or "premium support for moderate-income individuals," as the insurance lobbyists called them.

This was AHIP's opening offer to Obama: agreeing to guaranteed issue and community rating in return for subsidized insurance premiums, an individual mandate, and an employer mandate. By October, Obama and the Democrats were defending this very package among others, and railing against the "special interests" that were allegedly resisting Change.

"REFORM": AN IMMUNIZATION SHOT FOR HMOS

"I will never forget my own mother," Obama told the crowd in Portsmouth,

> as she fought cancer in her final months, having to worry about whether her insurance would refuse to pay for her treatment. And by the way, this was because the insurance company was arguing that somehow she should have known that she had cancer when she took her new job—even though it hadn't been diagnosed yet.
>
> So if it could happen to her, it could happen to any one of us. [12]

This is one of Obama's standard lines. It's a horrible image—a mother dying too young, and worrying about her insurance.

Obama is correct that insurers sometimes deny coverage unfairly—and that can kill you. But in that event, the House bill Obama so aggressively championed in summer 2009 would protect the insurer from liability.

Ask Florence Corcoran, a mother in Louisiana, about this shocking detail of federal health insurance regulation. Florence had serious problems late in her pregnancy in 1989.[13] In order to monitor her baby around the clock, her doctor ordered her hospitalized. He had done the same with her previous pregnancy, and when that baby had gone into distress a month before the due date, he performed an emergency C-section and delivered a healthy baby.

During her following pregnancy, though, the hospital sent her home after nine days. UnitedHealth, the insurance company that administered her benefits, refused to cover her hospital stay despite her doctor's orders and despite the experience with the first pregnancy. United said it would cover home nursing care for her, up to ten hours per day. Two weeks later, on October 25, 1989, baby Corcoran went into distress. No nurse was on duty at the Corcorans'. The baby died.

The Corcorans filed a wrongful death suit in Louisiana courts—and UnitedHealth won. The courts would not rule out United's responsibility for the baby's death, but that was irrelevant, they found. The Corcorans simply could not sue in state court because state law didn't apply to Florence's insurance plan.

Corcoran had her insurance through her job. That meant her insurance was regulated not under state law, but under the federal Employee Retirement Income Security Act of 1974 (ERISA). This law was billed as protecting workers and curbing the abuses of employers and insurers. But in practice, ERISA protected insurers. Section 514 of ERISA established that the law preempted all state laws when it came to most employer-based health-insurance plans. Other parts of the bill effectively immunized insurers from paying for harm they caused to customers.

This ugly aspect of ERISA is relevant to today's debate over healthcare reform. In general, it highlights how federal regulations supposedly protecting customers often protect the very business being regulated—remember the First Law of Obamanomics: "During a legislative debate, whichever business has the best lobbyists is most likely to win the most favorable small print." This turned out to be true of ERISA, a fact that does not give pause to today's reformers.

Specifically, in 2009, the House's reform bill explicitly preserved this extraordinary immunity for insurers. Congressman John Shadegg, an Arizona Republican, proposed an amendment in a committee hearing to end the immunity clause, but the committee chairman, Democrat Henry Waxman, pushed it aside, claiming a lack of jurisdiction.

Shadegg thinks the insurers insisted on preserving this provision. "I think they have an agreement with Mr. Waxman and with other Democrat proponents of the House bill that—at least for employer-sponsored plans—their immunity will continue," Shaddegg told me. And Waxman certainly didn't shun insurer attention: as of October 2009, he was the number three House recipient of HMO money.[14]

GUMMING UP COMPETITION

The argument for reform is certainly grounded in real problems: health insurers do frequently mistreat their customers, and they are rapidly raising their premiums. They get away with it because they don't have to compete.

In response, Obama would create a new government competitor—the public option—but leave in place the laws that kill private-sector competition. Lack of insurer competition is largely due to the prevalence of employer-based insurance, which serves 60 percent of Americans under age 65.[15] Although employer-based insurance seems normal to us, it's not—it's a function of Big Government policies that favor these policies over an individual market. Liberal blogger Ezra Klein explains the history:

> The Roosevelt administration had instituted wage and price controls to prevent profiteering. Excess profits were taxed at mind-bogglingly high rates. Wages were frozen so employers couldn't offer raises. But the government decided to exempt health benefits from these rules. So corporations took their wartime profits and plowed them into health care benefits. In 1953, with the war over, the IRS tried to overturn the rule. Congress overruled the IRS.[16]

And the insurers, engaging in the tried and true tactic of *Gumming Up the Works*, have defended these policies, because the policies mean the insurers don't really have to please their customers. Congressman Shadegg uses a simple comparison: if your car insurance goes up 50 percent, you find another car insurer. But if your health insurance goes up 50 percent, you don't have any say, because your employer bought the policy.[17]

Now, that's a bit of an oversimplification. You could change jobs, for instance, or convince your co-workers to lobby your company to switch insurers. But sticking the employer between the buyer and the seller does suppress competition, and that allows insurers to get away with more price hikes, more coverage denials, and more changing the rules mid-game. It's no coincidence that health insurance is one of the industries with the lowest customer satisfaction.

Klein, a dedicated supporter of President Obama's push for reform, outlined the problems of employer-based healthcare:

> Individuals don't know how much their employer is paying for health care. They don't know how much they're not getting in

wage increases. They don't know how much premiums are growing every year. (Out-of-pocket costs are a small fraction of total health care spending. ...) Protecting individuals from seeing the full cost of health care reduces the political pressure to reform the system. It leaves them more dependent on their employer and less able to start a new business or take a job with a small company.[18]

This system is also perpetuated through the tax exemption on employer-based health insurance. Almost any employer benefit of significant value is taxable with just a few exceptions—matching 401(k) funds, and some parking or transit fees. But the only benefit that is tax exempt with no limits is health insurance. The premiums you pay on every paycheck are pre-tax dollars, and the portion of the premium your employer pays is an untaxed benefit.

But you can't deduct your premiums if you find your insurance outside of your employer. That means the tax exemption effectively gives employer-based plans a competition-killing subsidy.

How much of a subsidy? The Joint Committee on Taxation estimated in 2007 that ending tax preferences for employer-based healthcare would raise more than $300 billion per year.[19] That means the tax exclusion is a $300 billion subsidy split between employers and health insurance companies.

So, insurers had successfully *Gummed Up the Works* to prevent real competition in health insurance, and during his campaign Obama savaged any proposal to remove the subsidies that were gumming up the works, as discussed in chapter two.

To summarize Obama's approach to health insurance reform: Obama ran on a platform of (1) introducing a government option to compete against insurers, (2) opposing an individual mandate, (3) subsidizing health insurance, and (4) preserving the tax subsidy for employer-sponsored health care. On points 3 and 4, he was on the side of the insurers—and on both points he persisted.

On points 1 and 2, Obama was at odds with the insurers—and on both those points he backed off.

THE DOCTOR CARTEL

At the heart of the call for reform is the cry to contain the soaring costs of healthcare. Politicians blame all sorts of culprits for the cost explosion: medical malpractice suits, unnecessary procedures, uninsured people using emergency rooms for primary care, "defensive medicine," lack of preventive care, and so on.

The McKinsey Global Institute in late 2008 compared U.S. healthcare costs to the rest of the West. Among other cost drivers, McKinsey found that "higher physician compensation adds $64 billion in costs to the US system."[20]

It's a little known fact that doctor salaries are kept artificially high because Congress and state governments effectively maintain a doctors' cartel. *USA Today* explained how it works:

> The government spends about $11 billion annually on 100,000 medical residents, or roughly $110,000 per resident. The number of residents has hovered at this level for the past decade, according to the Accreditation Council for Graduate Medical Education.
>
> In 1997, to save money and prevent a doctor glut, Congress capped the number of residents that Medicare will pay for at about 80,000 a year.[21]

Becoming a doctor wouldn't be easy in any event. But Congress, through funding a limited number of residencies, and state governments, through licensing laws, constrict the supply of doctors even more. And the powerful doctors' lobby—the American Medical Association—fights *for* these laws that constrict supply.

Forbes columnist and Reason Foundation senior analyst Shikha Dalmia makes an important point on this score:

> One way to relieve the shortage of providers that the medical industry has created would be for the AMA to abandon its aggressive game of turf-protection and allow nurses, midwives, physician assistants and practitioners of alternative therapies such as chiropractors, to offer standard treatments for routine illnesses without physician supervision. For instance, midwifery, once a robust industry in this country, has been virtually destroyed, thanks to the intense lobbying against it by the medical industry. In 1995, 36 states restricted or outright banned midwifery, even though studies have found that it delivers equally safe care at far lower prices than standard hospital births.[22]

The doctors' cartel is one of many existing forms of *Regulatory Robbery* that hurt our healthcare system and that Obama has steadfastly avoided fixing.

KEITH OLBERMANN: WORST FACT-CHECKER IN THE WORLD

An August 3, 2009, rant by MSNBC host Keith Olbermann was a quintessential example of *The Big Myth* that Big Government and Big Business are natural rivals, and that Republicans are the party of Big Business.[23] Although he was speaking in the context of the proposed government option for insurance—which the insurers really were opposing—Olbermann spoke in oversimplified black-and-white terms, as if the battle were simply reformers-vs.-industry. Here are a few of his assertions:

"The insurance industry owns the Republican Party."

If that's true, what's the word for the insurance industry's relationship to the Democratic Party? In the 2008 election cycle, employees and executives at HMOs gave $5.7 million to Republicans, but $8.6 million to Democrats. Republicans have never raised anywhere close to that amount from the HMOs.[24]

The most recent campaign finance numbers at the time of Olbermann's diatribe showed Democrats with nearly a two-to-one advantage in HMO fundraising in the 2010 cycle.

"Pharma owns part of [the GOP], too. Hospitals and HMO's, another part. Nursing homes—they have a share."

Hospitals and nursing homes, according to the Center for Responsive Politics, had given Democrats $2 million for the 2010 election at the time of Olbermann's screed—three times as much as they had given Republicans. Democratic Senate majority leader Harry Reid led recipients with more than four times the haul of the top Republican.

In the 2008 election, the Democrat advantage in hospital-and-nursing-home cash was $14.1 million to $9.0 million. Obama's $3.3 million from the industry was more than four times what McCain brought in and 50 percent more than what George W. Bush raised from these companies in both his elections combined.

"You name a Republican, any Republican, and he is literally brought to you by... campaign donations from the Health Sector. Sen. John Thune of South Dakota?"

John Thune was actually brought to you *despite* campaign donations from the health sector. Thune was elected to the Senate in 2004, when he beat Democratic minority leader Tom Daschle. That year, Daschle took in $720,000 from the health sector while Thune brought in only $480,000.

Check the donations of the political action committees in the sector: the PAC for AHIP, the industry lobbying group, gave Daschle $5,000 in 2003 and 2004—the most to any candidate—on top of a $2,500 gift two years earlier. AHIP's PAC gave nothing to Thune.

Blue Cross/Blue Shield PAC: $4,000 to Daschle, none to Thune. Aetna PAC: $3,000 to Daschle, nothing to Thune. UnitedHealth PAC: $7,000 to Daschle, the most any politician got from them that year—and $0 to Thune. Pfizer PAC: $2,000 to Daschle, nothing to Thune. Daschle's leadership PAC—DASHPAC—also pulled in $10,000 from UnitedHealth, $7,500 from the American Hospital Association PAC, $7,500 from the American Optometric Association, and smaller gifts from the PACs of the American Health Care Association, American Association of Nurse Anesthetists, Invacare, Amgen, Aetna, Medco Health, Blue Cross/Blue Shield of California, and AHIP.[25]

"The evil truth is, the Insurance industry, along with Hospitals, HMO's, Pharma, nursing homes—it owns Democrats, too. Not the whole party— Candidate Barack Obama got more than $18 million from the Health Sector just last year. And you can bet somebody in the Health Trust, somebody responsible for buying influence, got fired over what Obama's done.

"No, the Democrats are not wholly owned. Hundreds of Democrats have taken campaign money from the Health Sector without handing over their souls as receipts."

But Olbermann here misleads through lack of context. He appears to show balance by mentioning Obama's health sector haul, but he leaves out the real significance of that number: Obama's $19.4 million take was more than any candidate has ever received from the sector in any one election—by a long shot.[26] George W. Bush, with $10.4 million in 2004, is the only other candidate in history to have reached eight-figures in health-sector fundraising. The top ten Republican recipients of health sector cash in 2008 *combined* don't even equal Obama.

But the most telling comment is Olbermann's baseless assumption—he merely implies it, as if it's so obvious it doesn't need to be stated—that "what Obama's done" is detrimental to the health insurers, the drug makers, and the hospitals.

What Obama had already done by that point was to expand the State Children's Health Insurance Plan—a move supported by health insurers, drug makers, and hospitals, which all stood to gain more subsidies. As previously mentioned, he had also defended insurers' interests against John McCain's proposal to tax employer-based insurance. Moreover, Obama's healthcare reform, with its individual mandate, employer mandate, and ever-more health sector subsidies, was already shaping up to be a nice gift to the drug makers and the insurers, too. And by the time of Olbermann's rant, Obama was already backing away from the public option.

Imagine the outrage among the HMOs! *We donated to this guy, and now he's proposing to subsidize our customers and force everyone to buy our product!*

WAL-MART BECOMES A LIBERAL HERO

Wal-Mart, the largest U.S. employer besides the government, was one of Obama's many "unlikely allies" on healthcare reform. The company announced in early July that it was joining with a liberal group and a labor union to back the employer mandate— a federal requirement that all companies provide decent health insurance to workers.

One writer in *The Hill* newspaper exclaimed, "The decision by Wal-Mart to break away from the Chamber and its ilk marks the first visible crack in the business coalition on healthcare reform."[27] Somehow, every one of the countless Big Business embraces of Obama's Big Government policies is heralded as a groundbreaking surprise.

Wal-Mart was partnering with the Service Employees International Union and the Center for American Progress (CAP), a nonprofit organization dedicated to advancing Obama's agenda. Liberal writer Matt Yglesias, who worked and blogged for CAP, acknowledged that other businesses were supporting Obama on healthcare, declaring this "an important sign of change in the air."[28]

Presumably, Wal-Mart had "changed" from the previous summer, when Yglesias, working for the *Atlantic* at the time, wrote that Wal-Mart did business "like the mafia" and went around "break[ing] a few kneecaps" of its employees.[29] (Or maybe it was Yglesias who had changed—CAP, his new employer, had received at least $500,000 from Wal-Mart, according to Wal-Mart's website.)[30]

But, in an important way, Wal-Mart really hadn't changed at all. As early as 2006, Wal-Mart had been lobbying for this sort of government intervention into healthcare. Noting the "unlikely alliance" between the SEIU and Wal-Mart, a 2007 *Washington Post* article reported that Wal-Mart CEO Lee Scott had announced improved health coverage for employees, "but he also wanted help from government leaders and other groups to make substantive changes to the country's health policies."[31]

What sort of help? Government mandates that would pinch smaller competitors. Michael Cannon, a healthcare expert at the libertarian Cato Institute, in a 2009 blog post described his reaction when a Wal-Mart lobbyist told him in 2006 that the retailer supported an employer mandate:

I couldn't believe what I was hearing. Wal-Mart is a capitalist success story. At the time of our conversation, this lobbyist was helping Wal-Mart fight off employer-mandate legislation in dozens of states. Those measures were specifically designed to hurt Wal-Mart, and were underwritten by the unions and union shops that were losing jobs and business to Wal-Mart.

But it all became clear when the lobbyist explained the reason for Wal-Mart's position: "Target's health-benefits costs are lower."[32]

Wal-Mart was employing the *Overhead Smash*. Healthcare costs are one of the largest elements of a company's overhead. And Wal-Mart employs 1.4 million workers in the United States, compared to just 350,000 for Target. But Wal-Mart self-insures, meaning it acts as the health insurer to most of its employees, taking in the premium payments and paying the doctors. For most employers, this is a waste of resources, but Wal-Mart is large enough that it turns into a net savings by keeping out a profit-seeking middleman.

So Wal-Mart buys healthcare for its workers, which gives it another chance to do what it does best—getting low prices from its suppliers through its massive buying power.

Target can undercut Wal-Mart's healthcare costs only by offering inferior benefits—less coverage, higher premiums, and higher deductibles. If the government requires Target to offer the same benefits Wal-Mart does, it's raising Target's costs but not Wal-Mart's. Even if an employer mandate set a minimum benefit higher than Wal-Mart's current benefit, Target would suffer more than Wal-Mart—and that would be a net gain for Wal-Mart.

In this light, Wal-Mart's backing an employer mandate in health insurance starts to look like exactly the sort of cut-throat competition for which many liberals attack the retailer—but this time, rather than being maligned as "knee-capping," it is heralded as "change."

FLASHBACK TO HILLARYCARE: HMOS VS HARRY AND LOUISE

Throughout the 2009 healthcare debate, observers frequently recalled the role of "Harry and Louise" in killing Hillary Clinton's 1993 healthcare reform plan.

Harry and Louise were a fictional couple in television commercials who would sit around their kitchen table discussing Clinton's plan. Under proposed government programs and regulations, costs would go up and choices would contract, the ads warned. The everyman and everywoman concerns expressed by Harry and Louise stoked public skepticism of Clinton's plan and helped convince Congress to kill it.

Clinton had rolled out her plan in September 1993 with decent public support, but opposition grew as Congress debated the plan and Harry and Louise critiqued it. In a November 1993 speech, the First Lady used Harry and Louise as her foil, painting the ads as a Big Business ploy against the people:

> What you don't get told in the ad is that it is paid for by insurance companies who think their way is the better way. They like what is happening today.
>
> ...Now, they have the gall to run TV ads that there is a better way, the very industry that has brought us to the brink of bankruptcy because of the way that they have financed health care. It is time for you and for every American to stand up and say to the insurance industry, "Enough is enough. We want our health care system back."[33]

Drawing applause from the crowd of pediatricians, Hillary painted a useful and believable picture of reformers-vs.-industry—a theme Obama would trot out sixteen years later. But while Hillary was painting the industry with a broad brush, the truth of the matter was much less simple—and less useful to the Clintons.

The group running the Harry and Louise ads in late 1993 was the Health Insurance Association of America. So, yes, Harry and Louise did represent some health insurers—but not all of them.

A *New York Times* article in May 1993 explained the dynamic: "The five giants [Prudential, Cigna, Aetna, Metropolitan Life and Travelers] recently broke off from the Health Insurance Association of America, their longtime trade group in Washington, to form their own organization, the Coalition for Managed Competition, which is closer to Administration thinking on most issues."[34]

In short, the biggest insurers had become health maintenance organizations, or HMOs. Smaller insurers still operated as traditional insurance companies rather than healthcare managers. But healthcare managers were exactly what HillaryCare prescribed. The *Times* explained:

> Analysts predict that such a plan would drive tens or hundreds of thousands of health insurance agents out of their jobs and speed the pace at which Americans are compelled to join health maintenance organizations.
>
> In the end, they say, the health-care changes would also come as a tremendous boon to the industry's giants: Prudential, Cigna, Aetna, Metropolitan Life and Travelers as well as the nonprofit Blue Cross and Blue Shield plans. Those companies stand to benefit because they have already invested billions of dollars in health maintenance organizations, a way of controlling costs that is favored by the President's health policy planners.[35]

So the insurance industry was split. The big guys—the HMOs we now all know—wanted Hillary Clinton's "managed competition." The smaller guys wanted a free market. The smaller guys pooled their money and attacked HillaryCare, and Hillary fired back at "the insurance companies."

But when this story gets told today, it is upended to serve the interests of Big Government advocates—the story contrasts the supposed opposition of Big Business in 1993 to its more helpful role in Obama's reform efforts. This is the *Change-Is-in-the-Air* narrative. The *L.A. Times* was one of many outlets to tell the story this way:

> Some may find it hard to believe that the U.S. health insurance industry supports making major changes to the nation's healthcare system.
>
> The industry, after all, scuttled President Clinton's healthcare overhaul bid with ads featuring "Harry and Louise" fretting about change.[36]

This sort of faulty history is endemic in politicians' and journalists' discussion of Big Business and Big Government. Typically when Big Business lobbies for Big Government, the media don't notice. When the media do notice the dynamic, they declare it some sort of "strange bedfellows," "an interesting twist," or a dramatic shift from past industry behavior.

For pro-regulation and pro-Obama writers, this narrative is useful. It allows them to say, "This time things are different," "This time, everyone *knows* we need reform," or "Obama really is a uniter."

However, the "uniting" factor is not Obama, but the profit that his Big Government policies promise.

SCHIP: CORPORATE WELFARE "FOR THE CHILDREN"

Even before the heated healthcare reform battles of summer 2009, Obamanomics was at work in the health sector, expanding government and profiting Big Business.

One of President Obama's first actions in office was expanding a subsidy for drug makers and insurance companies. It's called the State Children's Health Insurance Program, or SCHIP.

Republicans created SCHIP in 1997 to cover health insurance for low-income children whose families were not poor enough to qualify for Medicare.[37] Although clearly a Big Government program (the federal government spent $40 billion on it in the first ten years), it was acceptable to Republicans for two reasons: (1) states administered the program; and (2) it subsidized private plans instead of putting additional Americans on government healthcare. Fighting off a single-payer plan or a government-run health system, such as Britain's, has been a consistent stance of the GOP as well as the health insurance industry.

The federal government covered somewhere from 65 percent to 83 percent of the cost of subsidizing the children's healthcare, with state governments picking up the rest.

As SCHIP's authorization expired in 2007, its reauthorization turned into a two-year skirmish between Democrats, who wanted to dramatically expand the bill to cover more people, and President Bush, who favored a more modest expansion.

In August 2007, Congress passed a bill to expand the program by loosening eligibility standards, providing incentives for states to enroll more customers, and making it easier for states to enroll higher-income families.[38] Funded by raising cigarette taxes, the measure was vetoed by President Bush, who argued the expansion violated the program's original purpose. Democrats passed it a second time, and Bush vetoed it again. Eventually Democrats settled on passing a temporary reauthorization of the program until March 2009, when there would be a new president. And sure enough, Congress passed a bill expanding SCHIP in January 2009, and President Obama signed it as soon as he took office.

Liberal MSNBC host Rachel Maddow commented on *Hardball*: "This is a bill that expands private health insurance for poor kids and pays for it by raising the cigarette tax. Like, you can't make this a prettier bill unless you added puppies to it or something."[39] And she was right. Those vetoes from Bush's pen—and the Republican votes to sustain them—opened up the GOP to relentless Democratic and media attacks as tools of Big Business. *Washington Post* writer Jeffrey Birnbaum claimed SCHIP was defeated by "the tobacco lobby and America's Health Insurance Plans [AHIP], the leading trade organization for health insurance companies."[40]

Birnbaum was correct that AHIP, the powerful Washington voice for health insurers such as Blue Cross/Blue Shield, Cigna, and United Health, was lobbying heavily on the issue of SCHIP expansion. But he apparently missed the fact that AHIP was among the earliest, most consistent, and most influential lobbyists *supporting* the expansion.

There was a kernel of truth in Birnbaum's claim: AHIP opposed one version of a SCHIP expansion because it was funded by trimming a subsidy to insurers called Medicare Advantage. But Birnbaum's column implied AHIP opposed SCHIP outright. This was objectively not the case.

AHIP had been pushing this policy since just after the 2006 election. Back then, AHIP was applauded by no less than House Speaker Nancy Pelosi, who declared, "There are parts of the proposal by America's Health Insurance Plans (AHIP) that I strongly endorse, particularly those relating to SCHIP and Medicaid."[41] Two weeks later, AHIP lobbied congressional staffers for the expansion.[42] When then-Congressman Rahm Emanuel in February 2007 introduced the "Healthy Kids Act" including SCHIP expansion and reauthorization, AHIP president Karen Ignagni stood on stage with the bill's sponsors and hailed the act.[43] And an

AHIP press release praised the Senate's approval of the bill in August 2007.[44]

It was the same with the drug makers. PhRMA published a "Platform for a Healthy America" in July 2008 which, among other things, called for just the sort of SCHIP expansion Democrats were pushing.[45]

But it took Obamanomics to deliver the industry's wish. President Obama signed SCHIP expansion in his first week in office. (The bill, of course, in no way cramped the existing Medicare subsidies for private insurers.) PhRMA applauded this event as a "tremendous victory for millions of low-income, uninsured American families, and, indeed, for all Americans—for we are the friends and neighbors of those who will be helped."

But of course, PhRMA is the *lobbyist* of those who will be helped. That is, drug makers like the program because it provides government subsidies for people to buy prescription drugs. If you can get taxpayers to funnel money to your consumers, why wouldn't you support it?

AHIP's stake in the fight is equally obvious. SCHIP is a subsidy for people to buy insurance. Expanding it expands the pipeline from taxpayers to HMOs.

But this entire public campaign by Big Business for SCHIP expansion was utterly ignored by nearly every newspaper. For example, the *Washington Post*, which carried Birnbaum's column blaming AHIP for SCHIP's defeat, never once, according to a Nexis search, mentioned that the bill had key support from the health insurance and pharmaceutical industries.

The *Post* did not completely ignore the lobbying effort in favor of SCHIP, though. In a January 19, 2009, piece titled "Children Get Into the Spirit of Promoting Health Reform," the *Post* reported how "almost 400 kids" had submitted artwork as part of a project to support SCHIP reauthorization. There was no word on whether any of those kids' college funds or inheritances were dependent on drug company profits.

Federal lobbying reports show a virtual army of big businesses pushing for SCHIP expansion. Drug makers and biotech companies that took the Obama–Emanuel–Pelosi side against Bush included Amgen, Abbot Laboratories, Eli Lilly, Pfizer, Bristol-Myers Squibb, Genentech, and others. Insurers who lobbied for the bill include Blue Cross and Blue Shield, Wellpoint, Cigna, Humana, Coventry Health Care, Assurant, United Health, and HealthSouth.

This sort of lobbying effort for a federal subsidy program might have garnered attention and scorn from the press were it not a bill "for the children."

To be sure, simply because Big Business stands to gain from SCHIP expansion doesn't mean it's bad. Kids being sick, after all, is a bad thing. Helping poor kids is good, too.

But there are costs to expanding the program. The obvious cost is expanding federal spending in a time of deficits. Federal spending on SCHIP had already doubled from 2001 to 2006, without even expanding eligibility.[46] And this increased spending wouldn't simply be the cost of insuring the uninsured: the subsidies would provide incentives for families (recall, this includes middle-class families) to stop paying for their own insurance and to stick taxpayers with the tab. The Congressional Budget Office wrote in 2007, "Some parents who would have otherwise had family coverage through their employer might decline it for their children—or might decline coverage altogether—if their children are eligible for SCHIP."[47] The CBO also noted SCHIP could encourage some employers to reduce their family health insurance coverage or end it altogether

But if families shift from paying for their own healthcare to having the taxpayers pay for their healthcare, that's just fine with the insurers, who get paid either way.

THE INSIDER INSIDE THE WHITE HOUSE

"They get the access while you get to write a letter," candidate Obama charged about the "special interests" and the lobbyists. "They think they own this government, but we're here today to take it back. The time for that politics is over. It's time to turn the page."

But Obama didn't turn the page. Instead, he brought in Tom Daschle.

A close confidant of the president, Daschle was introduced in August as "the architect of President Obama's health care plan."[48] Then Obama tried to appoint him secretary of health and human services. When Daschle's tax problems derailed his nomination, the president turned to him as an unofficial—but close—health-care advisor.

But Daschle has other interests as well: namely, he's a paid consultant at a lobbying firm representing some of the biggest insurers and other health sector businesses. The *New York Times* reported in August 2009 that the Obama administration doesn't seem particularly concerned about Daschle's close ties to corporate America:

> [Daschle] talks constantly with top White House advisers, many of whom previously worked for him.
>
> He still speaks frequently to the president, who met with him as recently as Friday morning in the Oval Office. And he remains a highly paid policy adviser to hospital, drug, pharmaceutical and other health care industry clients of Alston & Bird, the law and lobbying firm.[49]

Daschle is not technically a lobbyist—he hasn't registered under the Lobbying Disclosure Act. That means by law he cannot make "lobbying contacts"—speaking on behalf of clients to public officials about policy. But he can advise clients on strategies for lobbying. He can also advise his Alston & Bird colleagues—lobbyists—on how to lobby. Finally, he can still talk to government officials about policy—just not on behalf of his clients.

So, Tom Daschle works at a lobbying firm, gets paid by health industry clients for his work on health policy, and advises Obama on healthcare reform—but he's still not a lobbyist.

Allies of Daschle and the White House insist his advice to Obama is simply on behalf of the nation—not his clients. But *Times* reporter David Kirkpatrick noted an overlap in interests.

> Now the White House and Senate Democratic leaders appear to be moving toward a blueprint for overhauling the health system, centered on nonprofit insurance cooperatives, that Mr. Daschle began promoting two months ago as a politically feasible alternative to a more muscular government-run insurance plan.
>
> It is an idea that happens to dovetail with the interests of many Alston & Bird clients, like the insurance giant United-Health and the Tennessee Hospital Association. And it is drawing angry cries of accommodation from more liberal House Democrats bent on including a public insurance plan.[50]

Straddling the shriveling gap between the worlds of Big Government and Big Business, Tom Daschle is a natural fit to forward the Obamanomics agenda. And when Obama touted Republicans backing reform, he pointed to Daschle's Alston & Bird colleague Bob Dole—a healthcare lobbyist now—among other revolving-door Republicans like Bill Frist and Tommy Thompson currently in the pay of the health industry.

WHITHER OBAMACARE?

As this book went to press, the final shape of ObamaCare was not yet clear, but the trajectory was. As the *Times* reported, the White House was backing away from the proposals that would hurt the insurers (the government option, for instance), and pushing new proposals that would subsidize them (the individual mandate). Even the regulations that could reduce insurer profits were welcomed by the insurance lobby. Among other reasons, these regulations could keep out new competitors.

Again, Obama didn't set out to help the insurers. But as long as he insisted on Big Government as the means to reform, a corporate welfare package was inevitable.

CHAPTER 5

DREAMS FROM MY PHARMA

HEALTHCARE REFORM, STEM CELLS, AND OBAMA'S PRESCRIPTION FOR DRUG COMPANY PROFITS

"The reason that we're not getting things done," Barack Obama said in July 2007, "is not because we don't have good plans or good policy prescriptions. The reason is because it's not our agenda that's being moved forward in Washington—it's the agenda of the oil companies, the insurance companies, the drug companies, the special interests who dominate on a day-to-day basis in terms of legislative activity."[1]

This was a common Obama campaign theme, and the drug makers were a standard bad guy. Obama even aired a campaign ad focusing on their deal that forced Medicare to pay them higher prices. "The pharmaceutical industry wrote into the prescription drug plan that Medicare could not negotiate with drug companies," Obama said in the ad. He went on to highlight the pernicious effects of Washington's revolving door: "And you know what? The chairman of the committee, who pushed the law through, went to work for the pharmaceutical industry making $2 million a year."[2]

One year later, that same former committee chairman, Billy Tauzin, sat in the White House's Roosevelt Room with Obama's chief of staff, Rahm Emanuel, who was Tauzin's former congressional colleague. A handful of drug company executives were there, too.[3] Tauzin and Emanuel worked out a deal in which, in the words of the *L.A. Times*, the president gave "assurances that there would be no government price-setting in Medicare Part D, the drug program for seniors." In other words, Obama made the exact deal he denounced Republicans for having made—and sealed it with the same lobbyist he had condemned for going through the revolving door between politics and lobbying.

Tauzin in fact became a close Obama ally in the push for healthcare reform. By the end of fall 2009, Tauzin's lobbying group—the Pharmaceutical Researchers and Manufacturers of America—had lined up $150 million for ads on cable television supporting Obama's reform program.[4]

Candidate Obama had used drug makers as a symbol of corporate evil and lobbyist corruption. *President* Obama used them as a partner in the push for more government control over healthcare, even though that partnership meant higher prices for consumers, higher taxes, and more profits for an already lucrative industry.

Obama's gifts to pharmaceuticals went beyond the pay-offs to get them on board for "reform." The reform itself would increase their profits through subsidies funded by taxpayers and mandates imposed on individuals and employers. Even outside the reform debate, Obama helped the industry with his agenda of tearing down Bush-era pro-life regulations, including ethical limits on federal funding of embryo research.

After the drug makers proved a handy foil for Obama during the campaign, they also proved an indispensible partner once he was in the White House.

DRUG PUSHERS

Any industry worth its salt has at least one industry-wide lobbying group based in the Washington area. Oil companies have the American Petroleum Institute. Health insurers have a group called America's Health Insurance Plans. Airlines have the Air Transportation Association. These industry groups comprise much of the top echelon of "special interests" in Washington. They hire away the most influential congressional staff to press their case, and they spend millions every year on influence.

But the king of all the industry trade groups is the Pharmaceutical Researchers and Manufacturers of America, abbreviated as PhRMA and pronounced "pharma." In the first six months of 2009, PhRMA spent $13 million on lobbying.[5] The runner-up trade group was the National Association of Realtors, which spent $9.6 million. That is less than the lobbying spending of drug maker Pfizer, alone.

Led by Billy Tauzin, PhRMA employs more than twenty in-house lobbyists and also retains more than forty outside lobbying firms.[6] Their outside lobbyists include former senators Trent Lott and John Breaux,[7] as well as David Castagnetti, the former chief of staff for Senate Finance Committee Chairman Max Baucus.[8]

But that's just PhRMA. There's plenty more lobbying firepower in the drug industry.

First, there's the Biotechnology Industry Organization (BIO). At $3.7 million in lobbying expenditures in the first half of 2009,[9] it's one of the top players on K Street. Like PhRMA, BIO is run by a former congressman, Jim Greenwood, a Pennsylvania Republican whose pro-choice record meshed well with BIO's focus on subsidized embryonic stem-cell research. Then there are the impressive lobbying operations of the individual drug companies. With $11.7 million, Pfizer was the number four company overall in lobbying spending in the first half of 2009.[10]

All told, according to the Center for Responsive Politics, the "Pharmaceuticals/Health Products" industry has spent more money on lobbying since 1998 than any other industry. The industry's $1.7 billion—with a "b"—over that period outpaces the second-place industry (insurance) by a third. Drug companies have spent twice as much on lobbying since 1998 as have oil and gas companies. The drug industry's lobbying tab is more than the combined tab of telecoms, Wall Street, and the defense industry.[11]

While later chapters will argue that Goldman Sachs and General Electric are the quintessential "special interests," pharmaceuticals is the *industry* that's most enmeshed with Washington power. So, when Obama brags that he's working with "even the pharmaceutical industry,"[12] that's not saying much. Pharma is always working with politicians. That's why they get their way. And they're getting their way under Obamanomics.

The media, however, have not yet realized that. While attacking Republican opponents of healthcare reform as industry shills in July 2009, liberal writer Jonathan Chait asserted:

> It's not that every conservative apparatchik is walking around Washington toting a suitcase of Pharma cash and a conspiratorial grin. Intellectual corruption doesn't work that way. The health care industry has spent vast sums to influence politicians and opinion leaders, mostly on the right.[13]

There's some truth to that—the GOP *is* too susceptible to industry input. But if that's what concerns Chait, then he should denounce Barack Obama more than anyone. Obama raised more from the pharmaceutical industry in the 2008 election—$1.1 million—than did any candidate in history. He raised $3.57 from drug makers for every dollar John McCain raised. He raised more from the industry than George W. Bush did in both his elections combined. Executives and employees of Pfizer, the top giver in the industry, gave more than four times as much to Obama as to McCain.

Obama is the all-time champion of raising money from pharmaceuticals. This does not mean Obama is "owned" by the drug makers, or that he is doing their bidding. It does indicate, however, that he and the industry are on good terms, and it ought to discredit arguments that reform opponents are just Pharma shills.

THE DONUT HOLE

Since the election, Tauzin has morphed into the president's partner. He has been invited to the White House half a dozen times in recent months. There, he says, he eventually secured an agreement that the administration wouldn't try to overturn the very Medicare drug policy that Obama had criticized on the campaign trail.

"The White House blessed it," Tauzin said.[14]

The *L.A. Times* reported this part of the deal-making between the White House and the drug industry. The issue goes back to the bill Tauzin shepherded through Congress in 2003 that created a prescription drug benefit for Medicare.

The drug benefit effectively subsidizes drug makers by allowing seniors to stick taxpayers with the tab for their prescription drugs. Some Democrats had tried to control costs by allowing

Medicare to behave as an insurer does, or as Wal-Mart does, and negotiate an agreeable price. Just as Wal-Mart uses its massive buying power to get discounts, some lawmakers wanted Medicare to haggle as well. But Tauzin's bill ruled that out—the private insurers administering the program would negotiate the prices instead.

Ending this favor to drug makers was one of Obama's reform proposals: "Obama will repeal the ban on direct negotiation with drug companies and use the resulting savings," his campaign healthcare plan stated.[15] The change would cut costs for taxpayers by cutting into the profits of an industry that averages more than 15 percent profit margins.[16]

But the cash-cow of Medicare Part D was sacred for PhRMA. In fact, when the House Commerce Committee came out with its bill in late July, PhRMA voiced a rare complaint about reform legislation—because it would have allowed Medicare Part D price negotiation.[17]

But Obama was already asking the drug makers to make a sacrifice, and so Tauzin was in a position to make his own demands on the president.

Obama had declared a goal of finding hundreds of billions of dollars of savings in the healthcare system—private sector as well as government. He was calling on industries to develop proposals that would reduce costs. If Obama would drop the Medicare negotiation proposal, the drug makers had their offer—drug discounts for some seniors in the Medicare "donut hole."

Here's how the donut hole takes shape: Medicare Part D subsidizes the first $2,500 or so of a senior citizen's prescription costs in any year, with customers paying only a fraction. A second sort of subsidy covers "catastrophic" costs—expenses over $5,700 per year. In between, there is no subsidy—it's a "donut hole" where you're on your own. Tauzin's offer was to sell drugs to seniors in the donut hole at half off. The White House called it an "agreement by pharmaceutical companies to contribute to the health reform effort."[18]

Slate's Timothy Noah had a different view:

[I]n securing $80 billion in savings over 10 years, the White House is forgoing what could be as much as $156 billion over the same time period. That's what a 2008 report by energy and commerce's investigations subcommittee calculated to be the savings if Medicare were permitted to buy drugs at the same rates negotiated by the (much smaller) Medicaid program.[19]

And these donut-hole discounts really don't seem to be much of a sacrifice at all for drug makers, because of the odd pricing in the drug industry.

The saying in the industry is that the first pill costs a billion dollars, and after that they're a penny a piece. A company can spend hundreds of millions of dollars experimenting, developing, testing, and bringing a drug to market. Then they also spend hundreds of millions of dollars on all the drugs that don't work out. So coming up with a useful, safe, legal drug is very expensive.

But actually producing, packaging, and shipping the pill, for most drugs, barely costs a thing. Economists call this "high fixed costs and low variable costs." Another way of putting it: the marginal cost of each new pill produced and delivered is near zero.

Back to the donut hole. The relevant question is this: are the drug makers giving a discount to existing customers, or are they winning new customers with their low prices? The answer is probably a mixture of both. Seniors who could already afford their drugs would see their costs go down. Seniors who were saving money by leaving their less urgent prescriptions unfilled—or those who bought the generic version—would be more willing to buy Pfizer's drugs after the discount.

So some of those billions in discounts rope in new customers— new customers paying fifty cents for a pill that normally sells for a dollar, but which only costs the drug maker a penny to produce.

If drug makers simply announced they would charge more to people when they're being subsidized and less to people paying for it themselves, the companies could probably be sued for price discrimination. But when such an arrangement is hammered out with the White House—well, it's "reform."

BLAME CANADA

Americans pay much more for their prescription drugs than do people in other countries. We pay a market rate for our drugs while other governments set price controls. Drug makers are happy to sell into these price-controlled markets as long as they can charge sky-high prices here in the United States.

So Pfizer sells its drugs to Canadian retailers at low prices. If those retailers could then sell those drugs over the Internet into the United States or sell them to U.S.-based CVS stores, Americans could get huge discounts. But federal laws outlaw such "reimportation."

This was allegedly the subject of another Obama-Tauzin drug deal. According to the *L.A. Times*, Tauzin claimed Obama promised him not only to reject Medicare drug price negotiations, but also to abandon a campaign proposal to end the drug reimportation ban.[20] White House officials haven't admitted to making this offer, and it's impossible to know for sure because these talks were all conducted behind closed doors. But Obama has indeed stopped pushing to lift the reimportation ban, and the proposal is absent from all the Democrats' reform bills.

At the very least, we can conclude Obama didn't live up to his promise of transparency. During the campaign he vowed, "We'll have the negotiations televised on C-SPAN, so that people can see who is making arguments on behalf of their constituents, and who are making arguments on behalf of the drug companies or the insurance companies."[21]

Whatever Obama promised, it was enough to get PhRMA on board with "reform." And the provisions of the reform itself offer plenty of other sweeteners for the industry.

"REFORM" AND THE DRUG MAKERS

"And when you've got doctors, nurses, hospitals, the AARP," the president began, setting up the punchline, "and *even the drug companies*, as well as major employers like Wal-Mart, saying now's the time for us to bring about some change, I think it's time for us to bring about some change" [emphasis added].[22]

Apparently, we're supposed to be surprised the drug companies are signing onto "reform." And some indeed were surprised. Trying to make sense of it all, liberal columnist Paul Krugman wrote in May 2009, "What's presumably going on here is that key interest groups have realized that health care reform is going to happen no matter what they do, and that aligning themselves with the Party of No will just deny them a seat at the table."[23]

This *industry-just-wants-a-seat-at-the-table* line is a standard explanation by those who don't understand Obamanomics— writers who can't see that Big Government is often the easiest road to bigger corporate profits. You'd expect the esteemed Mr. Krugman, though, to get it—after all, he has a Nobel Prize in economics. But for liberals like Krugman, the *seat-at-the-table* explanation allows one to hold onto the gratifying myth that reform is a battle against Big Business.

The real dynamic, however, was obvious to those with their eyes on the bottom line. *La Merie*, a "business intelligence" publisher, observed that "Obama's new universal healthcare program will increase demand for drugs, both branded and generic, [and] reduce the need for free drug programs due to universal healthcare coverage."[24]

And indeed, Obama's reform offered myriad gifts to the drug makers. Let's start with the general proposition behind Obama's reform: get everybody on health insurance. Tauzin spoke about this on CNBC in March 2009:

> **Tauzin:** By and large, think about what this plan does. This plan talks about providing comprehensive health insurance to people who don't have it—that means to patients who can't take our medicines because they can't afford it. $650 billion spent to better insure Americans for the products we make. That ought to be a very optimistic and positive message for everyone who is interested in our sector of the economy.
>
> **Mike Huckman:** Just to clarify, then, are you saying that if there is some kind of universal health care plan where prescription drugs are more broadly available, and they're available at a cheaper price, that your sector may make up in higher prescription volume and sales what it might lose on price?
>
> **Tauzin:** Oh, absolutely, Mike. Think about this: Almost half of the prescriptions that are written today go unfilled. And they're unfilled primarily because people don't have adequate insurance—they have no insurance, or their insurance doesn't cover our products the way it covers hospitalizations. . . . We're going to quarrel over price controls . . . but we also believe more people ought to have good insurance.[25]

We heard the same note from David Brennan, CEO of Astra-Zeneca and new chairman of PhRMA, at PhRMA's 2009 annual conference: "I'm an advocate of free-market-based health care solutions. But," (when CEOs praise the free market, there's almost always a *but*) "within that framework, I support appropriate government efforts to protect people whose health care needs aren't met by the private marketplace."[26]

Those "appropriate government efforts" apparently include a few proposals included in the various reform bills. The first is expansion of Medicaid—which currently covers only the poor—to cover more people. Second is subsidizing the health insurance premiums of middle-class or poor people. Both these policies, in effect, force taxpayers to pay for the medical treatment—including the prescription drug purchases—of more people. This is good for PhRMA's member companies.

The third and fourth proposals that could expand insurance are the individual and employer mandates—federal laws requiring employers to offer health insurance to workers and requiring everybody to be insured. These mandates would set minimum standards for insurance—what the insurance must cover to fulfill the mandate. Tauzin is lobbying to ensure that prescription drug coverage is mandated.

Requiring everyone to pay for prescription drug insurance for themselves and their employees doesn't immediately drive money toward prescription drugs, but in the end it does. If I have a choice between buying prescription drug coverage or, say, signing up for Zip Car, I might choose Zip Car. Then when my doctor prescribes me a pain killer that costs $200 a month, I might pass and stock up on Advil instead.

But if Billy Tauzin and Barack Obama *force* me to buy the drug insurance, I'm much more likely to fill the prescription. It's a variation on the Obamanomics tactic called *Making an Offer You Can't Refuse.*

True, under Obama's reform Pfizer might only get $50 from me, but it will collect the other $150 from the insurance company. And even that $50 may be too much as far as the drug makers are concerned. "Quite frankly," PhRMA's Brennan said at the annual conference, "Americans deserve co-pay reform."[27] That means government should force insurers—both through the mandates and through regulation—to have lower prescription-drug co-pays.

"Reform," then, includes policies that both lure and force more people to buy prescription drug insurance. It appears, Mr. Krugman, that PhRMA doesn't just have a seat at the table—it's the guest of honor.

OBAMA ON THE PILL

Barack Obama promised he wouldn't take campaign contributions from lobbyists. And he meant it. At the end of each month, the campaign refunded thousands of dollars in lobbyists' contributions. One such donor was G. Lawrence Atkins, a lobbyist for drugmaker Schering-Plough. He had given $300 to Obama's campaign, and on May 31, 2008, the campaign returned it to him.[28]

Even if it hadn't been returned, Atkins' contribution would have been merely a drop in a very large bucket. But Atkins is worth noting because of the overlap between Obama's agenda—as both senator and president—and Schering-Plough's. According to Schering-Plough's disclosure form, in recent years Atkins lobbied on Medicaid issues, including "legislative proposals effecting Medicaid 'average manufacturers' price.' "[29]

One such proposal before Congress at the time was Senator Obama's "Prevention Through Affordable Access Act,"[30] a 2007 bill aimed at boosting the price Medicaid pays Schering-Plough.

Obama's bill never went anywhere until Obama became president. Then it was stuck in the 2009 omnibus appropriations bill, and Obama signed it into law.[31]

The liberal media hailed the measure as a victory for women's rights. "This victory for common sense follows a string of positive steps already taken by President Obama to dismantle his predecessor's assault on women's reproductive health and freedom,"[32] applauded the *New York Times* editorial page. Other standard media accounts claimed the measure "will allow pharmaceutical companies to once again supply college-health clinics with discounted birth-control pills and other contraceptives."[33]

But this is misleading. There was no law keeping drug makers from selling their contraceptives to college students at discounted prices—known as "nominal pricing." The problem for the drug makers was that, under a 2005 law, if drug makers offered students a discount on contraceptives, they would also have to slightly discount that same drug to Medicaid. Thanks to President Obama, they aren't "penalized" by Medicare anymore for offering college discounts.

While Planned Parenthood was the leading lobbyist for Obama's 2007 bill, the contraceptive makers also leaned on Congress for this favor, lobbying reports show. Schering-Plough particularly had skin in the game. The company makes NuvaRing, a contraceptive device for which there is no generic.

Recall the factors in pharmaceutical pricing discussed above. College girls might not buy the NuvaRing at all were it offered to them at full price, which means Schering-Plough is happy to discount it for them. Even a low price will cover the miniscule cost of production, and, hey, that's one more college-educated customer you've got on the hook before age twenty.

The government—Medicaid—is a different sort of customer. Medicaid is going to buy the products no matter what. The key here for Schering-Plough is getting the maximum price out of Medicaid. That is, out of the unwitting taxpayer.

Obama's 2007 "Prevention Through Affordable Access Act" offered Schering-Plough and the other name-brand contraceptive makers just what they wanted. When he signed it into law in 2009, it was another benefit of Obamanomics to the drug makers.

OBAMA "DEPOLITICIZES" SCIENCE BY EXPANDING THE GOVERNMENT'S ROLE

On a windy March day, Will Keating, a pudgy red-headed baby, stole the show on Capitol Hill.[34] During a press conference on stem cell research, Congressman Chris Smith, a pro-life New Jersey Republican, made the mistake of going on stage with the wee one, who got all the attention. Also getting plenty of attention that day was the stock ticker symbol STEM. More than 26 million shares of Stem Cells, Inc., sold in one day, boosting the stock price 43 percent.[35]

And these two—Will Keating and Stem Cells, Inc.—were getting noticed for the same reason.

Stem Cells, Inc., was rallying on President Obama's announcement that he was opening up billions of dollars of taxpayer funding for the sort of research on which the company depends for profits—research on stem cells harvested from human embryos. Obama's policy would not pay for the creation of new humans for use in experiments, but it provided funding for the destruction of healthy humans who happened to be suspended in the embryonic stage—the "byproducts of in-vitro fertilization," as Planned Parenthood puts it.[36]

Will Keating's parents also depended on the "byproducts of in-vitro fertilization," because Will was recently such a "byproduct." He had been created in a laboratory from the sperm and egg of a couple that, presumably, had trouble conceiving. But, apparently, that couple had chosen one of Will's tiny siblings, rather than him, to implant in the mother's uterus. Will was luckier than other embryos in the lab, however—he was adopted by the Keating couple and born to Mrs. Keating.

Pharmaceutical companies want to use embryos like Will Keating circa 2007 for research and development, and no federal law has ever prevented them from doing so. But Obama opened the spigot for taxpayers to fund research on Will's embryonic brothers and sisters.

"We need to give credit to the administration for living up to their promise to keep politics out of science," the *Washington Post* quoted one supporter.[37] It's an odd claim that increasing the federal role in embryonic stem-cell research is "keep[ing] politics out of science." Recall, research on human embryos and their stem cells never was illegal. Obama's move simply provided more taxpayer funding for the work.

It's also hard to buy the "depoliticizing science" spin when you realize this decision was a major lobbying priority for the biotech and pharmaceutical companies.

"We fully support and are enthusiastic about President Obama's decision to allow the [National Institutes of Health] to fund embryonic stem cell research," said Jim Greenwood, a former congressman who became the president of the Biotechnology Industry Organization.[38] The previous year, BIO (which has more than two dozen in-house lobbyists) spent $7.7 million on lobbying the federal government,[39] with stem-cell research on its lobbying agenda every quarter for three years.[40]

At the dawn of the Obama administration, BIO hired two Democratic lobbying firms: Peck, Madigan, Jones & Stewart;[41] and Bryan Cave, LLC.[42] Both firms lobbied on stem-cell funding among other issues. BIO's lobbyists at these firms included Jeff Peck, the former Democratic counsel for the Senate Judiciary Committee, and former Clinton White House lawyer Broderick Johnson.

During the Bush administration and the early days of the Obama administration, a handful of pharma and biotech companies lobbied on the issue, too. Novartis,[43] AstraZeneca,[44] and some smaller stem-cell companies all included stem-cell research on their lobbying disclosure forms.

Biotech is among the most politically active industries. But somehow, acceding to their lobbying demands counts as "depoliticizing science."

HARRY AND LOUISE ON DRUGS

"Well, it looks like we may finally get health-care reform," Harry, a sexagenarian-looking man says, handing the daily paper to his wife. "It's about time," Louise responds, "because every day, more and more people are finding they can't afford health care."[45]

This was the same couple that had starred in commercials in 1993 and 1994 dedicated to defeating HillaryCare. Their return to television ads—this time *supporting* reform—was supposed to mark that Change really had come to Washington.

The conventional wisdom on healthcare reform, as discussed in the previous chapter, was that industry used Harry and Louise in 1993 and 1994 to defeat reform under Hillary Clinton. But then the Hope and Change of Barack Obama—and the undeniable facts of the market—had brought industry on board. "The participation of Harry and Louise in this ad campaign clearly symbolizes how different the health reform debate is this year compared to the past," said one of the executives behind the ads.[46]

But this official history left out some important distinctions. Remember, the 1994 Harry and Louise ads were only backed by the mid-sized insurers—the rest of the healthcare industry was undecided or supportive of an increased government role. And in 2009, Harry and Louise ads were sponsored by PhRMA, the drugmakers' lobby.

So the real Change was this: in 2009, Harry and Louise actually *were* mouthpieces for Big Business. And, as typical, Big Business saw it would profit from Obamanomics. As the new Louise says, "A little more cooperation, a little less politics, and we can get the job done this time."

Obama was perfectly willing to provide the "little more cooperation"—payoffs to the drug industry for their lobbyists' early and vocal support of healthcare reform, including $150 million for ads supporting his reform.

THE BIG MYTH: RACHEL MADDOW EDITION

The Big Myth that obfuscates the true nature of Obamanomics is that Big Business always resists government intrusion. Reporters and pundits assume that corporate lobbying is always geared toward reducing regulation.

One would think all the events this book has discussed—all information in the public domain—would disabuse journalists of their misconceptions. But the Big Myth lives on because it's useful for liberals in defending Obama's healthcare reform, promoting Big Government, and bashing corporations.

For a textbook example of peddling the Big Myth, let's look at an August 2009 broadcast by MSNBC's Rachel Maddow. For many nights, Maddow had dedicated segments of her show to arguing that anti-ObamaCare protestors were corporate shills. Then, on August 6, Maddow reported the pro-free market group FreedomWorks—run by former House majority leader Dick Armey, a Republican—was encouraging its supporters to go to

congressional townhalls and was providing talking points against
the Democrats' proposals. Maddow tried to connect some dots:

> In addition to fronting that group, Dick Armey is a senior pol-
> icy adviser at a law firm called DLA Piper. DLA Piper just hap-
> pens to have received $830,000 this year, so far, from a giant
> pharmaceutical firm called Medicines Company. This after the
> $1.5 million Medicines Company paid Mr. Armey's firm last
> year.
>
> The fact that Dick Armey and FreedomWorks are standing
> alongside regular Joes like Rick Scott [a former doctor leading
> the opposition to reform bills] to lead the charge against health
> care reform—could be just a coincidence. Or it could be a stark
> reminder of who we're dealing with here. Who is actively
> organizing the campaign against health care reform?
>
> . . . These are the pros, very well-compensated pros. They do
> this all the time. It's a P.R. industry. It's a lobbying industry. And
> they have a clear vested financial interest in seeing that the
> health care industry is not reformed—not now, not ever.
>
> But the prospect of healthcare reform is up against, is a big,
> expensive corporate P.R. effort—and as I've said before, should
> be reported as such.[47]

The implication is clear: drug makers such as the Medicines
Company don't want reform, and they are sneakily undermining
it. But notice that Maddow offers no evidence or even argument
for this assumption. She isn't talking about opposition to any one
bill or provision, but about an overall "campaign against healthcare reform." Her segment ran after the *L.A. Times* had reported
on Obama's deal with Tauzin. Had she looked at the legislation,
she would know the bills included mandates and subsidies enriching the drug makers.

It's an absurd claim on its face, but Maddow views everything through the prism of the Big Business–hates–Big Government myth. The specific drug maker in question rebutted Maddow's claim three days later: "The Medicines Company has not opposed any of the pending health care reform bills, and has not in any way supported any efforts to disrupt open debate about health care reform."[48] Why would they?

And Dick Armey's lobbying firm? Healthcare reform caused a breakup there. Armey left DLA Piper a week later, and his old boss made it clear they didn't appreciate Armey's anti-ObamaCare work:

> Despite some unfounded media suggestions attempting to link DLA Piper to FreedomWorks' opposition to health care reform, the firm has not, on its own behalf, or on the behalf of any client, directly or indirectly opposed any of the pending health care reform bills. On the contrary, DLA Piper represents clients who support enactment of effective health care reform this year.[49]

Obama was a goose laying golden eggs for Pharma. And DLA Piper, with its health sector clients, didn't want anything to endanger that goose—especially not one of its own employees. Maddow was right that DLA Piper was involved in healthcare reform; she just didn't understand for which side it was working.

A PRESCRIPTION FOR PROFIT

"For those who fight reform in order to profit financially or politically from the status quo," the home page WhiteHouse.gov warned in July, "the president sends a simple message: 'Not this time.'" But what about those who lobby in favor of reform in order to profit financially—at taxpayer expense?

Obama appears to be saying, "You're in luck!"

Obama may not have set out to enrich drug companies or reward his donors, but that's the effect of policies that increase government control over the healthcare system. For one thing, Obama has been forced to cut deals with the drug makers in order to get his package through. But just as important, Big Government always tends to aid Big Business.

Rachel Maddow and Paul Krugman may not understand that, but Billy Tauzin does.

CHAPTER 6

THE GREEN RACKET

ENVIRONMENTALISM FOR PROFIT

"**I**f we are willing to work for it, and fight for it, and believe in it," Senator Obama told his fans after finally wrapping the Democratic nomination, "then I am absolutely certain that generations from now, we will be able to look back and tell our children that . . . this was the moment when the rise of the oceans began to slow and our planet began to heal."[1]

This was the promise of Obamanomics: if the right people got in power and used that power in the right ways, they could cure the world. Obama would heal not just the people on earth, but the planet itself.

The central struggle in Obama's fight to heal the planet has been curbing carbon dioxide and other greenhouse gas emissions that contribute to global warming. But the soaring rhetoric of candidate Obama has given way to the ugly truths of Washington

and the stubborn laws of Obamanomics. Climate change legislation has become a special-interest porkfest with the most well-connected companies lobbying for handouts. By summer 2009,
Obama was rallying America behind a bill whose provisions his
own budget director had earlier said would represent "the largest
corporate welfare program that has ever been enacted in the history of the United States."[2]

Other Obama environmental policies have also become corporate welfare boondoggles. And as government accumulates more
power under Obama, and as the special interests engage in *Regulatory Robbery*, small business, taxpayers, and consumers all face
higher prices, more regulations, and higher taxes.

THE CLIMATE RACKET

Scientist Bjørn Lomborg coined the phrase "Climate-Industrial
Complex." In an op-ed in the *Wall Street Journal*, Lomborg
wrote:

> Some business leaders are cozying up with politicians and sci-
> entists to demand swift, drastic action on global warming. This
> is a new twist on a very old practice: companies using public
> policy to line their own pockets.
>
> The tight relationship between the groups echoes the relation-
> ship among weapons makers, researchers and the U.S. military
> during the Cold War. President Dwight Eisenhower famously
> warned about the might of the "military-industrial complex,"
> cautioning that "the potential for the disastrous rise of misplaced
> power exists and will persist." He worried that "there is a recur-
> ring temptation to feel that some spectacular and costly action
> could become the miraculous solution to all current difficulties."

This is certainly true of climate change. We are told that very expensive carbon regulations are the only way to respond to global warming, despite ample evidence that this approach does not pass a basic cost-benefit test. We must ask whether a "climate-industrial complex" is emerging, pressing taxpayers to fork over money to please those who stand to gain.[3]

Obama's "spectacular and costly action" promising "the miraculous solution" to climate change is an ambitious new regulatory scheme called "cap-and-trade." The scheme's premise is that carbon emissions, especially from burning fossil fuels such as coal and oil, are leading to potentially catastrophic global warming. While some basic facts of this premise are undisputable—fossil fuel use adds to greenhouse-gas concentrations, which has a net warming effect—there are plenty of scientific reasons to question the dogma that we are causing radical climate change that will wreak havoc on the planet. Still, global warming alarmists like Al Gore insist that "the science is settled."

But even if you were to grant Al Gore and Barack Obama their premises on the causes and effects of climate change, there's even more reason to doubt the effectiveness of their proposed fixes—especially once you see how these policies have become special-interest porkfests.

The point of cap-and-trade is to lower the earth's CO_2 levels by forcing people to pay to produce or emit carbon. A carbon tax would be the most straightforward way to achieve this, but industry lobbyists and most politicians, including Barack Obama and John McCain, favor cap-and-trade. We can guess a few of the reasons.

First, cap-and-trade is not called a "tax," which makes it easier to sell, even though it functions much like a tax. Second—and probably more important—cap-and-trade necessarily involves more political tinkering and more lobbying.

Cap-and-trade requires an emitter to pay for his emissions with special permits, also called allowances or credits. Whoever has a permit can use it to pay for his emissions, or he can sell it to someone else who needs it—or to someone else who intends to sell it again. The government would not set the price of a permit—Washington would dictate only how many permits are in circulation, and the market would set the price.

But this basic groundwork leaves many questions—and corporate lobbyists are eager to help Congress and the Obama administration answer them.

First, which emitters will be covered? This is a key question, since every person emits carbon (by exhaling) or methane, as do cars, factories, landfills, farms, and just about every other living being or productive enterprise.

Then there's the fact that cap-and-trade will disadvantage American manufacturers—already struggling—compared to Mexican, Chinese, or Guatemalan manufacturers who don't have carbon caps. Are Congress and the president really willing to kill blue-collar jobs?

Things get even more fun when we talk about "offsets," which are practices that take greenhouse gasses out of the atmosphere. Since trees suck up CO_2, maybe the government should give you carbon credits for planting trees. But then should you have to spend the credits when the tree dies and decays, giving off much of the CO_2 it absorbed? If a forest fire wipes out your trees, will the EPA come and demand those credits back?

Then there are the two big questions: How many permits will the government create? And how will they initially be distributed?

As you would imagine, all these questions have been the object of the fiercest lobbying, providing brilliant opportunities for lobbyists and self-serving politicians to game the system. But Congress's attempt to answer the last question—how to distribute the permits—has shown most clearly that cap-and-trade is a corporate welfare porkfest of nearly unprecedented proportions.

CORPORATE GIVEAWAYS

The cap-and-trade bill that passed the House in July 2009, called Waxman-Markey, would give away 85 percent of all the emission permits in 2012, the first year the emissions caps would be in force. The bill would auction off the other 15 percent.[4] The EPA estimated that all the permits in 2012 would be worth $60 billion. That means the House passed a bill to give away $51 billion in assets.

Energy-intensive, "trade-sensitive" industries such as steelmakers, cement makers, and paper mills would get 15 percent of all the credits for free—an estimated value of $9 billion. Companies burning coal to make electricity would also get billions in free credits. Starting in 2014, oil refineries would pocket, at no charge, about 2 percent of all the credits. Electric utilities would also get 2 percent starting in 2014.

So, all these companies would need to "pay" for their emissions with permits, but they would get their permits for free, with the proportions determined by negotiations between lobbyists and lawmakers.

If permits worth $51 billion are given away for free, does this have any impact? Yes. Even if you got Super Bowl tickets for free, they would still be worth hundreds of dollars, because supply and demand—not the cost of acquisition—sets price. Imagine if your business wanted to start competing against Caterpillar—you would need to buy yourself some carbon credits, while Caterpillar would already have its credits for free. This new barrier to entry drives up costs.

So who ultimately will pay for this entire regulatory system? That's easy: the consumers will.

Gasoline, electricity, and heating oil will all become more expensive under cap-and-trade, and so will everything that is made or shipped using electricity, coal, gas, or oil—which is pretty much everything. Unsurprisingly, the Government Accountability Office found that regular people would end up paying the tab while corporations pocketed the profits: "Most of the benefits of freely allocated allowances will accrue to the shareholders of entities that receive them," the GAO wrote. "However, consumers are unlikely to see these benefits in the form of lower prices, since most covered entities will pass on costs associated with a cap-and-trade program, even when they receive allowances for free."[5]

Obama originally opposed giving away the credits. His budget director, Peter Orszag, told the House Budget Committee:

> If you didn't auction the permits, it would represent the largest corporate welfare program that has even been enacted in the history of the United States. All of the evidence suggests that what would occur is that corporate profits would increase by approximately the value of the permits.[6]

But Obama later endorsed Waxman-Markey,[7]which gives away 85 percent of the credits. Understandably, some of Obama's green allies did not like seeing their cherished anti-carbon regime transform into "the largest corporate welfare program" in U.S. history. Greenpeace announced, "Despite President Obama's assurance that he would enact strong, science-based legislation, we are now watching him put his full support behind a bill that chooses politics over science, elevates industry interests over national interest."[8]

After the House passed it, Obama praised the bill as "a historic piece of legislation."[9] And in terms of doling out corporate welfare, it certainly was.

ENTER THE LOBBYISTS

The biggest winners under Waxman-Markey would be the regulated electric companies, which would receive 30 percent of the free credits.[10]

The Edison Electric Institute, an association of electric companies, is at the core of the industry's influence. In the first quarter of 2009, EEI spent $2.6 million on lobbying, placing it 29th overall, just ahead of defense giant Boeing.[11] In the first half of 2009, the group retained about twenty outside lobbying firms[12] and employed about twenty in-house lobbyists.[13]

Energy and Environment Daily reported how aggressively EEI lobbyists labored for Waxman-Markey:

> Tom Kuhn, the group's executive director, stood in the doorway during the late night Energy and Commerce Committee markups in May. And EEI's senior vice president, Brian Wolff, a former top political adviser to House Speaker Nancy Pelosi (D-Calif.), worked the Capitol corridors, lobbying reluctant Democrats in the hours before the House adopted the bill on a narrow, 219–212 vote.[14]

This lobbying won the electric companies billions in free credits. The bill, however, required these utilities to pass this wealth down to consumers in order to dampen rate spikes. If this requirement actually works, it would reduce the effective tax hike of cap-and-trade. But by keeping electricity rates low, the requirement would also trample on the central environmental premise of the bill—promoting conservation by making people pay for their emissions.

It's hard to see how government will ensure none of this free money turns into higher executive salaries, a new water cooler, or some new parking spots at the electric corporate offices. Ultimately *you* will pay for all this, of course, because the cap will inevitably drive up prices throughout the whole economy, even if some players are getting the permits for free.

KING COAL PROFITS FROM CAP-AND-TRADE

American Electric Power uses more coal than any other consumer in the Western Hemisphere. And coal is the most CO_2-intensive source of electricity. So, if you buy Obama's rhetoric, it might seem inexplicable that AEP lobbied in favor of Waxman-Markey.

In September, Mike Morris—the president, chairman, and CEO of AEP—wrote a public letter declaring, "American Electric Power supports the American Clean Energy and Security Act." The company's second-quarter 2009 lobbying report states AEP lobbied on the bill, "for and against various provisions, generally in favor."[15]

Morris explained to *Forbes* how cap-and-trade with free credits means profits. AEP isn't worried about the costs of cap-and-trade, Morris said, because they'll mostly be passed on to consumers or covered by free credits. But the upside is that cap-and-trade will eventually allow AEP to charge much higher prices.

Here's how: regulators only allow utilities to make a slim profit on the energy they supply to customers. But when utilities have to make capital improvements—building new power plants or new transmission wires—regulators allow them larger margins. And Waxman-Markey, which requires utilities to use new sources of renewable fuels, would open that door. According to Morris, deploying carbon capture and storage technology would allow AEP to raise prices 30–50 percent.[16]

In short: building new infrastructure is where the profit is for utilities. If utilities just built and built with no consumer demand, though, regulators wouldn't allow the utilities to recoup the costs.

But if the federal government is demanding the new infrastructure, then the state regulators will have to go along and allow rate hikes. Once again, Obamanomics allows Big Business to get paid for building something nobody wants—and once again, consumers foot the bill.

Agriculture interests got their share of Waxman-Markey too, with the biggest prize, it seems, going to agri-chemical giant Monsanto. Rural congressmen led by Agriculture Committee chairman Collin Peterson, a Minnesota Democrat, raised concerns in June about the Waxman-Markey bill. Although farming was eventually exempted from the bill's emissions caps,[17] Peterson wanted more: he wanted farmers to earn offsets for adopting farming methods that kept CO_2 trapped in the soil. House Speaker Nancy Pelosi agreed to Peterson's demands.

As the liberal environmentalist website *Grist* explained, this was a big win for Monsanto. That's because one way of trapping CO_2 in the soil is by planting crops directly into the ground without plowing, a practice called "no-till." Monsanto just happens to make "Roundup Ready" seeds that can withstand the heavy herbicide doses no-till requires. And cap-and-trade rewards no-till farming with carbon credits. So the government will be providing farmers a big incentive to use Monsanto's product.[18]

And sure enough, Monsanto reported that it lobbied on climate change, with its lobbyists including Dean Aguillen, a former staffer for Speaker Pelosi.[19] Also, Novecta, a consulting and lobbying arm of the Iowa and Illinois Corn Growers Associations, lobbied Congress to grant offset credits for no-till. Monsanto helped Novecta with this lobbying push.[20]

Winning free permits isn't the only way to get rich off climate change—trading them can be profitable, too, for the well positioned. Goldman Sachs has been particularly aggressive in carbon-related investing. Goldman owns 10 percent of the Chicago

Climate Exchange (CCX)—a $24 million investment.[21] CCX bills itself as "the world's first and North America's only active voluntary, legally binding integrated trading system to reduce emissions of all six major greenhouse gases (GHGs), with offset projects worldwide."[22]

Obama's climate change regulations would make CCX no longer "voluntary" for the businesses covered by the regulations—good news for Goldman and others of that ilk. CCX's CEO, by the way, Richard Sandor, sits on the board of AEP.[23]

JUST DO IT

Nike makes good shoes, but its leadership in the U.S. sneaker market is largely a result of the company's image. Michael Jordan, Tiger Woods, the trademark "swoosh"—for Nike, image may not be everything, but it's the biggest thing.

So, when Nike gave up its seat on the U.S. Chamber of Commerce in protest over the Chamber's opposition to Waxman-Markey, it would have been easy to conclude the company was simply burnishing its green image. After all, the firm had already invested a small fortune to replace sulfur hexafluoride—a potent greenhouse gas—in its Nike Air shoes with nitrogen.

But some inconvenient facts belie Nike's green image: namely, Nike emissions from its "manufacturing and logistics" jumped 62 percent from 1998 to 2005, according to the company's own public reports.[24]

That's because Nike makes a vast majority of its apparel overseas, primarily in Asia. Conveniently, all these factories will be unaffected by Waxman-Markey. In contrast, Nike's competitor, New Balance, makes its best running shoes in New England. So Waxman-Markey would regulate New Balance's emissions, but not Nike's. In other words, Waxman-Markey would drive up New Balance's costs, but not Nike's.

Nike might really want to save the planet, but its support for climate change sure looks like a case of *Regulatory Robbery*.

BUY LOW, SELL HIGH

"On climate change," General Electric executive John Rice wrote to his colleagues, "we were able to work closely with key authors of the Waxman-Markey climate and energy bill, recently passed by the House of Representatives. If this bill is enacted into law it would benefit many GE businesses."[25]

This 2009 email reminded me of an internal email I read in 2002 from a different energy company discussing the Kyoto Protocol, a treaty effectively requiring cap-and-trade laws similar to Waxman-Markey. That email said, "This agreement will be good for Enron stock!!"[26]

GE plays a central role in lobbying for green laws that add to the firm's profits while bleeding consumers, taxpayers, and smaller competitors—so central that the company gets its own chapter in this book. But GE has plenty of company in seeking to cash in on cap-and-trade and other green legislation.

When operating within Green Obamanomics, an excellent corporate tactic is *Making an Offer you Can't Refuse*. While cap-and-trade drives money to "green" technologies that consumers and investors wouldn't demand in a free market, Obama has not hesitated also to use mandates to make people buy things they don't want. If you invested in that thing, Obamanomics spells profits.

A perfect example comes to us from Mark Patterson who, as of this writing, is the chief of staff at the Treasury Department.

Patterson used to be a lobbyist at Goldman Sachs, where he lobbied on the Energy Independence and Security Act of 2007 and on
Cellulosic Ethanol, an alcohol fuel derived from grass and other
plants.[27]

What is Goldman's stake in cellulosic ethanol? The firm just
happens to have paid $30 million in 2006 for a big stake in Iogen
Corp., a Canadian company specializing in cellulosic ethanol technology.[28] Commentators saw Goldman's investment as a sign that
cellulosic ethanol was a promising technology. But Goldman's lobbying record suggests that the firm saw ethanol's promise as con-
tingent upon government help. It's telling that Iogen set up its U.S.
headquarters in Arlington, Virginia, just across the river from the
capital.

Sure enough, the 2007 energy bill, which Obama voted for,
included a cellulosic ethanol mandate[29]—gasoline blenders were
required to buy certain amounts of cellulosic ethanol each year,
with the required quantity rising annually. The mandate adds to
the price of gasoline, and those profits go straight into Iogen's coffers—and ultimately into Goldman's coffers.

President Obama has called for more subsidies for cellulosic
ethanol, and corporate America is clearly listening. Tellingly, when
another biofuel company, Fulcrum BioEnergy, trumpeted its
advances in cellulosic ethanol in September 2009, the company's
CEO said, "This is just the type of program that President
Obama, Congress and the Department of Energy are calling for
to achieve the Nation's renewable fuel targets."[30]

Obama is also calling for a renewable energy standard, which
would be, in effect, a mandate for solar and wind power. Unsurprisingly, companies like Goldman, Duke Energy, and GE are
ramping up their investments in renewable energy.[31]

Obama needs mandates to get people to use solar and wind
energy because these power sources are more expensive than

electricity from coal, nuclear, or natural gas. If wind and solar electricity were the same price or cheaper, electric companies would use these technologies of their own volition.

For this reason, mandates mean higher prices for everyday people. But they also mean profits for the likes of Goldman, Duke Energy, and GE that invest in these technologies.

VAN JONES AND THE MYTH OF "GREEN JOBS"

Bins covered the factory floor, and the bins were filled with bolts—the really big kind of bolts that hold together oil rigs, bridges, and giant wind turbines. Factory workers, literally in blue-collared uniforms, assembled before President-elect Obama. It was a perfect photo-op for Obama to talk about jobs. [32]

After warning the factory workers that the recession could dry up wind turbine orders—half the company's business—Obama pointed across the Atlantic to give them hope:

> And think of what's happening in countries like Spain, Germany and Japan, where they're making real investments in renewable energy. They're surging ahead of us, poised to take the lead in these new industries.
>
> This isn't because they're smarter than us, or work harder than us, or are more innovative than we are. It's because their governments have harnessed their people's hard work and ingenuity with bold investments—investments that are paying off in good, high-wage jobs—jobs they won't lose to other countries.
>
> There is no reason we can't do the same thing right here in America. [33]

"Harnessed their people's hard work and ingenuity with bold investments," is another way of saying, "spent taxpayer money on subsidies to businesses that do what government wants them to do."

This is one of the core ideas behind Obamanomics: "green jobs." And while Obama didn't use those words at the Cardinal Fastener factory, it has been a major theme of his presidency. In fact, he even had a green jobs czar.

Van Jones was drummed from his czar post amid a public uproar about his associations, his signing a petition supporting September 11 conspiracy theories, and his vulgar insult of Republicans that made its way around YouTube. While these unsavory marks on his resume made him look like an extremist, Jones actually fit in perfectly with Obamanomics.

Jones is known among liberals for embracing a "market-based" or "business friendly" environmentalism.[34] In his 2008 book *Green Collar Jobs*, Jones wrote:

> So in the end, our success and survival as a species are largely and directly tied to the new eco-entrepreneurs—and the success and survival of their enterprises. Since almost all of the needed eco-technologies are likely to come from the private sector, civic leaders and voters should do all that can be done to help green business leaders succeed. That means, in large part, electing leaders who will pass bills to aid them.[35]

So Van Jones is hardly a Communist. He is instead a leading prophet of Obamanomics.

The "green jobs" idea is Obamanomics in all its glory: the notion justifies massive government transfers of wealth to industry and requires dramatic increases in government control over the economy for the putative purposes of helping the planet, the working man, and the economy.

While crunchier environmentalism aims to save the planet from rapacious industry, the environmentalism of Obamanomics is about helping business to help workers to help the planet. It's a way of getting Big Business on board with the entire green project, but it's also a way of getting regular people to care about the environment—which they don't, despite all the books, speeches, movies, and PowerPoint presentations by Al Gore in recent years. In a CBS/*New York Times* poll from June 2009, less than one percent of respondents named the environment as the most important issue. That poll has asked the same question every few months since March 2007, and the highest "the environment" ever polled was 3 percent.[36]

Naturally, if people don't care much about the environment, they don't want to make a lot of sacrifices for it. A May 2008 poll by the National Center for Public Policy Research found that 65 percent of likely voters were unwilling to pay any more for gasoline in order to reduce greenhouse gas emissions. Only 15 percent were willing pay an additional 6 percent or more.[37] Obama understands this, of course, which is why Green Obamanomics relies on coercive mandates and cap-and-trade to make people do things they don't want to do (reduce carbon emissions), and why it subsidizes Big Business to create things for which no one would pay full price (like electric cars, as described below).

This brings us back to green jobs. In August 2008, the Obama-Biden campaign pledged in an issue brief:

> Barack Obama and Joe Biden will strategically invest $150 billion over 10 years to accelerate the commercialization of plug-in hybrids, promote development of commercial scale renewable energy, encourage energy efficiency, invest in low emissions coal plants, advance the next generation of biofuels

and fuel infrastructure, and begin transition to a new digital electricity grid.

The plan will also invest in America's highly-skilled manufacturing workforce and manufacturing centers to ensure that American workers have the skills and tools they need to pioneer the green technologies that will be in high demand throughout the world. All together these investments will help the private sector create 5 million new green jobs, good jobs that cannot be outsourced.[38]

Obama used "green jobs" as a hook on which to hang subsidies for electric cars, green buildings, ethanol, clean coal, windmills, solar panels, and more. Of course, these programs all spell profits for battery makers, contractors, coal companies, politically connected investors, and others.

But profits generated through regulation and subsidies don't come from thin air—they come from higher prices and higher taxes. Every dime GE pockets in windmill subsidies is a dime a taxpayer could have spent stimulating some other portion of the economy. Every dollar Goldman Sachs makes in cellulosic ethanol subsidies is a dollar a taxpayer could have invested in a technology with more promise than squeezing fuel out of grass. And when our utility bills go up thanks to cap-and-trade, that's money an American family could have spent on books, vacations, or repairing broken doors. This simple economic principle undermines the idea of green jobs.

Obama, however, pointed to Spain as a success story worth emulating:

There is no reason we can't do the same thing right here in America. . . . In the process, we'll put nearly half a million people to work building wind turbines and solar panels; constructing fuel-efficient cars and buildings; and developing the new energy technologies that will lead to new jobs, more savings, and a cleaner, safer planet in the bargain.[39]

But the Spanish example actually teaches something else—that government only "creates jobs"—green or not—by taking money from more productive but less politically favored sectors of the economy. Spanish academic Gabriel Calzada Álvarez published a study in March 2009 finding that if Obama adopts the Spanish model, then for every renewable energy job created by government spending, "the U.S. should expect a loss of at least 2.2 jobs on average, or about 9 jobs lost for every 4 created, to which we have to add those jobs that non-subsidized investments with the same resources would have created."[40]

Álvarez's critics dismiss him as a global warming skeptic and opponent of energy regulation.[41] In other words, the man has an agenda that clashes with Obamanomics. But none of the critics have challenged his methodology, and his conclusion makes sense. "Green jobs" are created only through taxes or rate hikes. Those higher taxes and higher rates sap Americans of spending money, which destroys other jobs.

In a more damning conclusion, perhaps, Álvarez found that in Spain, "just one out of ten jobs has been created at the more permanent level of actual operation and maintenance of the renewable sources of electricity."[42] In other words, most of the "green jobs" were for building or installing the machinery to generate power. Once the solar panels are built and installed, once the ethanol distilleries are up and running, once the windmills are upright and spinning, there's not much work left to do. So some of those green jobs disappear.

This fact reflects a fundamental problem of Green Obama-nomics: instead of *adding* green energy to our current fossil fuel sources, it wants green energy to *replace* them. In other words, Obama is not trying to increase production, but change the manner of production. And maintaining current production levels with more jobs means un-automating things. Specifically, green jobs mean replacing the work carbon bonds used to do with work performed by people. You can see why this will raise rates for everyone who uses electricity.

Much of the increased costs represents dead-weight loss in the economy. But some of it represents profits for the well connected.

ALCOA: CARBON EXPORTER

"This is an extraordinary gathering," Obama declared in the Rose Garden. "Here we have today standing behind me, along with Ron Gettlefinger and leadership of the [United Auto Workers], we have ten of the world's largest auto manufacturers, we have environmental advocates, as well as elected officials from all across the country."[43]

Obama was announcing new federal mandates requiring automakers to increase the efficiency of their cars. This was supposed to show the president delivering on his promises of Hope and Change. "In the past," Obama said of the mandates,

> an agreement such as this would have been considered impossible. It's no secret that these are folks who've occasionally been at odds for years, even decades. In fact, some of the groups here have been embroiled in lawsuits against one another. So that gives you a sense of how impressive and significant it is that these leaders from across the country are willing to set aside the past for the sake of the future.[44]

As I watched the Rose Garden speech, I recalled Adam Smith's words:

> People of the same trade seldom meet together, even for merriment and diversion, but the conversation ends in a conspiracy against the public, or in some contrivance to raise prices.... But though the law cannot hinder people of the same trade from sometimes assembling together, it ought to do nothing to facilitate such assemblies; much less to render them necessary.

But Obamanomics is all about bringing them together. David McCurdy, president of the Alliance of Automobile manufacturers, raved that the Obama policy "launches a new beginning, an era of cooperation."[45]

The automakers didn't object to the new mileage mandates because they came paired with subsidies—financed by taxpayers. And because the mandates were industry-wide, new costs could be passed on to consumers.

But the benefits also went to companies that were not even in the Rose Garden, including Alcoa, one of the world's largest aluminum manufacturers. Alcoa supports higher fuel efficiency mandates for a simple reason: they push car makers toward aluminum frames, which are lighter and therefore more fuel efficient than steel ones. Alcoa is also a well-connected company. Jake Siewert, President Clinton's former press secretary, was Alcoa's vice president for "public strategy" until Timothy Geithner hired him at the Treasury Department in May 2009,[46] the same month Obama instituted his fuel efficiency standards. Alain Belda, Alcoa's board chairman, gave the maximum to Obama in the 2008 general election.[47]

So Alcoa, an Obama-connected special interest, lobbied for and profits from Obama's fuel economy policies. Why should we get upset, as long as it's good for the planet?

And there's the problem: Alcoa demonstrates how Obama's environmental policies are often undermined by Big Business involvement. Specifically, Obama's increased fuel standards may reduce greenhouse gasses emitted from the tailpipe, but the switch from steel to aluminum boosts emissions and energy use on the other side of the world.

Alcoa manufactures much of its aluminum in Australia. And making aluminum is much more energy intensive than making steel. Thus, in order to make cars run cleaner here, Alcoa is using more energy and giving off more CO_2 down there. And the company's lobbying efforts in Australia are markedly different from its lobbying efforts here. Check out the lead from this 2008 *Australian* piece about Alcoa's opposition to a proposed carbon trading scheme in Australia: "Australia's biggest alumina exporter, Alcoa, has warned that even a modest carbon cost on aluminium production could lead to plant closures in Australia and moves to higher-emitting plants in countries such as China."[48]

Do the added energy usage and emissions in Australia offset the gasoline savings up here? It's unclear. But certainly Obama's efficiency mandates are boosting emissions Down Under and boosting car prices here.

THE ELECTRIC CAR: A TRUE GOVERNMENT WINNER

Obamanomics is about Apollo projects and Manhattan projects. Big Ideas and Big Plans, implemented by Big Government, have always appealed to politicians, and apparently to Obama more than most. The new Big Idea in transportation: electric cars, a project that Obama has already supported with billions of taxpayer dollars.

Carmaker Tesla, in June 2009, got a $465 million loan from Obama's Energy Department to work on electric cars.[49] For the same purpose, the administration handed out even bigger loans to Ford ($5.9 billion)[50] and Nissan ($1.6 billion).[51] Ford President Alan Mulally praised the taxpayer-funded loan as "the kind of partnership that will help American manufacturing not just survive, but thrive."[52]

But if these were investments in electric cars and not handouts, then why couldn't the firms get the loans from a private investment firm? Why was the Obama administration the only willing investor?

The Energy Department did not disclose the terms of the loans, but the automakers indicated they were extremely favorable. A Ford spokesman said the interest rate on Ford's loan would be based on the current U.S. Treasury rate of 3–4 percent. "If it were at market rates it would be in the double digits," he noted. "That's a huge thing for us.'"[53]

So, while regular Americans were struggling under double digit credit card rates and resetting adjustable rate mortgages, their tax dollars were providing low-interest loans to automakers. Congress, at the time, was debating just which taxes to hike on the American people, but Obama was declaring these loans "will create good jobs."[54] This fails to acknowledge that this money was being taken from someone, who would have spent or invested it, thus creating jobs as well—though maybe not the kind of jobs Obama wanted.

And these loans came on top of the river of cash that Obama's stimulus directed toward electric cars. The stimulus appropriated $2 billion for "grants for the manufacturing of advanced batteries and components" for electric vehicles, including hybrids and plug-ins.[55] It also earmarked $300 million for the federal government to procure electric vehicles.[56] And government policies already in place or being considered before Obama's inauguration had created additional incentives, as did a host of other government subsidies.

To be fair, the electric car has plenty of arguments in its favor: no gas consumption, low pollution, no tailpipe emissions, and cutting edge technology. But when government takes money from taxpayers and "invests" it, the results are different from what would happen if government let people keep their own cash and invest or spend it as they please. Rather than millions of individuals judging for themselves what products are most desirable or what investments will be most profitable, you have a few people— Obama, his energy secretary, some congressmen, a few bureaucrats—making those decisions. It's called "picking winners and losers."

And the Obama administration has picked the electric car as a winner. To help meet Obama's goal of putting one million plug-ins on American roads,[57] the stimulus created special tax credits worth up to $5,000 for individuals or businesses that buy plug-ins.[58] And if you converted your regular car into a plug-in—an expensive process—the stimulus gave you a tax credit for 10 percent of the cost, up to $40,000 (meaning a maximum credit of $4,000).[59]

This ought to cause concern. If the cars are so promising, you'd think private money would line up behind them and they wouldn't need this sort of subsidy. But a deeper look at plug-ins suggests the benefits may be illusory.

PLUGGING INTO OBAMANOMICS

To begin with, the environmental benefits claimed for plug-ins are questionable. Plug-ins eliminate the need for gasoline, but you need electricity to power-up the battery. And there's a good chance that electricity will come from coal-fired plants, which generate about half of America's electricity.[60] So, while your subsidized plug-in car isn't burning any fossil fuels under the hood, it's probably burning fossil fuels on the edge of town. Environmentalists call this "the long tailpipe."

Is it better to run our cars on coal than on oil? There's no clear answer. For one thing, if it's greenhouse gas emissions you care about, coal-powered cars are more efficient than gasoline-powered cars. One study from U.C. Berkeley's Goldman School of Public Policy estimated that compact plug-ins charged by coal-fired plants cause about 4 percent less CO_2 per mile compared to a gasoline-powered car. Bigger cars save closer to 20 percent, while natural gas-charged plug-ins reduce CO_2 emissions by more than 50 percent.[61]

Also, burning fuels at night (when most people would be charging their cars) and outside of cities (where most power plants are) has a smaller impact than burning fuels during the day (when most people drive) and in town (where most driving occurs).

So there may be a net environmental benefit to plug-ins, but it's unclear how big. It is clear, however, that plug-ins are not the green elixir their backers claim them to be.

And plug-ins present numerous big problems aside from uncertainty over their environmental benefits. One looming problem for plug-ins is how to secure the lithium-ion batteries that power them. Lithium, like oil, natural gas, and coal, is a non-renewable resource—you can't plant lithium trees. And around half the world's known lithium reserves sit in a single country: Bolivia.

In 2009, the country's socialist president, Evo Morales, said he wanted to sell his lithium to the world—but he had his demands. First, the Bolivian government would always own the lithium, and would seize 60 percent of the earnings before the lithium even left the country.[62] Second, Morales wants lithium batteries, and even the cars themselves, manufactured in Bolivia. This considerably darkens Obama's vision of battery factories and electric car factories sprouting up and providing "green jobs" all over the United States.

In addition to the long tailpipe and dependence on Bolivia, the mass production of lithium-powered cars could pose other potential problems. Can plug-ins be used by people who don't have garages? Will quieter cars cause more accidents? How safe will the batteries be, considering they sometimes burst into flames, necessitating special federal rules for transporting them?[63]

We also have to consider pricing issues. Plug-in cars will drive up the price of electricity for everyone while applying downward pressure to the price of gasoline. This could shift costs from drivers to people who don't have cars—in other words, from wealthier people to poorer people. Keeping gasoline cheaper and providing seemingly emissions-free driving could spur more driving by both traditional drivers and plug-in drivers, exacerbating traffic and wiping out emissions savings from the electric cars.

Additionally, lithium prices will jump, leading to higher costs for the batteries in lap-top computers and cell phones, but also for glass and ceramics, whose manufacture involves lithium. These higher costs could shift some glass and ceramic manufacturing back to older techniques, which use more fuel and more toxins. Similarly, lithium is sometimes added to concrete in roads and runways to make them less likely to crack. Will a spike in lithium prices cause roadbuilders to use inferior materials?

Finally, environmentalists may be surprised to learn that mass-producing plug-ins would likely damage an environmentally sensitive area: Bolivia's Unuyi salt flats, which hold most of the country's lithium. According to the Associated Press, lithium mining there "would plant a substantial human footprint in one of the world's most remote places, a 12,000 foot high desert visited only by flocks of pink flamingos and occasional tourists."[64]

None of these negative side effects are guaranteed, and they may all be outweighed by the benefits of electric cars. But in addition to these *known* unknowns, as former Defense Secretary

Donald Rumsfeld put it once, there are the *unknown* unknowns. That is, we simply can't predict all the potential problems of the mass adoption of lithium-powered cars.

BIG IDEAS, BIG BUSINESS, BIG MISTAKES

As a cautionary tale, consider our recent history with fuel efficiency. To improve fuel efficiency in the late 1970s, our government, by means of the Clean Air Act, pushed on us the gasoline additive methyl tertiary-butyl ether, or MTBE. Today many states have banned MTBE as a carcinogen. So we replaced it with ethanol.

On a small scale, ethanol has benefits—we get it domestically, it helps farmers, and it burns cleaner than gasoline. But when the 2005 and 2007 energy bills created and expanded ethanol mandates and subsidies, a slew of unintended consequences appeared: the bills effectively polluted water supplies, expanded "dead zones" in the Gulf of Mexico,[65] accelerated soil erosion, encouraged deforestation overseas, drove up food prices and sparked "tortilla riots," and hurt ranchers. (Obama, however, still campaigned on outlawing all cars that couldn't run on fuel blends of 85 percent ethanol.)[66]

The lesson here: Big Plans can be dangerous. Where the free market consists of millions of little experiments, with the best rising to the top, government-picked winners enjoy immense demand and massive funding often before having proven themselves. This increases the odds of unpleasant surprises.

But Obamanomics is all about Big Plans, which satisfy the Man-on-the-Moon ambitions of all politicians. Every president wants his Hoover Dam or Eisenhower Interstate Highway System. They all want a big role, as Obama put it, in "remaking America."[67]

More important—and you see this when you reflect on ethanol, for instance—Big Plans are appetizing to Big Business. Handing out billions of dollars to anyone who can follow the politicians' marching orders guarantees the politicians will be showered with adoration—golfing trips to Scotland, campaign contributions, and the promise of a cushy lobbying job upon retirement.

And so we should be suspicious of big plans. Look, for instance, at the lobbying in recent years for those electric car subsidies. FMC Corporation is one of the world's largest lithium producers. The company began lobbying for lithium-battery subsidies on the 2007 energy bill.[68] FMC's outside lobbyists included Glenn McCullough, a former chairman of the Tennessee Valley Authority, a government entity. Between the beginning of 2007 and the middle of 2009, the company spent more than $4 million on lobbying.[69]

Altair Nanotechnologies is another lithium battery company. In 2007, it hired the Podesta Group, a lobbying firm started in 1988 by John Podesta—who later became Bill Clinton's White House chief of staff and the director of Barack Obama's presidential transition—and his brother Tony Podesta. Lobbying on Altair's behalf for lithium-ion funding are John Scofield, the Republican former communications director at the House Appropriations Committee, and Walter Pryor, former legislative director for Democratic senator Mark Pryor, who sits on the Appropriations Committee and the Commerce, Science, and Transportation Committee.[70]

International Battery, a lithium-ion battery manufacturer, hired former House minority leader Dick Gephardt on April 1, 2009, to lobby for federal aid for battery-powered cars.[71]

Search federal lobbying disclosure forms for "plug-in electric vehicles," and you'll see an interesting gang of corporations pushing the subsidies for this technology: Constellation Energy, the PPL Corporation, XCel Energy, Pepco, and the Edison Electric Institute.[72]

These are power companies, and they have obvious reasons for wanting more people to fuel their cars at the outlet as opposed to the pump. PPL gets much of its power from coal, as does Duke Energy, another company lobbying for plug-in subsidies.

Again, corporate profit isn't bad for America. But corporate profit through government mandates and subsidies doesn't create wealth, it redistributes it—often upward.

OBAMANOMICS AND PAST LESSONS

Once you consider the alliance of lobbyists pushing for electric car subsidies, and you see the porkfest cap-and-trade has already become, and you recall Adam Smith's warnings about business collusion, it's harder to believe that the current raft of environmental policies are crafted to serve the good of the planet or to achieve energy independence. That may have been their original intention, but once Big Business gets involved, the policies tend to be redirected to meet its needs.

The fact that lobbyists are pushing these subsidies and the promise that these businesses will profit don't mean the policies are bad. The potential problems this chapter has raised with plug-in cars don't necessarily mean these vehicles will be a bust. And our experience with ethanol shouldn't convince us that it's impossible to get off foreign oil.

But our experiences with past Big Ideas ought to give us humility. And the potential problems ought to give us pause. And the influence of companies standing to profit ought to make us skeptical about the latest Big Ideas, whether it's cap-and-trade or the plug-in car.

But Big Ideas, industry lobbying, and past failures don't function as red flags in Obamanomics—to the contrary, they are green lights.

CHAPTER 7

BIG GOVERNMENT AND BIG LABOR GET BEHIND THE WHEEL

OBAMA'S TAKEOVER OF THE AUTO INDUSTRY

B arack Obama used the power of the presidency to hand ownership of Chrysler to the United Auto Workers—a wealthy organization that spent nearly $5 million to help elect Obama president.[1] With Chrysler on the federal dole, taxpayers are now funneling money to the UAW, which in turn will spend money to re-elect Barack Obama.

Obama and his defenders maintain union ownership of the failed automaker is not only fair, but it's also the best outcome for the U.S. economy. Even if this was President Obama's motivation, the glaring appearance of impropriety is exactly the sort of thing candidate Obama had decried. The perception of Gangster Government[2] at work in the Chrysler deal fosters the very cynicism and distrust of government that Obama promised to dispel.

And then there's General Motors. Even after Obama—on behalf of the taxpayers—took ownership of the corporate titan, the company kept its in-house lobbying shop humming. The firm's second-quarter lobbying budget was only 1.4 percent lower than its first-quarter total.[3]

The Detroit takeover highlights the ethical minefield that Obamanomics creates. You can't have government ownership of business without introducing serious opportunities for corruption. First, government officials are spending an unlimited pool of other people's money, opening the door for graft. Second, no negotiation involving government can ever be fair because government has too much power.

A "car czar" has already resigned amid an unrelated corporate corruption scandal. And a lawyer for Chrysler's creditors has accused the White House of bullying and coercion. It wouldn't be surprising if the Detroit takeover became the source of serious ethical problems for the Obama administration—not because Obama is corrupt, but because corporate-government intimacy is a breeding ground for scandal.

But the Detroit bailout is not only Obama's baby. It began under George W. Bush, and Obama just took it to a new level. Because the auto bailout happened in the wake of the Wall Street bailouts, the radical nature of this development—the U.S. government nationalizing one of its largest manufacturers—was a bit obscured.

While unprecedented in its directness, Obama and Bush's takeover of a sizable portion of the auto industry fits into the pattern of Obamanomics: Big Government spending taxpayer money to save Big Business—all in the name of helping the economy, the workers, and even the environment.

THE CAR CRASH

Many things went badly for the auto industry in 2005–08, and specifically for General Motors and Chrysler.

Hurricane Katrina caused already rising gasoline prices to sky-rocket in fall 2005 to over $3 a gallon. Prices later eased, but they repeatedly hit $3 in 2006 and 2007, and then climbed above $4 in 2008. High gas prices, it appeared, were here to stay. Car sales took another hit when the housing collapse began dragging down the whole economy in 2006.

All automakers were suffering: in late 2008, Toyota reported its first loss in seventy years.[4] Detroit was hurting even worse, partly because of the economy and partly because of its own mismanagement and powerful unions. In 2006, none of *Consumer Reports'* top 10 cars were made by American companies.[5]

The 2007 energy bill, supported by then-Senator Obama, contained an auto industry bailout: it authorized $25 billion in direct loans for "reequipping, expanding, or establishing a[n automobile] manufacturing facility in the United States."[6] To back up those loans, Congress needed to set aside a few billion dollars to guard against default. As of September 2008, when Detroit's lobbyists hit Capitol Hill with a full-court press, the price tag for $25 billion in loans was about $7.5 billion in appropriations.[7]

There was some resistance on Capitol Hill to these loans, but Bush and McCain were both on board. Obama, meanwhile, wanted to double down, calling for $50 billion in direct loans to automakers. Obama's campaign proxies used this difference as a wedge for attacking McCain: "John McCain was late in coming to the game on the retooling loans," United Auto Workers President Ron Gettelfinger said, adding, "[H]e's never been clear from our standpoint about his level of support. Barack Obama came on board very early on the full $50 billion."[8]

In late September and early October, amid the turmoil of the Wall Street bailout, Congress approved and President Bush signed off on $25 billion in loans, at a low interest rate of 5 percent, for Detroit.[9]

After the election the Motor City came back for seconds, and Bush and Obama—just as they were when Wall Street came asking—were once again on the same side: pro-bailout. Bush for weeks leaned on Congress to pass another $25 billion bailout for automakers. President-Elect Obama seconded the call: "I believe our government should provide short-term assistance to the auto industry to avoid a collapse while holding the companies accountable and protecting taxpayer interests," he said.[10]

But there was more resistance this time. Congressman Ron Paul of Texas, for instance, gave a simple but important critique of the bailouts:

> In bailing out failing companies, they are confiscating money from productive members of the economy and giving it to failing ones. By sustaining companies with obsolete or unsustainable business models, the government prevents their resources from being liquidated and made available to other companies that can put them to better, more productive use. An essential element of a healthy free market, is that both success and failure must be permitted to happen when they are earned. But instead with a bailout, the rewards are reversed—the proceeds from successful entities are given to failing ones....It is obvious to most Americans that we need to reject corporate cronyism, and allow the natural regulations and incentives of the free market to pick the winners and losers in our economy, not the whims of bureaucrats and politicians.[11]

When Congress balked at a second bailout, President Bush tapped his slush fund. In a preview of a regular Obama practice,

Bush drew $17 billion out of the Troubled Asset Relief Program (TARP), the pool of made-up money created by the Wall Street bailout.[12] The auto bailout was the first sign that the TARP vote was something of a Gulf of Tonkin resolution for finance, giving Bush, and later Obama, wide latitude to spend the money however he wanted.

In exchange for the second bundle of cash, Chrysler and GM agreed to present the government with a restructuring plan. The plan was due in a few months, placing the companies in Obama's hands.

Early on, Obama's team concluded that GM and Chrysler must be saved at any cost.[13] It believed the firms' liquidation would ripple through the economy, shutting down factories, boosting unemployment, and raising welfare costs. While it's phrased in terms of concern for the broader economy and the working man, this corporate-safety-net thinking—also behind the Wall Street bailouts—is exactly the mindset that puts the government at the service of Big Business.

Rejecting the automakers' initial restructuring plans, President Obama countered with his own proposal: Chrysler would merge with Italian automaker Fiat, and Obama would give the United Auto Workers union majority ownership of the new company. GM, meanwhile, would become property of the U.S. government.

Just a few months earlier, this would have sounded like an unhinged power grab by a South American strongman. But Bush had already nationalized AIG and managed takeovers and mergers of other Wall Street banks. Why shouldn't Obama use the bailout to force his will on hapless automakers?

GANGSTER GOVERNMENT

Obama's attempts to exert strong government control over business inevitably clash with his calls for cleaner government.

That's because one participant in the negotiations—government— has the ability to make life unpleasant for anyone who doesn't go along. My colleague at the *Washington Examiner*, Michael Barone, calls this "Gangster Government."[14]

Thomas Lauria, a lawyer on the losing end of the battle over Chrysler, says he got a first-hand view of Obama's Gangster Government. A Florida-based attorney at White & Case, Lauria was a loyal Democrat, giving $10,000 to the Democratic Senatorial Campaign Committee in summer 2008.[15] One of his clients was Perella Weinberg, a hedge fund that had loaned money to Chrysler as a "secured creditor." This means when Chrysler went bankrupt, Perella should have been among the first to collect on its debts. But instead, the Obama administration made an offer to all of Chrysler's creditors—they would receive 29 percent of what Chrysler owed them, and the UAW would get majority ownership of the company.[16]

J.P. Morgan and other big banks went along. But they didn't really have a choice; these were TARP recipients which, by their bailed-out status, were already on the White House leash. However, some of the smaller creditors, including Perella, reportedly insisted on getting fifty cents on the dollar.[17] Lauria says the White House explained this was the sort of offer you can't refuse:

> One of my clients was directly threatened by the White House and in essence compelled to withdraw its opposition to the deal under threat that the full force of the White House press corps would destroy its reputation if it continued to fight.... That was Perella Weinberg.[18]

We know the Obama team was no fan of Lauria's. The White House had brought in bankruptcy lawyer Matthew Feldman, a donor to Joe Biden and Rahm Emanuel,[19] to serve on the auto industry task force. In an email that the *Wall Street Journal* obtained, Feldman called Lauria a "terrorist" for resisting Obama's offer.[20]

Lauria told ABC News it was car czar Steven Rattner who had threatened to sic the news media on him and his clients.[21] But President Obama had already begun the process of demonizing the recalcitrant creditors. During the negotiations, the president declared:

> While many stakeholders made sacrifices and worked construc-
> tively, I have to tell you some did not. In particular, a group of
> investment firms and hedge funds decided to hold out for the
> prospect of an unjustified taxpayer-funded bailout. They were
> hoping that everybody else would make sacrifices, and they
> would have to make none. Some demanded twice the return
> that other lenders were getting. I don't stand with them.[22]

There's something rich in hearing Obama—who clinched passage of the great Wall Street bailout and demanded doubling of the automakers' bailout—talking about "an unjustified taxpayer-funded bailout." What's more, the president was misleading Americans. "They were hoping that everybody else would make sacrifices, and they would have to make none," he said of the creditors. But the funds say they were only asking for fifty cents of every dollar they were owed. The White House hasn't denied that.

Obama's statement was a startling use of the bully pulpit and a clear demonstration of the problems of nationalization. Obama was, in one sense, a business negotiating with other businesses. But unlike the other CEOs, he was the President of the United States, with unlimited access to free media, an army of public relations agents at his disposal, and the full U.S. government at his call. Some parties didn't like his offer, and so he used the power of the presidency to malign them.

When Perella ultimately accepted Obama's "offer," the firm issued a statement denying that it had been coerced by the White House. A White House spokesman denied the charge, too. Lauria never backed off his claims, though. He continued to represent other holdouts, and he told a court that his clients had received death threats for clashing with the administration. In court, the holdouts charged, "The government exerted extreme pressure to coerce all of [Chrysler's] constituencies into accepting a deal which is being done largely for the benefit of unsecured creditors at the expense of senior creditors."[23]

Not everyone lost like the secured creditors did, however. And one of the biggest winners to emerge from the Chrysler bankruptcy just happened to be one of the largest donors to the Democratic Party.

BIG LABOR IS BIG BUSINESS

The United Automobile, Aerospace & Agricultural Implement Workers of America International Union, known as the UAW, is, in effect, a big business. And it is a big business that is very friendly to Barack Obama and the Democratic Party.

During the campaign, Obama decried "the lobbyists, and the special interests who've turned our government into a game only they can afford to play. They write the checks and you get stuck with the bills, they get the access while you get to write a letter; they think they own this government."[24] That's actually a fair description of the UAW. And Obama's restructuring plan gave the union majority ownership of Chrysler.

UAW operates a political action committee that in the 2008 election spent $13.1 million.[25] Let's put that in perspective by comparing it to other "special interests." If you take the PACs of Exxon, Halliburton, Peabody Coal, and Lockheed Martin, combine their 2008-cycle political spending, and *multiply it by four*, you get just over $13.1 million.

The UAW PAC spent $1.8 million on House races. More than 99 percent of that money went to Democrats. The PAC contributed to thirty-nine Senate candidates, only one of whom was a Republican—Arlen Specter, who soon afterward became a Democrat. The PAC also gave a quarter million to other PACs— every dime went to Democrats.

The largest single chunk of that $13.1 million was nearly $4.5 million in independent expenditures to support Obama for president, and another $420,000 in independent expenditures to attack John McCain.

You can look at the Chrysler deal this way: Obama flexed his political muscle to take wealth away from creditors and give it to a powerful entity that had spent nearly $5 million helping him get elected. Talk about writing the checks and getting the access.

And the UAW's $1.6 million lobbying operation in 2008, operating out of a beautiful $3.94 million townhouse in Washington, D.C.'s coveted DuPont Circle neighborhood, certainly didn't hurt the union's fortunes.[26] The UAW has plenty of cash for lobbying, since it sits on nearly $1.2 billion in investments—an endowment, in effect.[27] One of the operations funded by the endowment: Black Lake Golf Club, whose 18-hole course, according to the UAW, is "one of the finest anywhere in the nation."[28]

This was the special interest Obama favored over Chrysler's creditors. To be fair, the creditors may have been betting on a taxpayer bailout, and so there's not much reason to cry for them. But the Chrysler bailout highlights the pernicious results when business and politics mix.

GOVERNMENT MOTORS

GM's history is tied up with Big Government. The largest supplier to the allies during World War II,[29] GM successfully lobbied for the passage of clean air regulations in the 1970s after the company had perfected and patented the catalytic converter. In 1980, GM used the state of Michigan to get a Polish neighborhood near Detroit condemned and turned into a GM factory.

So, in some sense it was fitting when Obama announced the U.S. government was taking ownership of GM.

But it was also a shock. The United States has long had the reputation of a free-market economy. General Motors is one of the premier manufacturers in the country's history. And Barack Obama nationalized General Motors. This is what you expect in France—or Venezuela.

As with Chrysler, GM's intimacy with government raised some serious conflicts of interest. For one thing, there's the lobbying. GM spent $2 million on lobbying in the second quarter of 2008,[30] even though that was the quarter the company went into bankruptcy and was taken over by government. Every business should have the right to speak to lawmakers and policymakers. But should taxpayers really be forced to pay lobbyists' salaries when the lobbyists are asking for more of the taxpayers' money?

Additionally, for a government-owned enterprise, there's the awkwardness of doing business overseas. GM announced in August it planned to invest $1.2 billion in Mexico.[31] I guess you can call it foreign aid. But even more awkward might be the joint venture GM announced in late August with FAW Group, a manufacturer owned by the Communist government of the People's Republic of China.[32]

Building factories in Mexico and China might be the best business moves for GM, but any out-of-work automaker would be right to object that his tax dollars—back when he had a job—

were financing GM, and so GM shouldn't be spending that money overseas.

THE CAR CZAR

The Obama administration, many pundits joke, has more czars than Russia's 300-year Romanov dynasty.[33] The president named at least thirty-one men and women to manage policy and make official decisions in areas ranging from Sudan to executive pay.[34]

Czars don't have to go through Senate approval. That perk may have helped Steven Rattner, who managed the federal takeover of GM, the forced merger of Chrysler with Fiat, and the bankruptcy of both carmakers before resigning in July amid a corporate scandal.

Rattner was an appropriate pick as Obama's car czar because he had spent much of his career making money at the intersection of business and government—an intersection Obama and Bush turned into a full-fledged parking lot.

First, in picking Rattner, Obama wasn't calling in the help of an auto industry expert—he was giving a job to a Democratic moneyman. From 1990 to 2009, Rattner contributed more than $800,000 to federal campaign committees, with almost every dime going to Democrats—and the Democratic National Committee receiving most of the money.[35]

In 2004, Rattner contributed to Obama's Senate election. In 2008, he gave the maximum to Obama, contributed to the campaigns of Rahm Emanuel and Joe Biden, and gave $14,250 to the Democratic National Committee. He also contributed in the fall to all the most competitive Democratic Senate candidates.

Rattner might get a scolding at home if he wasn't giving to Democrats—his wife, Maureen White, is the DNC Finance Chair,[36] meaning she's the party's top fundraiser. She was a

Hillary Clinton backer early in the 2008 cycle,[37] as was Steve early on, but both jumped seamlessly over to Obama after he won the nomination. Each reportedly raised $100,000 for Obama's campaign.[38] After Obama was elected, Rattner gave another $5,000 to Obama's transition team.[39] Rattner, as *Business Week* put it, "has spent three decades cultivating relationships with people who matter."[40]

That's the man Obama chose to manage the auto industry: a well-connected Democratic moneyman. And Rattner's business record shows his expertise fits in well with Obamanomics: he knows how to turn public policy into private profit.

Rattner co-founded an investment firm called Quadrangle Group, and one thing Quadrangle invested in was legislation. On February 1, 2005, the company retained a K Street firm called Navigant Consulting to lobby the House and Senate on asbestos litigation reform.[41]

What was the firm's stake in asbestos litigation? Neither Quadrangle nor its lobbyists would tell me when I asked. But there's enough evidence out there to suggest a likely story. The firm invested heavily in bankrupt companies or companies facing serious solvency problems.[42] This is a risky world in which to play, but that's partly the nature of hedge funds.

Perhaps Quandrangle, as did other hedge funds, invested in companies facing asbestos lawsuits—this could be home builders or materials makers who were responsible for asbestos in homes or factories, or simply factories that had asbestos in them. The public knowledge of the lawsuits and expectation of huge legal costs had dragged the stock price low, giving the hedge funds a good price. These funds often made complementary investments in lobbyists, pushing legislation to reduce the companies' legal liability.

Quadrangle could have been making this play, or the opposite: lobby to get a favorable asbestos bill proposed in Congress, short the companies' stocks after their prices rise, then lobby to kill the bill.

In the asbestos-hedge fund-lobbying game, sometimes the lobbyists just acted as intelligence gatherers. Consider this, from a 2006 *Wall Street Journal* article:

> Some hedge funds, which tend to choose riskier investments that can yield high returns, saw the troubled asbestos companies as attractive. To weigh the value of their investments and decipher bankruptcy-court actions, hedge funds hired teams of analysts and researchers. When Congress began considering legislation to bail out the industry, the funds hired lobbyists to assess its prospects.[43]

Whatever Quadrangle's asbestos play was, it showed that Rattner, a political insider, aimed to turn government connections into profit.

Sometimes this business-government coziness borders on illegality, and Rattner's Quadrangle was caught up in two such flaps. One deal involved Rattner's firm financing the movie *Chooch*, a box-office bomb. Steven Loglisci was the producer. David Loglisci, Steven's brother, was the deputy state controller in charge of the state pension fund. The *New York Daily News* tells the story:

> David Loglisci got a money manager doing business with the pension fund to arrange a DVD distribution deal for his brother's film. The indictment doesn't name the fund manager.
>
> The film was distributed on DVD beginning in July 2005 by GoodTimes Entertainment, which at the time was owned by Quadrangle Group LLC.
>
> Quadrangle won $150 million in pension fund business in March 2005, just months before "Chooch" went to DVD.[44]

In a related case, the Securities and Exchange Commission alleges that a "senior executive" at Quadrangle—Rattner, according to the *Wall Street Journal*[45] and Reuters[46]—promised kickbacks to the man the city had hired to help it invest its pension-fund money. Sure enough, Quadrangle soon got an investment from the city's pension fund. As the New York pension fund scandal grew, Rattner stepped down from his czar post. But he remains well-connected—he is the personal money manager for New York City mayor Michael Bloomberg.[47]

Although Rattner himself has not been charged with any crime, these appearances of impropriety swirled around his business because he operated at the business-government intersection where half the parties are playing with other people's money. It's a recipe for corruption, and it highlights the contradictions of Obama's agenda: you can't increase government without increasing opportunities for corruption.

CASH FOR CLUNKERS

The Cash-for-Clunkers corporate welfare scheme, costing $3 billion in taxpayer money, captured every aspect of Obamanomics: big government, high spending, running up debt, rewarding special interests, claiming environmental benefit, claiming economic stimulus, and displaying ignorance of basic economics.

The idea was this: anyone buying a new car that got at least eighteen miles per gallon could get a taxpayer-funded voucher of $3,500 to $4,500 if she also traded in a car with sufficiently inferior fuel efficiency. The other condition: the dealer taking the "clunker" was required by law to destroy the car by pouring sodium silicate—known as "liquid glass"—into the engine.

This was unusual—a government program subsidizing destruction. But the destruction was the key to helping the "special interests" that were behind the bill.

It turns out the $4,500 subsidy itself may not have been a huge boon to the car dealers and manufacturers. The subsidy certainly drove buyers to the lots—in the first days of the program, dealers were overrun. In fact, the program quickly ran out of its $1 billion first tranche of funding. But did that mean additional sales?

Not really, according to at least one economic analyst. Economic modeler Macroeconomic Advisers, wrote:

> [W]e expect that roughly half of the 250,000 in new sales would have occurred in the months following the conclusion of the program, and the other half would have occurred during the program period anyway. Therefore, we do not expect a boost to industry-wide production (or GDP) in response to this program.[48]

In other words, Cash for Clunkers didn't generate new auto sales as much as it shifted them from Independence Day or Labor Day to the first week of August. The data confirmed this. GM's sales in September 2009 were 45 percent below its numbers for September 2008[49]—which was the industry's worst month in fifteen years. Chrysler posted a 32 percent drop from a year earlier, while Toyota and Honda both fell by double digits.

Those lucky enough to be in position to buy a car in August 2009 were subsidized by everybody else, but the customer didn't pocket the whole subsidy. With a $4,500 subsidy, a customer's price limit for a car goes up. That means the clunker cash gets split between the dealer and the customer. So, the dealer is getting a portion of the $4,500 subsidy, plus a few additional sales.

But for the dealer, the real subsidy came from the destruction.

Every Cash-for-Clunkers deal meant one drivable used car was destroyed and removed from the market. Diminishing supply drives up price. The price of used cars rises when the supply is reduced, but the price of new cars also increases. Raising the price of used cars makes people more willing to buy new cars (because there is less of a discount for the used cars), and thus drives demand on new cars—boosting their price.

So this was the heart of Cash for Clunkers: destroying cars to make other cars more expensive.

As a subsidy to automakers and auto dealers, the benefit is clear. But for the broader economy, the benefit is imaginary. Relevant here is the "broken window fallacy," explained by economists Frédéric Bastiat[50] and Henry Hazlitt.[51] This fallacy is the misguided notion that destruction can generate wealth. If a hoodlum smashes the baker's window with a rock, one might point out the glass worker now has new business, selling the window to the baker. The glass worker, newly enriched from the sale, might spend his profits on a new suit, thus profiting the tailor, who in turn buys a new chair, and so on.

But breaking the window doesn't, in fact, stimulate the economy. While it means a new suit for the glass worker, it also means the baker has to spend money on a window rather than on a suit. So the tailor is no better off than if the window weren't smashed, and neither are the folks who got the tailor's money. Maybe the tailor was planning on buying new shoes instead of a suit—in which case the broken window helped the tailor at the expense of the shoemaker. The only net difference is one less window and one more pile of broken glass in the street. Insofar as a window is better than a pile of broken glass, society is poorer.

Similarly, each Cash-for-Clunkers deal means America has one less drivable car and one more pile of scrap metal. Labor and energy went into turning the steel of that car into a frame, an engine, and a transmission, and that labor and energy is now scrapped. This is simple waste. Sure, much of the material could be recycled, but that takes more energy and labor. And of course, the added energy taken up in this build-destroy-build cycle mitigates the environmental gains of the program.

But Obamanomics counts this added labor as "creating jobs." If that's the case, though, why trash only clunkers? Why shouldn't Steve Rattner drive around American cities with a wrecking ball on the back of a truck, smashing people's cars and cutting the owner a check so that he can buy a new one? That would also spur auto sales and "create jobs."

FOLLOW THE LOBBYING TRAIL

While destruction and waste provide broad economic growth only in the fallacious world of Obamanomics, the destruction of Cash for Clunkers does provide some real benefits for a few— those "special interests" Obama supposedly was going to chase out of the temple. And these include more than just the car dealers and the automakers.

For example, look at Nucor Steel.[52] Nucor has a factory in Auburn, New York, that recycles scrap steel into sheet metal and other steel products.[53] Subsidizing the scrapping of cars forces the taxpayers to pay for Nucor's feedstock.

Nucor retained the K Street firm Wiley Rein, LLP, which lobbied for the company on a handful of issues, including Cash for Clunkers. One of the lobbyists on the account was Michael Bloomquist, who had been deputy general counsel for the House Energy and Commerce Committee.

Nucor's interest in this legislation could explain why New York senator Chuck Schumer was so enthusiastic to expand the program from $1 billion to $3 billion. Schumer, in calling for the extra $2 billion, said, "The bottom line is if it ain't broke, don't fix it."[54] Ironically, by this he meant taxpayers should continue subsidizing the destruction of working cars.

This tripling of the funding was needed because the first billion dollars was spent in a few days, highlighting the bad business sense so emblematic of Obamanomics. Not only did the immediate draining of the clunker cash show the inability of Congress and the White House to make proper budget estimates, it also reflected, as columnist Michael Barone put it, the government's inability to properly price things. If the goal was to drive as many auto sales and destroy as many used cars as possible, it's clear that $4,500 was not the optimal price to pay. Barone explained:

> Markets are good at price discovery; government isn't. If the House bill adding $2 billion in stimulus funds to the cash for clunkers program passes the Senate, the government will spend $3 billion for 750,000 trade-ins. If Congress had set the rebate at $1,333 instead of $4,000, it might well have had to spend only $1 billion for the same number of trade-ins. In which case Congress will have spent an extra $2 billion for no good reason.[55]

Once the clunker cash ran out, Congress rushed to add the additional $2 billion. The Obama administration, especially Transportation Secretary Ray LaHood, led the charge. While pushing for the new money—to come out of stimulus money, meaning it would be borrowed—Vice President Biden told the program's critics, "I think it would be hard to tell...the thousands of people who have just traded in gas guzzlers for more efficient cars that this is having no impact."[56]

Sure, but everyone who didn't participate in the program was paying for that benefit to the few who did. Particularly hard hit are lower-income people who can't afford a new car. The used car they might have bought has now been turned into a heap of scrap steel. It would also be hard to tell that person—who now can't afford a car because his tax dollars went to destroying the 2000 Volvo S80 he would have bought, while subsidizing his boss's purchase of a 2010 Toyota Avalon with a sunroof and variable-temperature heated leather seats—that the program is having no impact.

Recall Obama during the campaign: "What I do get frustrated with is an economy that is out of balance, that rewards a very few—with rewards that are all out of proportion to their actual success—while ordinary, hardworking Americans continue to get squeezed."[57] He seems to be precisely describing Cash for Clunkers.

The environmental benefits were probably overhyped, too. A *Business Week* analysis calculated that Cash for Clunkers reduced America's greenhouse gas emissions by a miniscule .04 percent.[58] But the claims of broad environmental and economic benefits didn't matter too much to the companies that profited from the measure.

Who lobbied for the bill? Of course the automakers were the most active, and the National Automobile Dealers Association pushed its members to call and write Congress in support of the program. In addition to Nucor, the U.S. Chamber of Commerce[59] and the National Association of Manufacturers[60] also supported the program.

Benefitting the special interests, increasing government, raising costs, spending taxpayers' money, and adding to the national debt, all for a program based on flawed economics and dubious environmental claims—that's Obamanomics.

CHAPTER 8

BARACK O'BAILOUT

OBAMA SAVES WALL STREET

Barack Obama was not the original author of the Great Wall Street Bailout of 2008. But he carried it across the goal line when he—perhaps alone—was in position to block it.

Later, when Obama became president, he brought with him one of the chief authors of the bailouts, Tim Geithner. Obama also reappointed the captain of the bailout ship, Federal Reserve Chairman Ben Bernanke. And one of the bailout innovators of the last twenty-five years, Larry Summers, sits in the West Wing. Unsurprisingly, Obama's team rolled out new bailouts in 2009, and its financial "reforms" would institutionalize them.

Obama, undeniably, is a Bailout President.

Even aside from the bailouts, Obama is cozy with Wall Street. He packed his administration with Goldman Sachs alumni, and he received more campaign cash from the finance industry than any politician in history. In supporting Obama, the industry is acting out of normal self-interest: it knows his plans for a robust federal involvement in Wall Street would actually end up helping the fat cats of Big Finance.

The Obama administration is from Wall Street, and Obamanomics is good news for Wall Street. On this score, at least, it's hard to see how, compared to Bush, Obama represents Change.

GEORGE W. BUSH AND THE YEAR OF THE BAILOUT

This book has focused on Obama's damage to the free market, small business, taxpayers, and consumers. But this criticism needs to be put in context. Everything Obama has done to grow government—to boost spending, hike taxes, and increase federal control over our economy—is the legacy of President George W. Bush.

Bush may never have brought our country this far down the road of Obamanomics—he may not have taken over the most important manufacturers, tied a tight harness around our energy companies, and turned the health sector into a managed economy—but with his flood of bailouts in 2008, especially the Great Wall Street Bailout, Bush got the tank of state rolling over the country's tradition of free enterprise—and Obamanomics is just the next gear.

Had Bush governed in 2008 according to the free-market principles he espoused for eight years, Obama wouldn't, politically, have been able to do what he has done. Capping Wall Street executive pay? That would have sounded downright Communist coming from Obama—had Bush not put these executives on the federal dole. Buying General Motors? Unprecedented, unconstitutional, and un-American—except that Bush bought AIG and expanded the Great Wall Street Bailout to Detroit. A $787 billion stimulus financed through borrowed money? Reckless beyond words—except that Bush had approved $700 billion in borrowing to finance his Wall Street bailout.

"I've abandoned free-market principles to save the free-market system,"[1] Bush said on his way out the door. If saving the free-market really was his aim, it's clear he misfired. Bush abandoned this country's free-market principles in the back alley. And when Obama took over the store, Rahm Emanuel went out back and tossed those principles in a dumpster that Tim Geithner drove to the landfill.

A voter asked me in the days before the 2008 election, "Do you think Obama is a socialist?" I had to answer, "Right now, it seems everyone in Washington is a socialist."

SECRETARY BAILOUT

Timothy Geithner, then-President of the Federal Reserve Bank of New York, was the key architect of Bush's early bailouts. Geithner's work impressed Obama, who later tapped Geithner as Treasury Secretary. This may have surprised some observers in light of Obama's continuous denunciation of Bush's economic policies as sops to the rich. But the appointment makes perfect sense: Geithner's resourcefulness in finding novel ways to expand government was just the quality Obama would need to implement his economic program.

Geithner revealed his inclinations early in the game. "The severity and complexity of this crisis," he told a crowd of Wall Street bankers in June 2008, "makes a compelling case for a comprehensive reassessment of how to use regulation to strike an appropriate balance between efficiency and stability."[2] With the Dow Jones Industrial Average still above 11,000 at the time, it would be months before the financial troubles became a meltdown.

But Geithner already saw big possibilities, declaring, "This crisis gives us the opportunity to bring about fundamental change" in Washington's relationship with Wall Street.

This was Obama's "Hope-and-Change" talk in banker-speak. Obama, after his election, would promise to "discover great opportunity in the midst of great crisis,"[3] and would describe his job as "remaking America."[4] Because our Founders didn't give the government the power to "remake" the nation, Obama would need someone like Geithner—someone who also wanted to seize crises to bring about dramatic change, even if some rules had to be bent along the way.

More important than his vision may have been Geithner's skills. He is an expert at gaming the bureaucracy and doing things nobody thought government could do—which may explain why Obama would go to the mat for Geithner's nomination while letting other nominees drop off upon the first bump in the road.

Geithner has exploited a seemingly impossible loophole in his hiring—naming a Goldman Sachs lobbyist as his chief of staff despite the president's restrictions on such hiring—and showed similar creativity in his taxes, which slowed down his confirmation as Treasury Secretary.

Crucially, Geithner's nose for loopholes might have been the key to Bush's bailouts, which required Enron-style gymnastics to execute.

HOW TIM GEITHNER BROKE THE BAILOUT DAM

There was a time when corporate bailouts were shocking to the U.S. media and the American people.[5] The Constitution didn't set up any mechanisms for the federal government to bail out private companies, and the unpopularity of bailouts has made Congress hesitant to change the law to allow them explicitly.

But bailouts have now become commonplace. Today, we all assume that more struggling industries will soon get on the federal dole, and in our next recession we can expect bailouts as a matter of course.

The sea change began in early 2008 with some crafty navigation of the law by Geithner in order to bail out Bear Stearns. In March 2008, Federal Reserve chairman Ben Bernanke and Geithner, who served on the Fed's Board of Governors, decided Bear Stearns needed a bailout loan. Because Bear Stearns was an investment bank and not a commercial bank, however, it was not regulated by the Fed nor was it eligible for a loan from the Fed.

Bernanke and Geithner could have called on Congress to pass an emergency bailout law, as Jimmy Carter did for Chrysler in 1979 and President Bush did for the airlines after 9/11—but that would involve messy politics and democracy-type stuff. Instead, Geithner, Bernanke, and crew dusted off Section 13(3) of the Federal Reserve Act—a special exception that allows a Federal Reserve Bank "in unusual and exigent circumstances," to lend money to non-banks.

To trigger this clause, a loan requires the approval of at least five members of the Fed's Board of Governors. At the time of the vote, however, the Board of Governors had two vacancies, meaning there were only five members total, and one member had not yet returned from a trip to Finland.[6] That posed no problem for Geithner, who exploited a loophole validating a measure if it's approved unanimously by all "available" board members.[7]

Having dispatched with little legal technicalities like voting, the Fed called on J.P. Morgan to buy Bear Stearns. The firm was willing, but it didn't want to own the "toxic assets" on Bear's books—it wanted the Fed to buy those.

Since the Fed isn't allowed to buy any assets at all, it needed another loophole. It came in the form of "Maiden Lane," a so-called special purpose vehicle, that pillar of Enron's financial shenanigans. The website Talking Points Memo quotes an expert on how this worked:

> Fed came up with this idea to start a shadow company, called a special purpose vehicle.... The deal then was JP Morgan put $1 billion into Maiden Lane, the Fed put $29 billion in cash into it. Maiden Lane paid Bear Stearns $30 billion, which went straight back to JP Morgan as this deal happened simultaneously to JP's purchase of Bear. So Morgan got $30 billion in cash ($29 billion net), and the Fed got stuck owning the crap but was legally only making a loan to Maiden Lane, who was the legal owner (Maiden Lane was incorporated not in NYC, but in Delaware to avoid paying taxes).[8]

So, while a few citizens' groups, left and right, have sued the Fed for its Bear Stearns bailout, it appears that Geithner, Bernanke, and the Fed always followed the letter of the law, even if they followed it somewhere nobody ever thought it could go.

GEITHNER AND BERNANKE GET CREATIVE TO BAIL OUT AIG

The skullduggery surrounding the Bear Stearns bailout demonstrates what sort of creature the Federal Reserve is: shadowy, powerful, and unaccountable. It's also clear what sort of operator Geithner is: determined, clever, and aggressive. These characteristics also shined through in the AIG bailout.

The Bush brain trust, with Bernanke and Geithner at the helm, wanted the government to buy AIG in order to bail out AIG's creditors, or "counterparties" as they put it. But no regular government agency could buy a private company without an authorization and appropriation from Congress.

Geithner's Federal Reserve Bank of New York, on the other hand, could make up money out of thin air (in a way, that's why

Congress created the Fed in the first place), but it still couldn't buy up companies. What to do? In the end, the New York Fed loaned AIG $85 billion (eventually, it would loan more), and in exchange, the federal government—but not the Fed—got 79.9 percent ownership in AIG. But the entire deal was so murky that nobody really knew who took ownership of AIG.

With the lack of transparency and oversight, it was inevitable that some scandal would ensue. This happened in March 2009 when news broke that AIG executives were poised to collect huge bonuses after running their company into the ground. The bonuses, in fact, were made possible by another Geithner loophole.[9] Obama's stimulus included a provision limiting employees' pay at businesses bailed out by government. Geithner's Treasury Department, however, inserted language exempting pre-promised bonuses from this restriction.

Taking a step back, the whole AIG bailout is akin to one big loophole. Bailing out AIG is really bailing out its counterparties, such as Goldman Sachs and Deutsche Bank. Before the Great Wall Street Bailout, AIG was a backdoor way to funnel cash, with no appropriations and no obvious fingerprints, to ailing Wall Street firms.

But the AIG bailout proved insufficient. Geithner, Bernanke, and then-Treasury Secretary Henry Paulson soon decided even more drastic measures were needed to save Wall Street. And Obama would prove their most important congressional ally.

OBAMA GUARANTEES VICTORY FOR THE GREAT WALL STREET BAILOUT

Barack Obama didn't write the Great Wall Street Bailout of 2008, but he guaranteed its passage, bringing his party with him.

In one sense, Obama was only one of a hundred senators voting on the Troubled Asset Relief Program (TARP), a bill that passed the Senate with seventy-four votes.[10] But Obama, more than anyone else in America, could have stopped this transfer of $700 billion from all Americans to the very Wall Street characters who had brought about the economic meltdown. Imagine if Obama—the Democrats' presidential nominee—had opposed TARP. His party, which held a majority in the Senate and House, would have largely followed suit. But instead Obama rallied behind Bush's bailout even while attacking the president for policies that "give more and more to the most" in the hope that "somehow prosperity will trickle down."[11]

Any politician would have done the same, given the dire circumstances, Obama's defenders argue. And to a large extent, they're right. Throughout the political spectrum, men and women shed their principles in fall 2008. Many conservatives embraced radical Big Government. Many laissez faire boosters couldn't let things be. Many progressives backed regressive wealth transfers. Just as there are, supposedly, no atheists in a foxhole, there are very few free-marketeers or anti-corporate crusaders during a financial crisis.

But Obama was supposed to be different—the harbinger of a new politics. In mid-2007, toward the beginning of his campaign, Obama declared, "We need a President who sees government not as a tool to enrich well-connected friends and high-priced lobbyists, but as the defender of fairness and opportunity for every American."[12] This was a major campaign theme, as Obama passionately vowed to break the "stranglehold" lobbyists and special interests exert on American democracy. He admonished corporate lobbyists that "a new day has dawned"[13] and warned of "a rude awakening" in store for the special interests that "think they own this government."[14]

And then the hour arrived, and Capitol Hill was bombarded with tens of thousands of citizen phone calls opposing TARP.

Indicating where public sentiment really lay, nearly every vulnerable member of the U.S. House from both parties voted against the bailout. But Obama ignored grassroots America and gave a few hundred Wall Street lobbyists what they wanted—he carried TARP across the goal line. In doing so, he confirmed that the special interests do indeed "own this government." He showed us just what sort of "new day has dawned": a new day in which Washington's devotion to Big Business is explicit rather than hidden.

Obama, McCain, and Bush all waved the bailout flag. They created the $700 billion, open-ended TARP bill, which could fairly be described—to borrow an Obama campaign phrase—as "a tool to enrich well-connected friends." And those well-connected friends on Wall Street breathed a sigh of relief.

Most of official Washington still argues that TARP saved us from a complete financial collapse. Of course there's no disproving that counterfactual, because all we can see is what happened post-TARP: a painful, but not catastrophic economic downturn, which is exactly what TARP opponents predicted would happen *without* a bailout.

And there's no reason to impugn Obama's motives. It's not likely he was bailing out Wall Street in order to reward his generous banker donors. (Though, if their generosity didn't make him vote Aye, it should have made him blush: he raised more from the industry than had any politician in history.)

Obama believes in Big Government. The lesson he drew from the economic meltdown was that government wasn't doing enough. He really was trying to save the economy by means of transferring regular people's wealth to Wall Street banks. He thought this was best for the country.

Regardless of motives, though, the lesson was clear: for the well-connected businesses important enough to pose "systemic risk," Obamanomics means never having to absorb your full losses.

OBAMA'S BAILOUTS

After becoming president, Obama bailed out more banks and even moved to institutionalize the practice.

In March 2009, Treasury Secretary Geithner announced the Public-Private Investment Program, or PPIP.[15] This is a double-shot bailout benefitting both banks and investors, with taxpayers serving as the involuntary co-investors and lenders.

PPIP aimed at helping banks unload two kinds of "toxic assets": loans that might never get paid back, and some complex investments whose values were unknown.

Under PPIP, Geithner's Treasury would go Dutch with any private investor willing to buy one of these scary loans. Then the Federal Deposit Insurance Corporation would come with its bailout cash: a loan for more than 85 percent of the purchase price. (The FDIC was established during the Depression to cover your deposits if your bank went under. Geithner turned it into a bailout lender.) Most important, the FDIC's loan was a "non-recourse" loan, meaning the borrowers could default and suffer no penalty except for giving up the collateral—in this case, the scary loan they just bought.

In practice, this scheme worked this way: a hedge fund buys a mortgage loan from Bank of America for $70. Treasury pays for half of it with taxpayer money. Then the FDIC finances six-sevenths of the deal, meaning the hedge fund and the Treasury have each put down $5 and the FDIC has floated a $60 loan. If the loan performs well, the hedge fund might be able to sell it for $100, in which case the investors—Treasury and the hedge fund—pay off the FDIC loan and split the $30 left over. So, for $5 plus some fees, the hedge fund walks away with $15—a 200 percent return on an investment that appreciated only 43 percent.

But if the mortgage holder defaults and the mortgage is worth only $40, the hedge fund simply walks away, the FDIC takes ownership of the mortgage, and the fund has lost only $5. Taxpayers have shelled out a $60 loan through the FDIC and a $5 invest-ment through Treasury. That $5 investment is gone, and in exchange for the $60 loan, the FDIC now has a loan worth only $40. So the PPIP bails out both the bank, which can now sell its mortgage at a subsidized price, and the investor (the hedge fund in the above example), which gets to offload its risk onto the tax-payers. Treasury established a similar program for "toxic" secu-rities, in which the Treasury, using borrowed money, acts as both the co-investor and the lender.

Think about the PPIP and then recall Obama's campaign-season attack on Bush and McCain's financial policies:

> Now, we also have to recognize that this is a final verdict on eight years of failed economic policies promoted by George Bush, supported by Senator McCain: a theory that basically says that we can shred regulations and consumer protections and give more and more to the most, and somehow prosperity will trickle down.[16]

Obama's plan sounds the same: bail out bankers and investors with taxpayer money, and hope that helps the broader economy.

BEN BERNANKE, CAPTAIN BAILOUT

On August 25, 2009, President Obama interrupted his vacation to nominate Ben Bernanke to a second four-year term as chairman of the Federal Reserve Bank. "Ben approached a financial system on the verge of collapse with calm and wisdom," Obama said, "with bold action and outside-the-box thinking that has helped put the brakes on our economic freefall."[17]

By "bold action," of course, Obama meant more than a trillion dollars in bailouts. By "outside-the-box thinking," he meant unprecedented and previously unimagined expansions of power by the Federal Reserve—all expansions that saved the big Wall Street banks at the expense of regular people.

Aside from Bear Stearns, AIG, and TARP, Bernanke initiated other "bold," "outside-the-box" bailouts that apparently struck Obama as signs of "wisdom." Bernanke's first bailout came in late 2007, when the housing crisis was beginning to hit, and worried banks were slowing their lending to other banks. Deciding to step in where banks were unwilling to go, Bernanke created a "Term Auction Facility,"[18] which would lend money—hundreds of billions of dollars created out of thin air—to banks every two weeks.

Come March, Bernanke invited Wall Street firms to this borrowing feast at the Fed and called this proto-Wall Street bailout the "Term Securities Lending Facility."[19] In July, Bernanke welcomed Fannie Mae and Freddie Mac to the Fed trough as well.[20]

When the Bush administration finally took control of Fannie Mae and Freddie Mac in early September, the Fed didn't play a direct role, but Bernanke applauded the move: "I strongly endorse both the decision by FHFA Director Lockhart to place Fannie Mae and Freddie Mac into conservatorship and the actions taken by Treasury Secretary Paulson to ensure the financial soundness of those two companies," he said.[21]

All this "outside-the-box thinking" was also outside the democratic process. This is the nature of the Federal Reserve. The Fed doesn't need Congress for its bailouts because the Fed doesn't need appropriations. The Fed makes its own money. No, it doesn't print bills. But when the Fed buys or lends money to a bank or a Wall Street firm, it isn't spending down its own balance. It simply conjures the money out of nowhere.

That's an incredible power, which is why the Fed has traditionally been contained to a limited role. Bernanke and Geithner dramatically expanded that role. And Obama applauded their "bold action." Since then, Obama has proposed giving the Fed even more power—which must be music to the ears of its most favored clients.

THE GOLDMAN CALF

Sherman McCoy set his sights too low.

The tragic main character of Tom Wolfe's novel, *Bonfire of the Vanities*, considered himself one of the "Masters of the Universe" because of all the money he controlled, the investment decisions he made, the businesses he propped up, and the businesses he helped sink. McCoy was a top Wall Street investment banker who, in his own self-image, made the world of finance move.

A banker at Goldman Sachs would adopt this same self-image only in a fit of self-pity. Goldman doesn't merely pull the levers of finance and commerce. Goldman, more than any other company, pulls the levers of government.

Consider this timeline: in 2007, Goldman reported net revenues of $46 billion, yielding profit of $11.6 billion[22]—the largest ever profit on Wall Street. In 2008, Goldman played a central role in the Wall Street bailouts, pocketing billions in bailout cash. In July 2009, Goldman posted second-quarter post-tax profits of $3.44 billion.[23]

In the context of Obamanomics, Goldman's role is notable. Obviously Goldman's campaign contributions to Obama—the firm was his top corporate source of funding—did not drive the AIG bailout, because Obama wasn't president yet, and Geithner and Bernanke weren't working for him. But in 2008 and 2009, Goldman helped transform the relationship between business and government. Goldman's tight ties to government indicate this firm may be the ultimate "special interest"—only General Electric could rival its claim. Thus Obama's coziness with Goldman is enough to puncture his insistence that he battles the powerful special interests.

First, let's start with Goldman's role in the AIG bailout. Consider this report from writer Joe Hagan in *New York* magazine, on the September 2008 meeting in which Bernanke, Paulson, and Geithner hatched the AIG bailout:

> At the meeting, it was hard to discern where concerns over AIG's collapse ended and concern for Goldman Sachs began: Among the 40 or so people in attendance, Goldman Sachs was on every side of the large conference table, with "triple" the number of representatives as other banks, says another person who was there. The entourage was led by the bank's top brass: CEO [Lloyd] Blankfein, co-chief operating officer Jon Winkelried, investment-banking head David Solomon, and its top merchant-banking executive Richard Friedman—all of whom had worked closely with Hank Paulson two years prior. By contrast, JPMorgan CEO Jamie Dimon did not attend. (Goldman Sachs has said that Blankfein left after twenty minutes, realizing he was the only chief executive present. But the person who was there says Blankfein was directly engaged in at least one full AIG meeting that Monday, appearing "ashen-faced" and "jumpy.")
>
> On the government side, Goldman was also well represented: Geithner himself had never worked for Goldman, but he was an acolyte of former Goldman co-chairman and Clinton Treasury secretary Robert Rubin. Former Goldman vice-president Dan Jester served as Paulson's representative from the Treasury. And though Paulson himself wasn't present, he didn't need to be: He was intimately aware of Goldman's historical relationship with AIG, since the original AIG swaps were acquired on his watch at Goldman.[24]

Goldman, it turns out, had a key stake in AIG's fate: it had $13 billion at risk in AIG credit-default swaps. That kind of loss, Hagan notes, "could have destroyed Goldman at that moment."[25]

So, when Geithner's New York Fed, through its special purpose entities, bought AIG with money it essentially created out of thin air, Bernanke and Geithner were diluting the value of every dollar you have earned and saved and funneling your wealth through their made-up companies, through AIG, and to Wall Street firms—Goldman Sachs most of all.

Bush, Bernanke, Paulson, and Geithner actually approved three AIG bailouts—the first in September and then two after the election—and then Obama, Bernanke, and Geithner approved a fourth in March 2009. How did AIG get so deep in the hole? *Time* magazine economics writer Justin Fox explains it this way:

> Essentially, AIG got into the business of insuring much of the world's financial system against the consequences of a global financial meltdown. It turned out to be incapable of delivering on that insurance—no private company could deliver on it, which is one reason why AIG's business of selling credit default swaps was a scam. And so government has stepped in as the ultimate insurer.[26]

So why did Goldman, supposedly brilliant, expose itself so much to AIG? It's reasonable, given the company's closeness to government, to conclude Goldman was counting on a bailout if things went badly.

So, when Obama speaks of special interests, Goldman should be the first that comes to mind.

THE GOLDMAN-OBAMA NEXUS

Goldman Sachs employees and executives gave $997,050 to Barack Obama's campaign.[27] Not only is that four times as much money as John McCain raised from Goldman—it's more than the combined Goldman haul of every Republican running for president, the Senate, and the House in 2008. Yes, Barack Obama, by himself, raised more from Goldman than did 500 Republican politicians running for federal office.

As a campaign advisor on economics, Obama tapped Warren Buffett, who also hosted a fundraiser for Obama. During the campaign and right before the bailout, Buffett invested $5 billion in Goldman, and explicitly stated he wouldn't have done so if he didn't expect government to act.[28] So, a top Obama advisor was betting on bailouts for Goldman, and Senator Obama played a key role in getting a bailout approved. Later, President Obama piled on with $30 billion more in AIG bailout money,[29] which was, largely, Goldman bailout money.

Come July 2009, Goldman was posting healthy profits, and so was Buffett. The *New York Post* reported:

> Goldman Sachs' remarkable comeback from the brink of financial Armageddon is adding luster to Warren Buffett's investment street cred—and more importantly, lining the billionaire investor's outsize pockets.
>
> Buffett's $5 billion investment in Goldman is yielding a paper return of more than $2.5 billion for his investment firm Berkshire Hathaway.[30]

Recall Obama's words: "We need a President who sees government not as a tool to enrich well-connected friends and high-priced lobbyists."[31]

Obama's West Wing also has deep connections to Goldman. First, there is Rahm Emanuel, the White House chief of staff. As noted in chapter two, Rahm got cozy with Goldman back in 1992 on Bill Clinton's presidential campaign—Rahm was Clinton's chief fundraiser, and Goldman became Clinton's top donor. The

Federal Election Commission criticized the campaign for some finance improprieties, including its acceptance of apparently prohibited discounts from Goldman. Meanwhile, Goldman paid Emanuel a retainer equaling about $35,000 a year for vaguely defined work at a time when the Clinton campaign was paying him just $60,000 to be its tireless full-time fundraiser.[32]

Next, there is Larry Summers, who runs Obama's National Economic Council. Summers, whom Goldman paid $135,000 for a single speech in 2008,[33] was the chief engineer in 1994 of the Mexican bailout. Goldman was the largest underwriter of Mexican financial deals back then,[34] and thus the bailout's prime beneficiary. Setting a precedent for the executive branch bailing out investors without approval from Congress, the Mexican bailout tapped an obscure "Exchange Stabilization Fund" in order to save the hides of the Wall Street firms that would suffer if the peso collapsed.

Third, Obama's deputy national security advisor is Tom Donilon, who came to the West Wing from law firm-lobbying firm O'Melveny and Myers. There, he represented Goldman Sachs among other clients.[35]

Over in Obama's Department of Treasury, there's also a strong whiff of Goldman in the air. Timothy Geithner never worked at Goldman, but he helped Summers in implementing the Mexican bailout, to Goldman's relief. Geithner also counted as a mentor Robert Rubin, who was a top Goldman executive before becoming Bill Clinton's treasury secretary. Geithner's right-hand man, Mark Patterson, as discussed in chapter three, was a lobbyist for Goldman until April 2008.

And Obama's pick as State Department undersecretary for economic, energy and agricultural affairs was Robert Hormats, a former Goldman vice president.

So Goldman, a preeminent "special interest," has unmatched access to Obama's White House. But the rest of Wall Street isn't left out.

OBAMANOMICS ON WALL STREET

Obama raised more money from the securities & investment industry—$14.8 million—than any candidate in history, according to the Center for Responsive Politics.[36] Hedge funds gave more than twice as much to Obama as to McCain.[37] Commercial Banks gave Obama $3.2 million, almost 50 percent more than they gave McCain.[38]

After Goldman, the industry's top political giver in the 2008 election was Morgan Stanley,[39] whose employees and executives gave Obama $515,000 compared to $273,000 for McCain.[40] The donations from executives illuminate the intimate political ties between Wall Street and Washington. For example, one of the donors was Thomas Nides, chief administrative officer at Morgan Stanley. Nides is an entrenched Democratic operative and money-man. He served as a staffer to Democratic house speaker Tom Foley, became chief of staff to Bill Clinton's U.S. Trade Representative,[41] then landed a senior vice president gig at Fannie Mae,[42] the government-sponsored enterprise that enriched many top Democrats while fueling the housing bubble. Now he's a Morgan Stanley executive, and he's given more than $76,000 to politicians, including the maximum to Obama in 2008.[43]

So it should be no surprise that Wall Street regards Obama as an indispensible ally. And Obama is indeed delivering numerous gifts to Big Finance, even aside from the bailouts.

For example, take a look at Obama's plans to create a Consumer Financial Protection Agency. Obama claimed this regulatory agency is "charged with just one job: looking out for the

interests of ordinary Americans in the financial system."[44] What
could be wrong with that? Obama spoke of borrowers duped by
lenders and realtors. He mentioned credit card holders fooled by
sudden rate explosions. And he proposed a slew of new regulations and new regulatory bodies to protect consumers from
unscrupulous lenders.

But the Independent Community Bankers of America objected
that the proposal would set one-size-fits-all regulations, disadvan-
taging the small bankers. For instance, Obama wanted to target
complex, "exotic" lending products that borrowers allegedly
don't understand. Community banks feared this would inhibit
their ability to tailor their loans to the particular needs of the communities they serve. [45]

In other words, Obama's plans to expand banking regulations
promote uniformity and punish creativity. That is good for big
businesses that specialize in mass-production and bad for small
businesses whose advantage is in local knowledge and uniqueness.
(The effect is similar to that of Obama's regulation of food and
toys discussed in chapter nine.) Although the 2008 meltdown was
caused by big banks—local banks generally weathered the storm
just fine—Obama's proposed financial regulations swept all of
them up together, punishing small businesses for the sins of Big
Business.[46]

Even Obama's proposals to regulate banker pay could play to
the advantage of the big bankers. Just ask Todd Edgar, a commodities trader at J.P. Morgan in Britain. Barclays Capital offered
him and his team about 30 million pounds to come over to Barclays. How did J.P. Morgan react? It called on the government's
Financial Services Authority to block the offer.[47]

Consider this example in light of Goldman's influence here in
America. What will happen when some smaller bank tries to hire
away Goldman's top talent? A Goldman executive calls Rahm

Emanuel, who calls the pay czar, who tells the smaller bank to back off before things get ugly.

This helps to explain why Goldman Sachs CEO Lloyd Blankfein has endorsed detailed federal regulation of banker pay.[48]

REGULATORY ROBBERY

One of Obama's favorite campaign themes was attacking Bush for deregulation, which Obama blamed for the Wall Street collapse.

When Obama proposed increased regulation of Wall Street, he found Wall Street's lobbyists on his side. Obama proposed that the Securities and Exchange Commission "should be given new tools to increase fairness for investors." These would impose on broker-dealers—the people who actually buy or sell your stock for you—the same fiduciary responsibilities investment advisers have. In other words, you could sue your broker if he wasn't looking out for your interests. Reuters reported in July, "The Securities Industry and Financial Markets Association (SIFMA) said it backs the proposal to 'provide clarity to consumers while expanding investor protection to a broader range of personalized investment advice.' "[49]

Why does SIFMA, the lobbyist for stock brokers, investment banks, and other investment businesses, want more regulation of brokers? Part of it is the *Confidence Game*. Regular people have lost faith in Wall Street, probably for good reason. If Wall Street can get Obama's stamp of approval, maybe folks will come back. Another part of it is *Gumming Up the Works*—more regulation impedes competition, protecting the incumbents from new entrants.

But the most important part of Obama's regulatory push may have been his plan to, in effect, make permanent the "too big to fail" doctrine that protects Wall Street's giants.

In September 2009, on the anniversary of the collapse of Lehman Brothers—the spark that ignited the 2008 stock market collapse and financial panic—Obama travelled to Wall Street with some proposed regulations. He presented the speech as tough talk, and much of the media reported it as such. The *Washington Post* dutifully ran the headline, "Obama Gets Stern with Wall Street."[50]

Obama said he wanted to end the notion of any company being too big to fail. But those who listened closely took away a different message: Obama was really proposing to *institutionalize* bailouts for the largest financial institutions. Obama proposed special regulations for larger banks, to be designated as "Tier 1" financial institutions. The clear context of these rules was, "If we're going to bail you out, you have to play by our rules."

Paul Volcker, the former chairman of the Federal Reserve and a financial advisor to Obama, testified before Congress that Obama was creating new "moral hazard" with this Tier 1 designation. "Whether they say it or not, that carries the connotation in the market that they're too big to fail," Volcker testified. And this implication could lead to future crises being worse: "The danger is the spread of moral hazard could make the next crisis much bigger."[51]

If that next crisis hits during Obama's presidency, there's little doubt he will cite it as proof of the need for even more regulation. And, as always, Big Business will be ready and willing to help him craft his new proposals.

BIG GOVERNMENT IS GOOD FOR WALL STREET

Obama's actions in the finance sector are all geared toward increasing government and helping those on Wall Street who are most politically connected. But I wouldn't argue this is cronyism. I don't think he's enriching Goldman because Goldman financed

his campaign. Obama's enriching of Goldman is simply a consequence of Obama increasing government's role in Wall Street.
Obama believes in Big Government, and Big Government is good
for Wall Street's biggest players.

Conservatives like to think of Wall Street as a bastion of capitalism, but that image ignores the ways in which our financial sector depends on government protection. Federal financial
regulation is, for the most part, about boosting "investor confidence." And, even before the bailouts, Washington was funneling
money to Wall Street with the combination of high tax rates and
IRAs or 401(k)s—*give your money to Morgan Stanley or lose 25
percent of it*. Obama has proposed to make investment in 401(k)s
automatic.

So, Wall Street wasn't buying off Obama with those millions in
contributions. They were investing in Obamanomics—and that
investment is paying off.

CHAPTER 9

OBAMANOMICS HELPS GOLIATH

REGULATING SMALL BUSINESS OUT OF BUSINESS

The Rose Garden was splendid on a perfectly temperate summer day in 2009. The president's rhetoric was nearly as delightful as the weather.

"When I ran for President," Barack Obama said on stage, surrounded by well-dressed, well-behaved children, "I did so because I believed that despite the power of the status quo and the influence of special interests, it was possible for us to bring change to Washington. And the progress we've made these past five months has only reinforced my faith in this belief."[1] He then rattled off his triumphs over "the influence of special interests":

Despite the influence of the credit card industry, we passed a law to protect consumers from unfair rate hikes and abusive fees.

173

Despite the influence of banks and lenders, we passed a law to protect homeowners from mortgage fraud.

Despite the influence of the defense industry, we passed a law to protect taxpayers from waste and abuse in defense contracting.

And today, despite decades of lobbying and advertising by the tobacco industry, we've passed a law to help protect the next generation of Americans from growing up with a deadly habit that so many of our generation have lived with.

Obama that day was signing the "Family Smoking Prevention and Tobacco Control Act,"[2] which gave the Food and Drug Administration (FDA) authority to regulate tobacco advertising, sales, and manufacturing.

Obama invited to the Rose Garden the head of non-profits dedicated to stamping out smoking, including the crew from the Campaign for Tobacco-Free Kids. It was a wonderful image: well-meaning and hard-working public servants, together with self-sacrificing non-profit laborers, had battled the lobbyists of a wealthy and ruthless industry. And in the end, the good guys beat Big Business. Or so the story went.

Many news outlets dutifully reported this narrative. Kelly Wallace, filling in for Katie Couric, reported, "While the bill has its critics in the tobacco industry, supporters applaud the efforts to improve public health and to try to keep cigarettes out of the reach of young people."[3] The American Cancer Society, in a message titled "Thank Washington for kicking Big Tobacco's butts," had a similar take on the bill:

It wasn't easy, but Congress and the President are standing up to Big Tobacco with an exceptional new law that makes it harder for tobacco companies to push their product.

... As it turns out, there's one thing more powerful than slick cigarette lobbyists—the voices of real people from all across the country fighting for change.[4]

This was the same theme Senator Ted Kennedy's office sounded when the Senate passed the bill: "Miracles still happen.... The United States Senate has finally said 'no' to Big Tobacco."[5] Likewise, Iowa Democratic senator Tom Harkin claimed, "This bill is about standing up to the power of Big Tobacco."[6]

But people who really believed Big Tobacco had suffered a blow might have been confused if they checked the website of Philip Morris, the largest tobacco company in the world. As Obama signed the bill, the top headline on the company's homepage blared, "Philip Morris USA Supports Federal Regulation of Tobacco." The website proclaimed, "Philip Morris USA has supported legislation that would provide for tough but reasonable federal regulation of tobacco products by the Food and Drug Administration for more than eight years."[7]

Similar headlines on the website made clear the position of Philip Morris's parent company, Altria. "Altria Group Supports Enactment of Tobacco Industry Regulation," said one. "Altria Group Supports Senate Approval of Tobacco Industry Regulation," declared another. And ten days before the president signed the bill, Michael Szymanczyk, chairman and CEO of Altria, sent Obama a letter supporting the act. "We applaud this important and historic legislative achievement," he gushed.[8]

This surely didn't jibe with President Obama's tale of a tobacco lobby fighting tooth and nail against regulation. Was Philip Morris simply trying to put on a good face after losing its battle?

Not at all. In fact, Altria and Philip Morris supported the bill from the start. According to National Public Radio, the company even helped author the bill the president had cited as a victory over the tobacco lobby.[9]

Philip Morris's seemingly inexplicable campaign for stricter tobacco regulation reportedly began over a decade ago. According to *Roll Call* newspaper, "Altria executive [Mark] Berlind first laid out a case for supporting federal regulations in a 23-page internal memo dated Oct. 1, 1998."[10] The company began actively working for regulation in 2000, just after Bush's inauguration.[11] Come 2004, when the Family Smoking bill was first proposed. Altria's annual report included this passage:

> ALG and PM USA endorsed federal legislation introduced in May 2004 in the Senate and the House of Representatives, known as the Family Smoking Prevention and Tobacco Control Act, which would have granted the FDA the authority to regulate the design, manufacture and marketing of cigarettes and disclosures of related information.[12]

But Philip Morris didn't just "endorse" the bill in 2004—the firm toiled for its passage. An Altria spokesman told the *Richmond Times-Dispatch*, "We spent a lot of time and effort on it. We think it's very important to the industry as a whole. We don't have any regrets about pursuing it."[13]

That year, Altria spent $13.4 million lobbying the federal government,[14] which comes out to $95,714 every day Congress was in session. The company employed more than twenty outside lobbying firms, a majority of which lobbied on FDA regulation of tobacco or the tobacco buyout bill, which was one vehicle that year for the FDA regulation legislation.[15]

One firm was particularly explicit about its lobbying activities on Altria's behalf. Lobbyist Rick Murphy, former staffer for Republican senator Judd Gregg, chairman of the Senate's Health

Committee, wrote on his lobbying disclosure form that he was "Working to have tobacco products regulated by the FDA."[16]

The Senate in 2004 passed the Family Smoking legislation, but the bill died in the House. Senator Harkin told the *Washington Post* at the time that President Bush had convinced House members to kill the bill. "I lay this right at President Bush's door," Harkin said, "He concurred with Big Tobacco."[17]

The *Post* didn't dispute Harkin's claim, because it seemed natural that Big Tobacco would resist Big Government regulation. But if Bush really killed the bill, he was, in fact, battling the biggest tobacco company in America.

THE MARLBORO MONOPOLY ACT

Philip Morris *is* Big Tobacco. The nation's top cigarette seller, the firm often sells more than all other cigarette companies *combined*. In the fourth quarter of 2008, for instance, Philip Morris cigarettes accounted for 50.4 percent of all cigarettes sold in stores.[18] In fact, 41.6 percent of all U.S. cigarette sales in that quarter were Marlboros, a Philip Morris brand. That means Marlboro, on its own, outsold all brands from R.J. Reynolds, the second-biggest cigarette producer.

Its enormous size and market dominance help explain why Philip Morris would welcome FDA regulation. Recall the First Law of Obamanomics: regulations almost always hurt smaller companies more than bigger ones. The tobacco industry is no exception. For example, the FDA, under the Family Smoking bill, could require cigarette makers to measure the amount of certain ingredients in the smoke. Altria's 2007 annual report revealed that Philip Morris supports these regulations. Why? Because the company already conducts most of these tests.[19] In other words, mandating the tests imposes new costs only on the firm's rivals.

The FDA, under the Family Smoking act, will also severely limit all cigarette advertising. That will give a big advantage to Marlboro, whose name is universally known, over lesser-known smaller brands and potential start-ups: Marlboro would get to save nearly all its advertising budget, while locking in its dominant market position.[20] Already in 2007, even before the bill's passage, Altria reported that "Marketing and selling expenses were lower, reflecting regulatory restrictions on advertising and promotion activities."[21]

Experts agreed this bill would help Philip Morris and Altria. "This puts Philip Morris absolutely in control of the American market," Alan Blum, director of the Center for the Study of Tobacco and Society at the University of Alabama, told the *Richmond Times-Dispatch*. "This means Marlboro is king."[22]

Michael Siegel, a professor at the Boston University School of Public Health, told *Slate*, "It is a dream come true for Philip Morris. . . . First, they make it look like they are a reformed company which really cares about reducing the toll of cigarettes and protecting the public's health; and second, they protect their domination of the market and make it impossible for potentially competitive products to enter the market."[23]

This is a typical effect of Obamanomics: the president pitches Big Government as a way to curb the excesses of Big Business, but the regulations actually prop up those Big Businesses at the expense of the smaller guys. And in this case, industry consolidation also hurts tobacco farmers, both big and small, who are made more dependent on a single corporate customer.

In light of these facts, it's hard to accept Obama's claim that he had battled the "lobbying and advertising by the tobacco industry" in passing this bill. Yes, most of the smaller tobacco companies—perceiving how this would give Philip Morris a competitive advantage—opposed the regulation, calling it "The Marlboro

Monopoly Act."[24] Philip Morris, however, comprises a majority not only of the cigarette market, but also of the tobacco lobby Obama was supposedly fighting. Between the beginning of 2003 and the middle of 2009—just about the entire time the "Family Smoking" bill was on Capitol Hill—the tobacco industry spent $162 million on lobbying. Altria's lobbying accounts for a *majority* of that: $88 million.[25]

At the beginning of 2009, Altria employed sixteen outside lobbying firms in addition to its impressive in-house lobbying shop.[26] In the following months, the company took on four more lobbying firms, three of which were lobbying on the Family Smoking bill.

So when President Obama signed the bill in June 2009, he should have had a Philip Morris executive or lobbyist on stage with him. Of course, he didn't. He had a dozen kids as his props, instead. Keeping Big Tobacco, the bill's true champion, out of sight allowed him to continue attacking it:

> When [Congressman] Henry Waxman first brought tobacco CEOs before Congress in 1994, they famously denied that tobacco was deadly, nicotine was addictive, or that their companies marketed to children. And they spent millions upon millions in lobbying and advertising to fight back every attempt to expose these denials as lies.
>
> Fifteen years later, their campaign has finally failed. Today, thanks to the work of Democrats and Republicans, health care and consumer advocates, the decades-long effort to protect our children from the harmful effects of tobacco has emerged victorious. Today, change has come to Washington.[27]

America's biggest tobacco company spent millions in a successful lobbying effort to secure favorable legislation—it's not clear what had actually changed.

THE WASHINGTON TOY STORY

Many industries have analogies to the Family Smoking bill—regulations, pitched as consumer protection, that function as Big Business protection. In Obama's first year, we've already seen this in toys.

Candidates will make some overblown promises during campaign season. Obama, for instance, pledged a few days before Christmas 2007, "I would stop the import of all toys from China."[28] "The year of the recall," as some people called it, saw recalls of Dora the Explorer and Barbie dolls due to excessive lead in the toys' paint. Mattel, the largest toymaker in the world, recalled more than two million toys. All the recalled toys were made in China, turning the situation into a triple opportunity for Obama, who got to (1) assail the Bush administration's incompetence, (2) pledge to keep kids safe, and (3) sound a protectionist note—important during a Democratic primary.

But Obama quickly backed off his sweeping pledge to keep out Chinese toys. After all, that would have banned 80 percent of the toys on the market.[29] Instead, he supported a bill called the Consumer Product Safety Improvement Act (CPSIA). This bill passed Congress in July when Obama was on the campaign trail, so he missed the vote. But he issued a joint press release with another Democratic senator reading, in part, " 'Keeping America's children safe from dangerous products must be a top priority' said Senator Obama.... 'I urge the President to sign this bill into law as quickly as possible.' "[30]

When Obama entered the White House, he made enforcing this law a priority. His nominee to head the Consumer Products Safety Commission, Inez Tenenbaum, testified during her confirmation hearings that "one of the things that is urgent is the full implementation of the Consumer Product Safety Improvement Act which you passed last year."[31]

Although standing up for child safety is a pretty safe bet politically, this bill isn't all puppies, rainbows, and smiling babies. Like most Washington regulation, it has a sordid backstory. And, as with most instances of Obamanomics, Big Government has been a boon for Big Business and a bane to smaller competitors.

The story revolves around Mattel, whose reputation suffered a blow with the recall scandal of 2007—it's hard to generate worse PR than you get for selling over-leaded toys to kids. Mattel responded to its critics by immediately instituting a new testing regimen for its toys and by working to standardize and streamline the process.[32]

While Mattel was investing in its factories, it was also investing in Washington. The company had spent a steady $120,000 per year on lobbying from 2002 through 2006,[33] but the number ballooned to $540,000 in 2007, the year of the recall. In 2008, its lobbying expenditures hit $730,000—more than six times what the company had spent two years before.[34]

In August 2007, during the recall scandal, Mattel retained the lobbying firm Johnson, Madigan, Peck, Boland & Stewart.[35] The company's lobbyists included Sean Richardson and Sheila Murphy, who had recently been the chief of staff and legislative director, respectively, for Democratic senator Amy Klobuchar. A month later, Klobuchar became a co-sponsor of CPSIA.

The bill imposed new but bearable costs on Mattel. Perhaps more important, it promised to provide a government stamp of approval on Mattel's toys which had—justly—earned the distrust of consumers. CPSIA established a principle that any children's product was guilty until proven innocent—or in this case, unsafe until proven safe. The bill required every manufacturer of children's products to submit its products to third-party testing for lead and other toxins before selling them. It also promised to crack down on second-hand sales of products violating the new lead standards.

The law sent shivers through the world of thrift stores. Products that were perfectly legal to make and sell in 2008 might be outlawed in 2009. "This has gotten so serious, and it is so frightening, because we serve consumers that sometimes have no other way to clothe their children," said Adele Meyer, executive director of the National Association of Resale and Thrift Shops. She added, "You could wipe out a whole industry."[36]

Thrift stores didn't have a powerful lobby in Washington, but they had plenty of public sentiment behind them. In its final days, Bush's CPSC tried to allay the fears:

> The new safety law does not require resellers to test children's products in inventory for compliance with the lead limit before they are sold. However, resellers cannot sell children's products that exceed the lead limit and therefore should avoid products that are likely to have lead content, unless they have testing or other information to indicate the products being sold have less than the new limit. Those resellers that do sell products in violation of the new limits could face civil and/or criminal penalties.[37]

You got that, Salvation Army? The bill doesn't require you to test your products for lead. But if you sell a product with 301 parts per million of lead—even if nobody gets sick—you could get sued or go to jail.

And small craftsmen were threatened by the testing requirement. Every manufacturer, including grandpa in his woodshed, would need to submit its products to an accredited outside testing facility. This would be costly and burdensome. But written into the law was a provision that, while common sense, seriously favored mass-producers. Look at this guidance from the CPSIA:

If your products need to be tested, and they are materially identical and made in the same fashion with no change in assembly, equipment used, etc., then a single sample may be all that is necessary for testing purposes. A change in materials or design can be enough to alter testing results.[38]

So if you're rolling 10,000 petroleum-based Barbies off an assembly line in Shanghai, you need test only one. If you're making ten sets of children's rosary beads to donate to the kids in your parish receiving their first communion, you also need to test one—unless these rosaries are unique, or if you made some at home, some at your office, and some while visiting your grandchildren. In those cases, you need to get each one tested—not just each rosary, but each *component*: the little beads, the big beads, the crucifix, and the string.

Like Philip Morris's position on the Family Tobacco act, this was Mattel's *Overhead Smash*—crowding out smaller competitors and potential start-ups by lobbying for stricter regulation.

Obama's CPSC, to its credit, moved fairly quickly to exclude certain safe materials from testing requirements.[39] And come late August—six months after the law took effect—the government lifted the testing burden on Grandpa's all-wood, unpainted chair—depending on what sort of screws, nails, or joinery he used.

But the CPSC issued another, crucial exemption: the commission voted unanimously in July to allow seven manufacturer-owned or run testing facilities to conduct their own testing without going to a third-party tester—all seven were Mattel factories or Mattel subcontractors, including plants in Indonesia, China, and Mexico.[40] Now, this exemption was not given out lightly. Mattel spent considerable resources developing its own testing facilities, which the company "firewalled" to protect it from corporate influence.

Mattel, through extraordinary effort and expenditure, had earned the right to test its own products. The company made its case to the CPSC, and the CPSC agreed.

There's no evidence of cronyism or any sort of wrong-doing here, and the law explicitly provided for such exemptions. But this episode gets at the heart of the problems with Obamanomics.

First, Mattel had already begun developing its own in-house testing regimen before the CPSIA even passed. We also can tell—thanks to their lobbying filings—that Mattel had significant input into the bill's drafting. The relationship was probably a two-way street: Mattel lobbyists guided the bill's testing requirements to match the company's testing plans, and lawmakers' demands on testing helped shape Mattel's testing process.

And after the law went into effect, the world's largest toymaker had decent access to Obama's CPSC. One day in late August, according to CPSC notes, Mattel executives met with CPSC Chair Inez Tenenbaum and other CPSC commissioners, at the request of Mattel executive Jim Walter.[41]

Do you think grandpa in the back shed would get meetings with three CPSC commissioners? No, Mattel was exploiting the First Law of Obamanomics: "During a legislative debate, whichever business has the best lobbyists is most likely to win the most favorable small print." Playing the *Inside Game*, Mattel found it easier to follow all the rules because it was there as the rules were being drafted.

Also, consider that no small manufacturer could afford to build its own in-house testing facility. This was all typical of Big Government, one-size-fits-all regulation: the smaller businesses, many serving the poorer communities, don't have their own K Street lobbyists (and certainly not a former chief of staff and a former legislative director for a U.S. Senator). And they get steamrolled.

As a footnote, days after Mattel's testing exemption became public knowledge, CPSC launched a sting operation. As CPSC described it:

> As part of a campaign called Resale Roundup, the federal government is cracking down on the secondhand sales of dangerous and defective products.
>
> The initiative, which targets toys and other products for children, enforces a new provision that makes it a crime to resell anything that's been recalled by its manufacturer.[42]

So, when Obama bragged of battling those evil special interests, it seems he wasn't talking about Big Business as much as Big Yard Sales.

GASTROBAMANOMICS

"There are certain things that we can't do on our own. There are certain things only government can do," President Obama said in a weekly radio address in March 2009. "And one of those things is ensuring that the foods we eat—and the medicines we take—are safe and don't cause us harm."[43]

Obama was touting his nominations to the Food and Drug Administration and to a special Food Safety Working Group. Among the names put forward in those days was Mike Taylor, whom Obama named to head the working group and later tapped as the senior advisor for food safety at the FDA.

Taylor, perhaps, is the most prolific practitioner of Obamanomics the food world has ever seen. After graduating law school in 1976, Taylor soon went to work in Jimmy Carter's Agriculture Department.[44] When Ronald Reagan took power, he left for a pri-

vate law firm called King and Spalding, serving clients such as the
biotech giant Monsanto. In 1991, Taylor returned to government
as deputy commissioner for policy at the FDA.

Under President Clinton, Taylor remained at the FDA for a
while and then returned to the Agriculture Department to run the
Food Safety and Inspection Service. There, he continued his Big
Business–Big Government regulating record. Taylor, in his own
words, "led the development of new safety requirements for meat
and poultry."[45] The program was called "Hazard Analysis and
Critical Control Points," or HACCP.

HACCP shows us proto-Obamanomics in action; a September
2008 study by Michael Ollinger, a USDA researcher, found the
largest 20 percent of beef producers paid an extra 1.7 cents per
pound thanks to the regulation. The smallest 20 percent paid an
extra 7.8 cents per pound. With hogs, the costs were 1.3 cents per
pound for the big guys and 6.6 cents per pound for the little ones.
The per-pound regulatory burden for chicken: 0.8 cents for big
producers and 3.8 cents for small producers.[46] Ollinger drew the
obvious conclusion: the regulation "favors large plants over small
ones."[47]

This was a statistical confirmation of the Second Law of Obamanomics: "Regulation adds to overhead, and higher overhead
crowds out smaller competitors and prevents startups from entering the industry."

Think about the costs of starting a lemonade stand compared
to the cost of starting an airline. It's not hard to see why there are
so many more lemonade stands than there are airlines. Each regulation of an industry pushes the industry one step further away
from the lemonade stand and one step closer to the airline—which
means less threat of new entrants and a harsher environment for
smaller competitors.

So, Taylor's leadership in government food safety regulations was one of favoring mass production and government control over smaller food producers. And after his agency created these rules, Taylor cashed out. He went to work for his old client, Monsanto, as vice president for public policy—that means he was the firm's top lobbyist. Taylor, like so many Obama appointees, embodies "the revolving door between K Street and the Executive Branch" that Obama pledged to "close."[48]

Monsanto is reviled in many pockets on the Left. The name is synonymous with genetically modified foods (more generally, genetically modified organisms, or GMOs) which some people argue are unsafe. Monsanto, of course, doesn't believe GMOs are unsafe. And neither does the FDA,[49] the National Academy of Sciences, the American Dietetic Association, the American Medical Association, the Royal Society of London, the Brazilian Academy of Sciences, the Chinese Academy of Sciences, the Indian National Science Academy, or the Mexican Academy of Sciences.

Nonetheless, Monsanto's lobbying operation, under Taylor's command, pushed for new regulations requiring federal approval before a GMO could be legally sold in the United States. Why would Taylor and his colleagues lobby to burden their own company with a costly new set of mandates? It's the *Overhead Smash* again: the FDA estimated a company entering the GMO market would spend 34 percent more time complying with the regulation than would a current participant such as Monsanto.[50]

This is also the *Confidence Game*. As Senator Dick Durbin, an Illinois Democrat, put it in a letter supporting the rule, "Public confidence will be well-served by changing the status of pre-market reviews from voluntary to mandatory."[51] In other words, Monsanto and Taylor knew federal regulation would amount to a government stamp of approval on food some consumers might find scary.

A pattern is clear: whether in the private sector or the government, Taylor pushed regulations that increased government control over our food producers in a way that aided the biggest companies. Taylor was a practitioner of Obamanomics. That makes it unsurprising that Obama lured him back through the revolving door.

THE OBAMNIVORE'S DILEMMA

One of Taylor's first tasks at the FDA was, on Obama's behalf, to lobby the House Agriculture Committee to pass food safety regulation. On July 16, 2009, Taylor endorsed a handful of food-safety bills before Congress, including the Food Safety Modernization Act (HR 875) and the Food Safety Enhancement Act (HR 2749).[52]

Both these bills were inspired by a series of outbreaks of food-borne illnesses. In late 2006, hundreds of Americans were infected by the e coli bacterium transmitted through spinach and lettuce. Then in 2008, more than 1,000 became sick from salmonella poisoning.[53] This time peppers were the culprits, and tomatoes were also a suspect. In 2009, nine people may have been killed by salmonella in peanuts.[54]

According to Obama, these outbreaks were part of "a troubling trend"[55] that demanded quick government action. Food-borne illness would be yet another crisis which Obama's White House would use as a lever to ratchet up federal power—and once again, Big Business would be the White House's partner.

HR 875 and HR 2749 would both create a slew of new regulatory burdens on food factories and both large and small farms. Hurting smaller farms and local agriculture, the bills lumped farms in with food-processing factories and HR 875 labeled them both "food production facilities."

The bills would force food processors and farms to open their property and their records up to the FDA. Both bills would also require farmers to keep intricate records. HR 2749 would, according to one Republican summary of the bill, "regulate agricultural production practices, effectively telling farmers how to farm."[56]

You can imagine the burdens such regulations would place on small farms. Too busy planting, growing, harvesting, and selling your food to update your written food-safety action plan? The Feds could shut you down. Use traditional measures to protect your crops? The FDA might force you to modernize.

Groups representing farmers' markets and organic produce rallied against the bill. "Anywhere food is produced," warned Debbie Stockton of the Farm-to-Consumer Legal Defense Fund about HR 875, "the federal government can send someone out to the farm and tell them how to run things."[57] As for HR 2749, it would "break the backs of small farmers."

But the big guys liked these bills. Lobbying for one or both of the food safety bills were Kraft Foods, General Mills, Kellogg, Pepsico (maker of Frito-Lay brand snacks), the Grocery Manufacturers Association, and the National Restaurant Association. Kraft's lobbyists on the issue included William Lesher, a former assistant secretary at the Department of Agriculture.

Once again, both the *Overhead Smash* and the *Confidence Game* were at play. When the House debated HR 2749, the bill's sponsor, Congressman John Dingell of Michigan, bragged that "we have brought in industry, which supports the bill," and that Americans would "know that the foods that we are bringing into this country and that are being made available to the American people are in fact safe."[58]

Another reason Big Business liked the bill: a sweeping federal regulation of food safety could wipe out some of the "private-sector regulation" that irks the biggest growers. Testifying to Congress,

Drew McDonald, vice president for safety at Taylor Farms, the world's largest salad producer, explained that he supported a uniform, government-endorsed food safety standard. This, he argued, would eliminate the hassle of different customers insisting on their own safety audits.[59]

Compare this to President Obama's claim that "only government" can enforce food safety. Here, you have private sector buyers, in order to protect their customers and their reputation, enforcing their own food safety regulations on their suppliers. The single largest supplier doesn't like these private rules, in part because different buyers have different standards and different tastes. Such diversity whittles away the advantage the salad king gets from being one of the biggest salad producers on the planet.

So Big Business wants to prohibit buyers from exercising their own judgment about what's safe and what's not. This is the *Confidence Game* taken to a whole new level: if government says it is safe, you *must* consider it safe.

But it's not illegitimate to have different standards of safety. Some buyers might want their salad chemical-free, or locally grown, or organic. Others might want to know no rabbits were shot to protect their carrots. The problem for Big Business is that varied consumer demand—varied private-sector "regulation"—makes it harder to mass-produce crops.

In addition to the big producers, some big buyers also lobbied for the stricter federal standards. Here's an anecdote from the *San Francisco Chronicle*:

Dick Peixoto planted hedges of fennel and flowering cilantro around his organic vegetable fields in the Pajaro Valley near Watsonville to harbor beneficial insects, an alternative to pesticides. He has since ripped out such plants in the name of food safety, because his big customers demand sterile buffers around his crops. No vegetation. No water. No wildlife of any kind.[60]

The big buyers, who enforced such sterility through their market clout, saw the regulation as a way to offload enforcement costs to the government. Food writer Michael Pollan told the *Chronicle*, "Sanitizing American agriculture, aside from being impossible, is foolhardy."[61]

But that's what the Obama-backed food safety regulation aims to do. The results reduce diversity in our food supply and in our farms. What's more, in doing so, "food safety" regulation could make our food *less* safe. As *Chronicle* writer Carolyn Lochhead put it:

> An Amish farmer in Ohio who uses horses to plow his fields could find himself caught in a net aimed 2,000 miles away at a feral pig in San Benito County. While he may pick, pack, and sell his greens in one day because he does not refrigerate, the bagged lettuce trucked from Salinas with a 17-day shelf life may be considered safer.[62]

According to a report from the Centers for Disease Control, "An increasingly centralized food supply means that a food contaminated in production can be rapidly shipped to many states causing a widespread outbreak."[63] But increasing centralization is precisely what Obama's food safety regulations will create. Like most regulations, they will pinch smaller businesses and enhance the market share of the mass producers. And fewer producers and more centralization mean less competition—and more health risks.

As this book went to press, HR 875 and HR 2749—with Obama's endorsement—were still working their ways through Congress.

OBAMANOMICS' VICTIMS

We all suffer when taxes go up, prices go up, and choices are limited by government intervention in the economy, but nobody suffers as much as the small businessman. That's why small toy-makers, second-hand stores, local and organic farmers, and a galaxy of other small enterprises are the most acute victims of Obamanomics.

People often assume that laissez-faire economics is the cause of monopoly, consolidation, and Mom 'n' Pop being driven out of business. But it's really the Laws of Obamanomics that achieve those outcomes. The real lesson of Obamanomics is this: be big or go home.

CHAPTER 10

GENERAL ELECTRIC

THE FOR-PROFIT ARM OF THE OBAMA ADMINISTRATION

"[W]e are going through more than a cycle," Jeff Immelt, CEO of General Electric, wrote to shareholders days after Obama's inauguration. "The global economy, and capitalism, will be 'reset' in several important ways. The interaction between government and business will change forever. In a reset economy, the government will be a regulator; and also an industry policy champion, a financier, and a key partner."[1]

General Electric is a sprawling, complex corporation with many diverse businesses. The company makes light bulbs and refrigerators, sure, but it also has a finance arm, a transportation arm, a healthcare arm, a communications arm, and more. The above letter from Immelt reveals what these arms all have in common: they all reach out for government favors.

Look at any major Obama policy initiative—healthcare reform, climate-change regulation, embryonic stem-cell research, infra-structure stimulus, electrical transmission smart-grids—and you'll find GE has set up shop, angling for a way to pocket government handouts, gain business through mandates, or profit from govern-ment regulation.

GE has long been plugged in to Washington power—the policy proposals in George W. Bush's 2007 State of the Union address, for instance, looked like they were lifted straight from a GE annual report. You might call GE a "powerful special interest," particularly when you consider that since 1998, the firm has spent more on lobbying than any other company.[2]

But Obama has not knocked this special interest off its influen-tial perch. Indeed, the Obama era is proving to be the salad days for GE. Rather than chasing out this lobbying powerhouse, Obama has proven, to use Immelt's words, to be an unprecedented "cham-pion," "financier," and "partner" of the corporate behemoth.

Once a week, Immelt enjoys a phone call with top White House economic official Austan Goolsbee.[3] Immelt also sits on Obama's Economic Recovery Advisory Board. It reminds one of the Wash-ington Obama derided in 2006: "The American people are tired of a Washington that's only open to those with the most cash and the right connections."[4]

Obama raised more money from GE in the 2008 election than had any previous politician—by a long shot.[5] The company has an army of K Street lobbyists that includes Linda Daschle,[6] wife of Obama confidant Tom Daschle, the former senator.

These details would be enough to show the company is cozy with the Obama administration, but there's one more arm to the GE leviathan that takes this partnership to a new level. It's called NBC Universal.

Although there are rumors of an imminent sale, as this book goes to press GE owns NBC Universal, which means GE owns the television networks NBC, CNBC, and MSNBC. So Keith Olbermann, the strident liberal with partisan blinkers who serves up a pound of name-calling vitriol for every ounce of fact—he's an employee of GE. Rachel Maddow, the fastest-rising left-winger on television—she works for GE. And of course, there's Chris Matthews, who admitted on air that when listening to Obama, he "felt this thrill going up my leg"[7]—he's one of GE's most public figures.

When you read this chapter, and learn just how dependent GE is on government favors, and just how significant is the overlap between GE's business and Obama's policy, you might consider in a new light Matthews' post-election declaration that it's his job to do "everything I can to make this thing work—this new presidency work."[8]

Given NBC's willingness, well before Obama's election, to turn to advocacy that would aid other GE businesses—like its "Green Week" and "Earth Week" programming—it's not a stretch to see Olbermann, Maddow, Matthews, and their MSNBC and NBC colleagues as GE public relations officials. And given GE's intimacy with government and with the current president, it's also not a stretch to call GE the for-profit arm of the Obama administration.

A SPECIAL INTEREST FINDS A SPECIAL CANDIDATE

"The intersection between GE's interests and government action is clearer than ever."[9]

With this note, a GE executive solicited his colleagues to contribute to the GE Political Action Committee, or GEPAC. The email, from GE vice chairman John Rice, explained:

GEPAC is an important tool that enables GE employees to collectively help support candidates who share the values and goals of GE. While we must continue to engage elected officials to help them better understand our various businesses and how legislation affects our Company and our customers, we must also make sure that candidates who share GE's values and goals get elected to office.[10]

"Candidates who share GE's values and goals" is one way of putting it. "Politicians who support subsidies for our businesses" would probably be more precise. And campaign contributions are not merely a way of helping agreeable candidates win; they are also a way of making certain politicians more agreeable.

The fundraising letter draws a clear line from campaign contributions to lobbying success: "Our Company is heavily impacted by a number of issues pending in Washington this fall," it states. Obviously, money raised in August can't affect who is in Congress that same fall—but it can make current lawmakers more receptive to GE lobbyists.

GE clearly knows campaign contributions matter toward shaping policy. So how have GEPAC, employees, and executives spent their political money?

This is becoming something of a refrain in this book, but given the false conventional wisdom about Obama's reliance on small donors, it bears stating again: Barack Obama raised more money from GE in 2008 than any other politician has ever raised in an election.[11] Sure, he raised nearly twice as much money as John McCain overall, but GE donations favored Obama ($461,030) over McCain ($93,622) by a lopsided margin of nearly 5-to-1.[12]

Obama didn't accept PAC money, and so all of that $461,030 was from employees and executives at GE. Those executives included Dan Henson, president and CEO of GE Capital, the investment arm of GE. Henson gave Obama the maximum contribution in both the primary and general election, and then also contributed to the Obama Victory Fund, a DNC fundraising committee.[13] Eric Luftig, the marketing manager for GE Healthcare, gave $6,000 to the Obama Victory Fund.[14] And GE Aviation senior executive Muhammad Al-Lamadani maxed out to Obama in the primary.[15] Other top GE officials bankrolling Obama included Bob Corcoran, head of the GE Foundation;[16] Pamela Daley, senior vice president for corporate business development;[17] and Ronald Pressman, President and CEO of GE Real Estate.[18]

Obama's haul from GE was more than the combined contributions of GEPAC, employees, and executives to the top twenty-eight Republican recipients of GE money.[19] And GEPAC also gave $15,000 to the DNC—a de facto contribution to Obama—and nothing to the RNC (although GE gave $30,000 each to the Senate and House campaign committees for both parties).[20]

Other GEPAC recipients include Senator Ken Salazar, now Obama's secretary of the interior; Congresswoman Hilda Solis, now Obama's labor secretary; and Congressman Rahm Emanuel, now Obama's White House chief of staff.[21]

So GE doesn't seem to have been worried by Obama's vows to clear the "special interests" out of Washington. To the contrary, if political donations are an indicator, the firm saw something in Obama that it liked very much.

KINGS OF K STREET

Let's recall some of Obama's Hope-and-Change talk from the campaign trail:

The cynics, and the lobbyists, and the special interests who've turned our government into a game only they can afford to play.

They write the checks and you get stuck with the bills, they get the access while you get to write a letter; they think they own this government, but we're here today to take it back. The time for that politics is over. It's time to turn the page.[22]

If you wanted a quantitative definition of "special interests," or wanted an objective way to measure just which companies are "get[ting] the access," one place to begin might be lobbying expenditures. And special interest No. 1 by this standard would be General Electric.

GE spends more on lobbying than any other corporation in America. According to the non-partisan Center for Responsive Politics, GE is the top-spending company from 1998 through the middle of 2009. At nearly $184 million, GE spent 30 percent more on lobbying than runner-up AT&T,[23] and has spent about 50 percent more on lobbying than have Blue Cross or Exxon. Altria, the parent company of tobacco giant Philip Morris, has spent less than half what GE spends.

Through the first six months of 2009, GE was in third place with $12.3 million in lobbying costs, placing the company behind only Exxon and Chevron.[24] But for the second quarter alone, GE once again topped the standings, spending $7.2 million on lobbying—that's $163,636.36 every day Congress was in session.[25]

About thirty men and women make up GE's official platoon of corporate lobbyists.[26] This in-house government-affairs office includes well-connected Republicans and Democrats. Eric Pelletier was George W. Bush's deputy assistant for legislative affairs. Nancy Dorn was Bush's No. 2 budget official before cashing out as a GE lobbyist.

Senior Manager for Government Relations Joshua Raymond is another "revolving-door" type. He worked in President Clinton's Office of Management and Budget right out of Columbia

University, served briefly on Capitol Hill, then left for K Street. After six years of lobbying, he returned to the Hill as chief of staff to Congressman Chris Murphy, a Democrat on the Energy and Commerce Committee. From there GE hired him.

Then there are the outside lobbyists: approximately twenty K Street firms GE retains to do its bidding on everything from taxes to fighter jets and from MRIs to climate change.

Some of GE's hired guns are big names. Republican former Senate majority leader Trent Lott and his lobbying partner, former Democratic senator John Breaux, are GE lobbyists.[27] Former House minority leader Dick Gephardt lobbies on behalf of GE's NBC Universal division.[28] Former senator Don Nickles, who chaired the Budget Committee earlier this decade, advocates for GE on tax law.[29] And Linda Hall Daschle advances GE's case on high-speed rail and freight rail.[30]

So GE, to borrow a phrase from candidate Obama, is one of those "special interests who dominate on a day-to-day basis in terms of legislative activity."[31] But the company still finds a welcome mat in Obama's Washington.

ECOMAGINATION

"I like to describe it as 'A Funny Thing Happened on the Way to the End of Last Year,'" said GE executive Steve Fludder in early 2009. "All of a sudden green is relevant."[32]

Speaking at the Goldman Sachs Fourth Annual Alternative Energy Conference, Fludder was talking about U.S. demand for GE's green products. Obama's election, he posited, meant "North America is going to be on a par with Europe very quickly in terms of commitment." His meaning was unmistakable: because of Obama, the United States will soon subsidize alternative fuels as much as Europe does. And that means big money for GE.

Fludder is the vice president in charge of "Ecomagination," GE's initiative for green technology and green businesses. Profiting while helping the planet is great—capitalism at its best. But invariably, Ecomagination involves government funding. GE doesn't like to use the word "subsidy," though. For example, the preface to the 2008 annual Ecomagination report—the first report issued in the Obama era—brags about "GE's growing partnerships with...governments."[33] The report contains a letter by Immelt and Fludder that features a flurry of similar euphemisms about GE's success in "shar[ing] our insights" with various governments. It also includes this interesting passage: "Beyond the immediate goals of the stimulus programs, ecomagination also has provided us with the opportunity to work with global thought leaders and legislators to craft longer-term policies designed to accelerate innovation and spur action."

In other words, dressing oneself in green garb gives the company an even better seat at the table when it comes to crafting new subsidies and spending programs. Government is, always was, and must be central to Ecomagination's promise of making *green* yield green.

Immelt tipped off the central role mandates and subsidies would play in Ecomagination by holding the 2005 launch event not at corporate headquarters in Connecticut or the media hub in New York, but on Pennsylvania Avenue in Washington, D.C.— the boulevard that runs from the Capitol to the White House. "It's no longer a zero-sum game," Immelt said at that event. "Things that are good for the environment are also good for business."[34] But he added that this would only succeed if GE could "work in concert with government."

Some Ecomagination projects could actually be profitable in their own right, such as energy-saving technologies. But, as discussed in chapter six, GE's alternative energy sources could not compete without government subsidy, mandate, or regulation.

And the Ecomagination project that's 100 percent dependent on government is the effort to make companies pay GE for the right to burn their own fuel.

TURNING GREENHOUSE GASES INTO GREENBACKS

"On climate change," GE vice chairman John Rice wrote in his August 2009 fundraising letter for GEPAC, "we were able to work closely with key authors of the Waxman-Markey climate and energy bill, recently passed by the House of Representatives. If this bill is enacted into law it would benefit many GE businesses."[35]

Chapter six explained how the push to curb greenhouse gasses has become a massive corporate welfare boondoggle. GE is at the forefront of this scheme. It was a founding member of the U.S. Climate Action Partnership (USCAP), a lobbying coalition of environmental non-profits and some of America's largest corporations.[36] The partnership was a driving force behind the policies that ended up in the Waxman-Markey climate change bill.

While some companies might have joined USCAP in an effort to foster good will or ward off particularly damaging regulations, GE was playing for bigger stakes—lobbying for cap-and-trade is GE's way of trying to hit the jackpot.

Note the bills on which GE has lobbied since late 2008, according to the firm's disclosure forms: the American Clean Energy and Security Act, Greenhouse Gas Registry Act, Climate Stewardship Act, Safe Climate Act, Climate Stewardship and Innovation Act, Global Warming Pollution Reduction Act, Electric Utility Cap and Trade Act, Global Warming Reduction Act, Federal Government Greenhouse Gas Registry Act, Low Carbon

Economy Act, America's Climate Security Act, and Lieberman-Warner Climate Security Act.[37]

You see a theme here.

There are many ways in which GE profits from climate change regulation. The first place to look is Greenhouse Gas Services (GHGS), a joint venture between GE and power company AES. Hoping to become the broker in greenhouse gas allowances under a future cap-and-trade scheme, the company aims to help other firms lower their greenhouse gas emissions.[38] It makes money by developing wind- or solar-generated electricity, and by partnering in projects to remove greenhouse gasses from the air by planting trees or by capturing gasses emitted from landfills.

For instance, in Caldwell County, North Carolina, lies a closed-down landfill called Mount Herman. Bacteria in landfills produce methane, a greenhouse gas more than twenty times as potent per volume as carbon dioxide.[39] So GHGS announced in late 2008 that it was setting up equipment to capture the methane coming from this dump. The methane then "will be destroyed by flare or converted to a fuel source to power a new research greenhouse."[40]

Even if it does sell the methane as fuel, this project couldn't make money without the inclusion of greenhouse gas credits. And that's where Google comes in. Google, it turns out, is paying GHGS to capture the methane. Google has no connection to the Mt. Herman landfill, but the company is hoping the project will burnish its green credentials. In return for Google's financing, GHGS will issue Google 110,000 tons of token "carbon credits."

This explains GE's enthusiasm for a cap-and-trade scheme: if the company can make money now issuing purely symbolic carbon credits, imagine the possibilities if carbon credits become mandatory—and a GE joint-venture is the broker. With so much money riding on government action on climate change, it's no wonder GHGS has its headquarters next to the capital in Arlington, Virginia.[41]

That's just one way GE would profit from Obama's green legislation. In July 2009, Reuters reported on another goody the Waxman-Markey bill holds out for GE:

> The bill passed by the House of Representatives included incentives that would pay manufacturers of super-efficient appliances for every unit they sell until 2013.
>
> For instance, GE would get about $75 for every super-efficient dishwasher, about $200 for every such refrigerator, and up to $300 for hot water heaters.[42]

The measure also would create a renewable energy standard—a mandate that power producers get a certain percentage of their power from renewable sources. Obama campaigned for this proposal,[43] which would be a boon for GE's massive investment in wind energy.

ECOMAGINATION = SUBSIDYMAGINATION

"We've proven that green investing is good investing," said CEO Immelt in a 2009 CNBC interview after his first quarter earnings report.[44] He was touting GE's recent contract to provide "smart meters" to the City of Miami as part of Miami's "smart grid"—a $200 million, stimulus-funded program to make electricity transmission more efficient. President Obama is a big advocate of smart grids; shortly before his inauguration, he pledged to begin building one across the entire nation.[45]

This was music to Immelt's ears. If enough cities sign up, he marveled on CNBC, a government-sponsored smart grid "is a

$3, $4, $5 billion—multiple billion—opportunity for GE."[46] Speaking as part of GE's "Earth Week" programming highlighting environmental issues, Immelt was also using the opportunity to pump up his company's stock. At no point in the interview did "Squawk Box" host Joe Kernan issue the standard disclaimer— that GE owned CNBC, meaning Kernan was interviewing his boss.

But hostess Becky Quick eventually asked an insightful question: "How important is the government's involvement in projects like these?" Immelt responded, "I don't think the administration has the luxury of not focusing on this right now." In other words—subsidies are essential to projects like these.

The other aspects of "Ecomagination" also require—and, under President Obama, increasingly receive—subsidies.

GE Capital has invested $70 million in a company called A123 systems that creates lithium ion batteries.[47] Why is this a promising investment? The Ecomagination annual report explains, "As emissions standards and fuel availability become more serious issues facing the automotive industry, manufacturers have turned to new advancements in the electrification of vehicles."[48]

Translation: President Obama's move to unilaterally hike federal fuel economy mandates makes it potentially profitable to make cars that run on batteries—which means demand for batteries.

GE is also building a factory in upstate New York that makes high-tech batteries.[49] This factory is being built with $15 million in subsidies from New York taxpayers,[50] but GE is also eyeing direct grants from the Obama administration. "We believe this is just the type of proposal envisioned for federal stimulus funding," GE executive Todd Alhart said.[51]

GE also wants to use high-tech batteries to power trains— another business that would be financed by Uncle Sam. In April 2009, Obama announced plans to spend $8 billion in stimulus money on expanding the nation's high-speed rail infrastructure, but also requested another $5 billion from Congress.[52] In June, GE retained lobbyist Linda Hall Daschle to lobby on Amtrak, high-speed rail, and freight rail, federal lobbying filings show.[53] More on this below.

Another government-funded GE project is wind power. "Our wind business is handsomely profitable," Ecomagination boss Fludder said in May.[54] You would think a "handsomely profitable" venture wouldn't need federal subsidies, but the stimulus made wind projects eligible for $6 billion in federal loan guarantees.[55] The stimulus also provided a three-year extension of the Production Tax Credit, which reduces taxes on wind power by 2.1 cents per kilowatt-hour of electricity.[56]

Additionally, the stimulus included a new tax break called the Investment Tax Credit, which allows a company setting up windmills any time before 2013 to reduce their taxes.[57] Note that GE can pocket this credit even if the windmills don't produce significant electricity. But it gets sweeter, as the American Wind Energy Association explains: "The ITC then qualifies to be converted to a grant from the Department of Treasury. The Treasury Department must pay the grant within 60 days of an application being submitted."[58]

So, it's not really a tax credit—it's a welfare payment from the Treasury that taxpayers finance even if the windmill never produces enough juice to power a light bulb.

But U.S. taxpayers aren't footing the entire bill—GE has convinced other governments to kick in as well. Bloomberg News reported in September, "General Electric Co., the biggest maker of power-generation equipment, is reviving its Indian wind-turbine business after a four-year absence because the government has improved incentives."[59]

Fludder, however, says, "I'd prefer not to think of words like 'subsidies' and that type of a construct. I think it is more supporting the creation of scale."[60]

GE's lobbying reports, of course, show that GE has been extremely active in encouraging government to "create scale."

TURNING OUT THE LIGHTS

"I live paycheck to paycheck," Robert Pifer tells me. He's a bit over six-feet tall, bald, with a tattoo wrapping around his left bicep. "So what am I going to do when I'm earning eleven dollars an hour?"

Pifer, standing outside the employees' entrance to the Winchester Bulb Plant in Virginia, will lose his job in July 2010.

Manufacturing has been crumbling across America for decades, with the blue-collar jobs—often paying more than $20 an hour—being flushed to low-wage countries like Mexico and China. Sure enough, Pifer's job—making light bulbs for General Electric—is, more or less, going to China. Two hundred men and women are losing their jobs in Winchester.

Also in July 2010, GE plans to close a factory in Lexington, Kentucky, where a hundred employees made the glass casings of the light bulbs. In Niles, Ohio, another hundred GE workers are slated to lose their jobs when the company closes down its glass factory.[61]

The humble light bulb is the emblem of GE, which makes these closings a stark symbol of the U.S. recession. In announcing the factory closings in July 2009, GE blamed "energy regulations" that would make their light bulbs obsolete.[62] "Government did us in," barked Dwayne Madigan, a worker at the Winchester plant.

Did the Obama administration really undermine GE? On the surface, it seems so. On the campaign trail, Obama had pledged to outlaw incandescent light bulbs.[63] He also voted for the 2007 energy bill, which included efficiency standards that made it illegal, beginning in 2012, to sell the kind of bulbs made in Lexington, Niles, and Winchester. Once he took office, Obama accelerated the process with a June 2009 rule by his Department of Energy that set new efficiency standards for light bulbs

Simply blaming the plant closures on the government, however, ignores a key player in these events: GE itself lobbied *for* the 2007 provision that will effectively outlaw its own light bulbs. Thomas Edison, founder of GE, invented today's incandescent bulb—and a century later his company lobbied for the bill that killed it. The Associated Press reported in 2007, "GE's Earl Jones, senior counsel for the company's consumer and industrial business, says the goal is to agree on efficiency standards that reduce greenhouse gases and cut energy consumption, but also 'satisfy basic consumer interest in the quality of light in their home and at work.' "[64]

In 2007, when Congress passed these efficiency standards, the existing replacement for the regular incandescent was the compact fluorescent lamp, or CFL. Those are the spiral-shaped bulbs that advertise, for instance, the brightness of a 60 watt bulb for only 13 watts. These bulbs are unpopular for various reasons: they're expensive, contain potentially dangerous mercury gas, are slow to reach full brightness, lose their longevity when they're frequently turned on and off, and many people don't like the light quality.[65]

But GE manufactures CFLs, and it can make a lot more money selling them for $5 than it can selling fifty-cent incandescents. A Winchester worker explained the company's dilemma to me: "GE doesn't make the money on an incandescent they can make on the fluorescents. . . . How do you get people buy it if they don't want to pay for it?"

The answer: *Regulatory Robbery*. GE lobbied for standards that would outlaw the cheaper bulb. And conveniently, GE doesn't make the CFLs in Winchester. It makes them in low-wage China[66] and the Philippines.[67]

By blaming the light bulb law, GE tried to deflect anger about 400 layoffs. If Immelt (or "E-Melt," as Winchester workers pronounce it), a CEO on Obama's Economic Recovery Advisory Board, was simply moving 400 jobs to Asia in the midst of a recession, that might not play well politically. But if it's an unfortunate consequence of a green policy, then it's out of Immelt's hands.

Adam Morroni was a temp worker at Winchester Bulb in August 2009. He hoped to land a full-time gig there, which would double his pay to more than $20 per hour, but the plant-closing announcement killed that plan. When I asked him about the light bulb regulations that were closing the factory, he brought up a fair question: "What about the people who can't afford them . . . who shop at the dollar store?"

The workers at Winchester are very well versed in the evils of the CFL, which they see as killing their jobs. But these workers are not like the fabled Luddites, who lost their jobs due to technology. Nor are they victims of unfettered capitalism or free trade. They are victims of Big Government. More specifically, they are victims of Big Government–Big Business collusion. In other words, they are victims of Obamanomics.

Environmental and labor laws would make it difficult for GE to make the CFLs here. As the *Times* of London noted about CFL factories:

Large numbers of Chinese workers have been poisoned by mercury, which forms part of the compact fluorescent lightbulbs. . . . Making the bulbs requires workers to handle mercury in either solid or liquid form because a small amount of the metal is put into each bulb to start the chemical reaction that creates light.[68]

But the CFLs may not even be the real issue in the long run. The real issue seems to be this: back when it was lobbying for the light bulb law in 2007, GE was developing high-efficiency incandescent light bulbs that would match CFL efficiency standards. Of course, involving years of research and development and incorporating "new materials," the bulbs would cost much more than tradi-tional incandescents.[69]

Discussing this technology, the *New York Times* called the light bulb law "a case study of the way government mandates can spur innovation." But the *Times* had it backward. GE and its cohorts figured out how to make these bulbs, and *then* they lobbied to outlaw the cheaper, lower-tech bulbs. It's not government spurring innovation. It's innovation—that meets no market demand—spurring lobbying.

And it's just the sort of scheme that thrives under Obamanomics.

TRAINS, EMBRYOS, AND MORE

President Obama appeared with Vice President Joe Biden and Transportation Secretary Ray LaHood alongside a map depicting a network of high-speed passenger rail lines crossing the nation. "What we're talking about is a vision for high-speed rail in Amer-ica," Obama said. He added:

> Imagine boarding a train in the center of a city. No racing to an airport and across a terminal, no delays, no sitting on the tar-mac, no lost luggage, no taking off your shoes. [Laughter.] Imagine whisking through towns at speeds over 100 miles an hour, walking only a few steps to public transportation, and ending up just blocks from your destination. Imagine what a great project that would be to rebuild America.[70]

After the Hope came the call for Change:

There's no reason why we can't do this. This is America. There's no reason why the future of travel should lie somewhere else beyond our borders. Building a new system of high-speed rail in America will be faster, cheaper and easier than building more freeways or adding to an already overburdened aviation system—and everybody stands to benefit.[71]

He was talking about $13 million in federal spending on this rail vision. So, it was clear *someone* would benefit. One month later we got a hint of who it would be: "GE has the know-how and the manufacturing base to develop the next generation of high-speed passenger locomotives," said Lorenzo Simonelli, CEO of GE Transportation. "We are ready to partner with the federal government and Amtrak to make high-speed rail a reality."[72]

GE was rolling out its next generation locomotive "before a crowd of employees and public officials," the *Erie Times-News* reported. One month later, GE Transportation hired Linda Daschle, wife of Obama confidant Tom Daschle, to lobby on train issues.

This was typical—an Obama policy pronouncement in close conjunction with a GE business initiative. It happens across all sectors of the economy and in all corners of GE's sprawling enterprise.

Here's another example: on March 9, 2009, Obama issued an executive order extending federal funding, through the National Institutes for Health, for research on stem-cells derived from human embryos.[73] Where President Bush had opened federal funding only for stem-cells that had already been harvested from embryos (and those stem cells can be used to create new stem cells), Obama was allowing scientists who harvest stem cells from healthy embryos (thus killing the embryos) to get NIH funding for the research on those new stem cells.

Obama's executive order went into effect July 7, 2009. A week earlier, GE had announced that GE Healthcare and embryonic stem-cell giant Geron "have entered into a global exclusive license and alliance agreement to develop and commercialize cellular assay products derived from human embryonic stem cells (hESCs) for use in drug discovery, development and toxicity screening."[74] Geron described itself as having "core expertise in telomerase and human embryonic stem cells."[75]

Obama sent money to an industry, and GE hustled to make sure the company was there waiting.

The GE–Obama "partnership" may even extend to the realm of foreign policy. In September 2009, President Obama acceded to a long-term Russian demand to cancel U.S. plans to place missile-defense installations in Poland and the Czech Republic. Many Republicans and hawkish commentators assailed Obama for showing weakness. Not everyone was disappointed, however. Reuters reported, "Investors could see some long-term trade and other benefits if a U.S. move to back away from a missile shield in Eastern Europe yields improvements in relations with Russia."[76] Then Reuters revealed a telling detail: "Shortly after the pullback on the shield programme was announced, Russia's government said Prime Minister Vladimir Putin would meet several U.S. executives on Friday from firms including General Electric."

Obama acts, GE profits.

OBAMANOMICS ON THE AIRWAVES

MSNBC host Chris Matthews provoked some derisive commentary when he declared during the 2008 Iowa caucus that

Obama had been "almost delivered to us."[77] When five weeks later Matthews gleefully described the thrill Obama sent up his leg, he cemented the view that MSNBC was not just a left-leaning network, but that it was in the bag for Obama.

MSNBC, along with NBC and CNBC, is owned by GE. The company's sprawling nature and the larger-than-life personae of Matthews, Keith Olbermann, and Rachel Maddow make it easy to overlook just what is going on here. So it's worth stating plainly: a company dependent on government for its profits is operating three major television stations, one of which overtly and stridently promotes the agenda of the current president and the party in power.

There's no need to read minds and posit that Jeff Immelt is deliberately using MSNBC as a propaganda tool to secure GE-friendly profit. The simple facts of the matter raise glaring conflicts of interest that clash with journalistic ethics.

Aside from MSNBC's Obama boosterism, there's the green agenda advanced by all three networks in their annual "Green Week" every spring and "Earth Week" every fall. Exhorting viewers to reduce their carbon footprints, the networks rally for greenhouse gas restrictions with alarmist reports on melting snow in South America (with no complementary report on the cooling oceans)[78] and dubious predictions that oceans "could rise at least 200 feet" due to global warming.[79] Every viewer they convince with their one-sided reporting is another likely ally in GE's lobbying push for cap-and-trade.

And sometimes Green Week is more explicit in advocating policies, like Immelt's touting of the Smart Grid, discussed above. Likewise, one morning Tom Brokaw reminisced on NBC about the marvelous achievements of the first Earth Day. "It was a massive success," Brokaw explained, because "the Clean Air Act, the

Clean Water Act, the Endangered Species Act quickly followed. President Nixon created the Environmental Protection Agency."[80]

Media accounts have surfaced—and the full stories are still murky—of other conflicts of interest on GE's television networks. There was the *New York Times* report that GE executives had told Olbermann to go easy on his conservative rival on FOX News, Bill O'Reilly, as part of a deal in which O'Reilly would cease his on-air attacks on GE: "Over time," the *Times* reported, "G.E. and the News Corporation concluded that the fighting 'wasn't good for either parent,' said an NBC employee with direct knowledge of the situation."[81] Olbermann denied he was part of any deal, but liberal media critic Glenn Greenwald noted the host had not mentioned O'Reilly's name a single time after the reported deal had been struck.[82] (After the *Times* report appeared, both personalities resumed their mutual attacks.)

For its part, the Obama administration has not hesitated to appeal to its GE friends for a favor. As Howard Kurtz reported in the *Washington Post*:

> In the days before President Obama's last news conference, as the networks weighed whether to give up a chunk of their precious prime time, Rahm Emanuel went straight to the top.
>
> ...Instead of contacting NBC, Emanuel went to Jeffrey Immelt, the chief executive of General Electric.
>
> ...Whether this amounted to undue pressure or plain old Chicago arm-twisting, Emanuel got results: the fourth hour of lucrative network time for his boss in six months.[83]

In this case, Immelt reportedly delegated the decision to his NBC chief, but *Slate*'s Greenwald has documented a history of top-down control of the television stations. He writes, "GE isn't even bothering any longer to deny the fact that they exert control over MSNBC's journalism."[84]

Then there was this *New York Post* report:

> The top suits and some of the on-air talent at CNBC were recently ordered to a top-secret meeting with General Electric CEO Jeffrey Immelt and NBC Universal President Jeff Zucker to discuss whether they've turned into the President Obama-bashing network, Page Six has learned.
>
> "It was an intensive, three-hour dinner at 30 Rock which Zucker himself was behind," a source familiar with the pow-wow told us. "There was a long discussion about whether CNBC has become too conservative and is beating up on Obama too much. There's great concern that CNBC is now the anti-Obama network. The whole meeting was really kind of creepy."

This story is questionable, since the article and its follow-ups had only one—anonymous—source for these allegations, and the company denied the account. But the tale certainly fits a pattern that, at the very least, raises questions about the editorial independence of GE's television networks.

THE SPECIALEST INTEREST

In a tournament for the title of the quintessential "special interest," the finalists would be Goldman Sachs and General Electric. GE's boardroom doesn't have the revolving door that connects straight to the West Wing as Goldman's apparently does, but on the other hand, Goldman doesn't own three television networks. And Exxon and Pfizer probably make the semifinals, but the breadth of GE's lobbying gives Immelt the edge.

So any claim that Obama battles the corporate lobbyists, or that Obamanomics is about curbing the power of special interests, should be measured in part by studying Obama's dealings with GE.

Yes, Obama has sparred a bit with GE on occasion. For instance, he has opposed funding a second engine for the Joint Strike Fighter—an engine GE would make. He also called for spending cuts on medical equipment—a direct threat to GE Health. In the latter case, however, GE reacted by unveiling its "Healthymagination" initiative as a cost-savings plan. As the *New York Times* put it, "General Electric is shifting the strategy in its $17 billion-a-year health equipment and technology business, seeking to broaden its reach with more lower-cost products."[85]

As GE argues, its relationship with the government is a "partnership"—they won't always agree, but they learn how to get along.

Recall Immelt's prediction that Obama's presidency would "reset" the economy and the relationship between business and government. This "reset" economy is bad news for the workers at Winchester's bulb plant and for taxpayers in general. But for GE shareholders, who have suffered for a couple of years, Obamanomics indeed provides Hope—and lots of it.

CHAPTER 11

FIGHTING OBAMANOMICS

A NEW AGENDA FOR SMALL GOVERNMENT, SMALL BUSINESS, AND FREE COMPETITION

I t's easy to despair. Fighting Big Government is hard enough. Having to fight Big Business at the same time makes it even more daunting. Making matters tougher still, not only is the media—as a class—disposed to love Barack Obama and his agenda of Hope and Change, but major media players also have corporate interests tied up in his policies.

What is a frustrated taxpayer to do? What is a small businessman, feeling crushed by the unholy alliance of Leviathan and Megacorp, to do? What is the mother, terrified of the debt her children will inherit from Obamanomics, to do? What is the consumer, forced through government-inflated prices to subsidize energy companies, health insurers, and ruthless drug makers, to do?

As overwhelming as Obamanomics can seem, an effective response is possible. But that's not what the Republican Party is trying today. Instead, the GOP is attacking Obama as anti-business, and at times is proposing me-too Big Government policies.

The appropriate response to Obamanomics is a consistent rejection of government as a solution to our problems. But it is also a clear-throated attack on the misdeeds of Big Business. Attacking corporate evil should not be the sole province of the Left. Conservatives and free-market advocates should get in the game too, because, frankly, Big Business is not the friend of limited government and low taxes.

This chapter will lay out an agenda, with specific policy proposals, general principles, and new ways of talking about the issues. But first, it's worth learning from some recent history.

THE ROAD NOT TAKEN

Obamanomics—together with the Bush bailouts—has already reshaped our government and our economy, profiting the well-connected companies and unions while constraining our liberty, hiking our taxes, raising our prices, and saddling our children with unimaginable debt. And as Obama has said, he is just getting warmed up.

It didn't have to be this way.

Let's step back in time to fall 2008: after a summer of housing bailouts and bank failures, Lehmann Brothers and Merrill Lynch both collapse in mid-September. The Federal Reserve and the Bush Administration, using legal, regulatory, and financial jujitsu, bail out insurance giant AIG in an effort to stabilize the investment banks hurt by the billions they hold in worthless housing-related debt and securities.

When that doesn't work, the stock markets continue to fall, and Goldman Sachs pleads for more help. Fed Chairman Ben Bernanke and Treasury Secretary Henry Paulson announce they want to create a $700 billion bailout of Wall Street, borrowing the money from future taxpayers in order to buy bad assets from banks. It is an unprecedented, open-ended intervention into the U.S. economy: a financial Gulf of Tonkin resolution, creating a slush fund for the president to give private businesses billions of dollars that don't really exist.

Senator Obama, the Democratic presidential nominee, announces his support for Bush's bailout, and in the same breath he assails Bush and the GOP for ideological adherence to "deregulation."

Advisors tell Republican presidential nominee John McCain he needs to support the bailout or the stock market will plunge even further and credit will evaporate. Nobody will be able to borrow, we'll fall into a deflationary spiral, and it will be a new Great Depression. In order to avoid looking like a "me-too" bailout supporter, he needs to make a bold move, suspend his campaign, roll up his sleeves, and sit down at the table to help draft the bailout himself.

Now, as we stand at this terrifying fork in history, let's take a stroll down the road not taken. Let's imagine how things might have been different.

While discussing the bailout with the administration, McCain's fabled independent streak rises up inside him. He reiterates his good-government, anti-corporate-influence sentiments and notes how Goldman embodies the revolving door of business and government. He walks out of the meeting, flies to Ohio, and launches into the following speech at a campaign rally:

> Our economic crisis is real and requires action. But what the president and Senator Obama have proposed—borrowing nearly $1 trillion from our children and grandchildren and handing that money to the very financial institutions that created this mess—is unconscionable, unconstitutional, and un-American.

Treasury Secretary Paulson, a former executive at Goldman
Sachs, came to the U.S. Senate and told us we had no time to
lose, we have to *act now* and give the administration the power
to create—out of thin air—hundreds of billions of dollars to
give to Goldman Sachs and any other corporation the administration thinks needs it. And now, Warren Buffett, the richest
man in America and Barack Obama's economic advisor, has
invested $5 billion in Goldman on the expectation of a tax-
payer-funded bailout.

I say Secretary Paulson's friends at Goldman have had their
chance. I say the "Masters of the Universe" on Wall Street
have shown their true colors. I say Warren Buffett's investments are doing well enough. These millionaires don't need
your money. These millionaires don't deserve your money.
Barack Obama and George W. Bush think they do. I say, *over
my dead body.*

McCain flies to Wall Street and addresses the stock exchange
the next day.

To the traders, the analysts, the brokers, the CEOs, and the
managers: I have always defended your right to make a profit.
I do not think, as my opponent does, that Congress and the
White House need to make more of your decisions for you. I
believe that your pursuit of profit has helped make this country
more prosperous.

But you are not entitled to the money that the auto mechanic
in Sandusky earned today replacing carburetors. You have no
just claim on the wages of the school teacher in Dubuque. The
doctor in Jacksonville owes you nothing.

The doomsday threats of your friends in Washington tell us
only one thing: that Wall Street is terrified about the future of

Wall Street. "Wall Street must be saved," we're told, "or the whole economy will collapse." This is an argument unworthy of this symbol of capitalism.

When the buggy-whip makers saw their industry collapse at the dawn of the automobile, and when the men of Bethlehem Steel saw their jobs evaporate under the heat of globalization, Wall Street's was the loudest voice crying, "Progress! Change! Laissez-Faire!" Today, it is Wall Street that is impeding progress and free enterprise, either through hubris or naked self-interest.

Perhaps you are so vain that you think America cannot function if you slow down. Perhaps you think Americans who don't work on the southern tip of this island couldn't build a home or feed a family without you. It's true that a world with less debt and less stock trading would be a different world. But you are the last people who should be arguing that our government must protect us from the invisible hand of the free market.

Maybe you just want our money. Well, get in line. Get in line behind all the special interests in Washington that come to us with their palms up looking for their ethanol subsidies, their sugar tariffs, their drug subsidies, their bridges to nowhere. Get in line behind these subsidy-sucklers, and I'll tell you what I have always told them: Get Lost!

Then McCain gets on the train back to Washington and takes to the Senate floor, where he knows a strong majority of senators are ready to follow Paulson and Bernanke's marching orders.

This is known as the world's greatest deliberative body, yet we are being told we have no time to waste—that we must pass this unprecedented and unpredictable bill without a moment's reflection.

I don't say we should do nothing. I say, we should not do *this*—we should not simply give the president $700 billion to use as he sees fit. We should not bail out Wall Street. And we certainly should not do it without negotiation and debate.

When Wall Street and the White House tell us it is urgent to give more power to the White House and more money to Wall Street, some skepticism is called for.

McCain rallies his allies—on the Left, such as Senator Russ Feingold, and on the Right, such as Senator Jim DeMint. They grind Paulson's fast train down to a halt. They paint the debate as one of socialism versus the free market, but also as a debate between Goldman Sachs and the working man.

McCain conducts his campaign from the Senate floor. CNN and FOX News tune in to a McCain filibuster, and soon so do ABC and CBS. McCain and his allies sound a populist note— "Do not rob from the middle class to give to the rich"—and a free-market note—"Washington does not know how to run an economy."

Soon, McCain has persuaded forty comrades to join him. The vote comes up, a majority support the bailout, but they can't get sixty votes to invoke cloture. The bailout stalls. The House votes it down the next day, waving McCain's populist, free-market flag. Obama spends the final five weeks attacking McCain as Hoover, doing nothing in the face of a crisis. McCain spends those weeks attacking Obama as a corporate socialist.

Maybe McCain gets trounced as the stock market falls and CNBC blames it on the lack of a bailout—but then he's no worse off than what actually happened.

But it's not impossible to imagine that this Hail Mary pass pays off. Maybe America sees one campaign as the campaign of Wall Street and Big Government. It sees the other as the campaign of Joe the Plumber and individual enterprise.

THE PARTY OF THE WORKING MAN

This piece of fiction does not reflect a longing for a McCain presidency, but instead it reflects a way of thinking and speaking that could have nipped Obamanomics in the bud—and how it can be fought in the future.

The Republican Party could become the party of the working man. It would take some serious work, but it wouldn't require compromising any conservative principles.

One of the hardest parts of transforming the GOP into the party of the little guy will be rhetorical. Republican politicians are used to describing themselves as "pro-business." This is a fine term, depending on how they use it. Do they mean they believe business—big and small—is crucial to America's strength or prosperity? Do they mean government shouldn't interfere with business? Are they defending profit and the pursuit of profit as moral, noble, and beneficial to the society? In all those senses, Republicans and conservatives should be "pro-business."

But "pro-business" policy recently has meant something different—that government should help business. In this sense, the bailouts were "pro-business," the stimulus was "pro-business," and corporate welfare is "pro-business." In other words, nowadays "pro-business" really means "pro-existing-businesses," "pro-businesses-with-good-lobbyists," and typically, as this book has shown, "pro-Big Business."

This stance has two deadly flaws, one political and one policy-wise. Politically, it lends truth to the Democratic attack that Republicans are stooges of Big Business. On the policy score, this coziness with Big Business often results in Big Government which, in the long run, hurts the economy.

I am not a partisan Republican—I've spent most of my adult life as a registered independent. And before Obama was in power, Republicans were far too willing to use Big Government to aid Big Business.

But the Republican Party is the only place to look for a response to Obamanomics. Democrats are in charge now. Wall Street, the insurers, the drug makers, the automakers, the energy companies, and GE have all latched onto the Democrats, and their hooks are sunk in deep.

The GOP, on the other hand, is deep in the woods. Its donors are abandoning it. Many of its pro-Big Business lawmakers are resigning and becoming lobbyists. The Republican Party is desperately in need of a new direction. This book can point the way.

TIME TO BREAK UP WITH BIG BUSINESS

Michael Steele, chairman of the Republican Party, took to the press in July 2009 to rebut President Obama's push for healthcare legislation loaded up with taxes, regulations, mandates, subsidies, and new government programs. Among his critiques of Obama was a sensible conservative objection—politicians don't understand industry, and political "solutions" often reflect this ignorance. But, as the *Pittsburgh Tribune-Review* reported, Steele then proposed his own dubious process for "reform":

> Having Congress reshape health care puts "the wrong people at the table," Steele said. He said stake holders—"doctors, lawyers, health care employees, insurance companies"—should develop a solution and present it to Congress, rather than the other way around.[1]

This reflects a depressing naïveté. First, industry already has a seat at the healthcare reform table, as chapters four and five demonstrated. Recall the meetings at the White House enjoyed by leading healthcare executives and lobbyists. Billy Tauzin, the drug industry's lead lobbyist, has been to the White House at least five times, while Karen Ignagni, the top lobbyist for the HMOs, has also visited multiple times. And second, nobody should want industry writing their own regulations, because the biggest, richest companies with the most lobbyists inevitably get what they want at the expense of their smaller competitors.

Steele's position also plays bad politically. Everyday Americans don't like the idea of Big Business calling the shots. Meanwhile the Big Business fat cats know the Democratic Party is the place to go these days to advance industry's agenda. So, Steele turns off regular people without even winning over the elites. "Let industry call the shots!" is just not a winning message.

Indeed, throughout the healthcare debate in 2009, there was an interesting set of priorities among some Republicans and conservative activists. Republican objections to Democratic "reform" proposals focused on opposing a government-run HMO (the "public option") and—oddly for a supposedly "small-government" party—on denouncing some of the cost savings proposed for Medicare and other taxpayer-funded healthcare programs.

Less ammunition was spent attacking new healthcare subsidies, taxpayer funding of abortion, the mandate that all individuals carry health insurance, or the mandate that most employers offer health insurance for their employees. In other words, GOP and conservative concern seems focused on the liberal proposals that bother the drug makers and the HMOs, while concern is more muted on those ideas the industry supports.

For instance, included in Obama's $787 billion stimulus bill was $1.1 billion for "comparative effectiveness research" on healthcare treatments. This elicited Republican warnings about "rationing" healthcare. The idea was that CER, combined with a federal takeover of the healthcare sector, would mean that grandma can't get her new hip, no matter what she's willing to pay, or even that the child with Down Syndrome can't get any expensive life-saving or pain-reducing treatments.

Senator Jon Kyl, a conservative Republican from Arizona, proposed a bill prohibiting the government from using CER "to deny coverage of an item or service under a Federal health care program"—that means Medicare and Medicaid. A Kyl spokesman said the bill aimed to ensure CER "wasn't used to ration care based on cost."[2]

But conservative concern about rationing should focus on government intrusions in private transactions—not on the government reducing its own spending, which is what Kyl's bill would actually curb.

Let's put it another way: if, as proposed, government more heavily regulates private insurers and funnels customers to them through "exchanges," it's possible bureaucrats could prevent insurers from covering certain procedures—and *that's* rationing.

Under Medicare and Medicaid, though, the government is already deciding which treatments to cover, because the government (that is, the taxpayer) is footing the bill. Kyl's bill doesn't prevent "rationing," it prevents the government from using all available information to figure out the best way to spend money. So Kyl's measure would just force taxpayers to continue wasting money.

This hardly sounds like a conservative priority. It sounds instead like a drug company priority, a doctor priority, or a hospital priority, because the businesses that stand on the receiving end of Medicare and Medicaid spending don't want that pipeline of taxpayer dollars constricted at all.

There are many potential explanations for this dynamic, but liberal writer Jonathan Chait hit on one of the primary ones in a July article in the *New Republic*:

Conservatives certainly have understandable ideological reasons to oppose the Obama health care reform as a whole. It's the particulars of their opposition that arouse curiosity. The right has presented its opposition to health care reform as principled disagreement with "big government." But opposing "big government" can mean different things. Does it mean opposition to regulation? To spending? To the direct funding of public services as opposed to via private sector middlemen? The Republican Party and its ideological allies have defined it increasingly as whatever suits the profitability of the health care industry.[3]

Now, Chait is not particularly sympathetic toward conservatives or the GOP,[4] and his article did not discuss the Democrats' collusion with the drug industry on healthcare reform. But his explanation here carries some truth:

Health care is an issue where precious few conservatives have paid any attention to the details of policy. And the industry is a natural ally of the conservative goal of preventing single-payer health care. So the industry has managed to define its self-interest as the conservative position on health care.[5]

This is often how Republican and conservative opinion is formed: look at whom Ralph Nader or Michael Moore want to drive out of business, and ask them what they think is the best policy. As long as the answer isn't downright Communist, defer to them.

This book has made clear, though, that the Big Business agenda is anything but a free-market agenda. Conservatives and Republicans need to start from principles of limited government rather than from the standpoint of being "pro-business."

ATTACK CORPORATE WELFARE

Republicans and conservatives are reluctant to criticize big-government boondoggles as "corporate welfare." This past summer, I told a former top staffer to a Republican senator I was writing a book attacking corporate welfare, and he responded, "Well, that's not very conservative."

Maybe it's because they don't want to bear even the faintest similarity to those politicians on the Left who attack business for simply earning a profit or exercising its own will outside the wishes of the bureaucrats and the unions. Or maybe it's because some of them really *are* owned by Big Business.

But it's time to pull out the "corporate welfare" club and use it to pound Obamanomics to a pulp.

The problem with policies like cap-and-trade isn't simply that they hurt the economy: it's that taking money from regular families and giving it to General Electric is immoral. It's Robin Hood in reverse. And the problem with ObamaCare isn't simply that it raises healthcare costs and taxes, but that those added costs and taxes will line the pockets of already flush drug companies.

It's important to point out who's getting rich off Big Government as a way of defusing two favorite claims of the Left often parroted by the media.

First, the Left attacks the Right, the GOP, and anyone who espouses free-market policies as shills for Big Business. This attack is overused, but it is not ineffective. Americans know that the political class is not free of ulterior motives, and the Left's narrative—that opposing regulation and taxation is a way of serving Big Business donors—is a believable one for many people.

Read the Democrats' attacks on the House floor during debate on the Waxman-Markey global warming bill. Here's freshman congressman Jared Polis of Colorado:

> I'd just like to reiterate the scale of this issue, and say that I find it truly troubling that when we are faced with overwhelming credible and independent scientific evidence, and we can see the effects of a changing climate in our daily lives, the delusion it takes to drum up facts and figures paid for by oil companies and promote those as if they were science is truly reaching a new low.
>
> ...Don't buy the falsities that big oil and big energy companies are spending millions to promote.
>
> ...It's time we take a significant step forward, shaking the special interests and act boldly for the good of our country.[6]

California congresswoman Lynn Woolsey sounded the same note:

> Now, it's never easy to change the status quo. There's a lot of money out there for people who would continue the practices that we know are harmful to all of us. And we all know how that money can be used to muddy the issues and derail the will of the people.
>
> The plain fact of the matter is this: Without this bill, without a strict regime for controlling carbon emissions, Big Oil and Big Coal Win. And the environment, endangered species, our kids, our grandkids, you, and I will be the losers.[7]

But the Democrats get to have it both ways. Congressman John Dingell of Michigan pointed to the U.S. Climate Action Partnership and marveled that *even industry* supported the bill:

The legislation before us is largely based on the recommenda-
tions of USCAP, a diverse group of environmental groups and
industry with a shared desire for a commonsense bill to address
climate change.

One might ask why such a diverse group would agree on a
matter like this. Well, the answer is three-fold:

1. There is scientific consensus that we need to address climate change quickly and effectively.

2. We need, and industry needs, certainty. Without this certainty, expansion and new investment is not going to happen.

3. Actions by the Supreme Court which led to the recent
endangerment finding by EPA makes it critically important we
act. If we do not, we will face regulation under the Clean Air
Act—and I assure you, the Clean Air Act was not designed to
regulate greenhouse gases.[8]

Dingell's explanation for corporate support of this measure—
this bill provides regulatory certainty and saves us from the rav-
ages of climate change—went unchallenged by Republicans in the
floor debate. Not one Republican pointed out (a) that Democrats
like Woolsey and Polis were being supremely misleading by painting the anti-cap-and-trade side as the ones serving Big Business
profit; or (b) that Dingell was ignoring the real reason companies
like GE and Goldman Sachs support this bill: it funneled taxpayers' and ratepayers' money to their corporate coffers.

The only attack on this bill as a pile of corporate giveaways came
from liberal Pete Stark, a Democrat from the San Francisco Bay:

This bill unfortunately continues the Congressional tradition of
subsidizing the fossil fuel industry. Only this time it is cloaked
in the disguise of environmentalism and the subsidies come in
the form of free allowances, institutionalization of the "clean
coal" fiction, and the gutting of EPA authority.[9]

Now, there's no reason to impute bad motives to the lawmakers. There's little evidence Democrats supported cap-and-trade in order to please their donors at Goldman and GE. The impetus behind cap-and-trade is probably a blend of the politicians' impulse to "do something," a sincere concern about global warming, the politicians' hunger for more power, and the calculation that a major "win" for Obama will help the Democratic Party.

But the motives of the bill's corporate backers are also relevant, because private profit through government intervention always involves somebody else's loss—in this case consumers' and taxpayers'.

On climate change, why don't Republicans say, "This bill raises your costs in order to enrich General Electric and Goldman Sachs, who are already taking your money through the Wall Street bailouts"? On healthcare, why don't Republicans say, "This bill taxes you and gives the profits to Pfizer and Aetna"?

This probably strikes some Republicans as unseemly or excessively "populist." But "populist" should not be a dirty word. It means championing the working man. Although populism may have taken some unsavory forms in the past, today the way to fight for the working man is to battle against the growing plague of corporate socialism. In other words, *free-market populism* is the answer—in both politics and policy—to Obamanomics.

POPULIST LIBERTARIANISM

In most respectable Republican and conservative circles these days, both the terms "populist" and "libertarian" have bad connotations. And those who call themselves populist or libertarian rarely see much common ground with the other. But Obamanomics demonstrates there is an overlap—fighting against Big Government is often the only way to look out for the interest of the common man.

Today, a fusion is needed between these two camps. Populists—people who distrust elites and care deeply about the middle-class—need to embrace more libertarian economic policies. And libertarians—people who distrust government and jealously guard individual liberty—need to embrace populist rhetoric and goals.

Populists need to realize that Big Government always has and always will end up serving the demands of those with the best connections and the most lobbyists—and that isn't Mom 'n' Pop. And libertarians need to realize that defending the profits of big corporations is good in the abstract, but politically, it alienates regular people in defense of a class that doesn't share the free-market philosophy. In short, Big Business is no friend of libertarians.

And those conservatives and Republicans who consider themselves neither populist nor libertarian—and who may consider both distasteful, dogmatic, or demagogic—need to realize that now is not the time for luke-warmness. Obamanomics wields the awesome combined power of the state, the corporation, and the media. All free-market adherents should unite to resist this juggernaut, which shows no respect for the traditional limits on government.

Obama's agenda—which is GE's agenda, Pfizer's agenda, and Goldman Sachs' agenda—is bold. The response needs to be equally bold.

THE DOUGHERTY DOCTRINE

Before getting into the specifics, I want to address a problem endemic with proposals to "fix the Republican Party," which, I suppose, this section amounts to. Authors and pundits often seem to fall into the trap of arguing that whatever policy they favor most is also the policy that would win.

Just before the 2006 elections, my friend and fellow journalist Michael Brendan Dougherty covered a panel of libertarians, social conservatives, GOP operatives, and movement conservatives. Everyone knew the GOP was about to go down in flames, and everyone had a theory why. "At the end of the day," Dougherty wrote of the panelists' presentations, "the arguments all seem to boil down to something similar: If it were more like me, the Republican Party would be better off. It's failing because it's like you."[10]

We call this insight the Dougherty Doctrine. I myself probably can't help but fall into the same trap, but I am wary enough of it that I don't believe all my preferred policies are or can be political winners. Some forms of corporate welfare, although I believe them to be destructive, are popular. For instance, repealing the tax deduction for interest on home mortgages would be good policy. The deduction, the Holy Grail attained by the National Association of Realtors after intense lobbying, drives up housing prices, distorts the economy, and results in higher deficits and higher marginal income tax rates. But politically, it would most likely be suicide to propose eliminating it.

That said, some issues that may not be winners on their own could still form part of a powerful platform if presented in the right context and in the right terms. I propose here a platform that battles the entrenched powers—political and corporate—in order to build a level playing field on which the regular guy can compete and thrive.

THE NEW AGENDA

The underlying policy principle of free-market populism is rejection of government control of the economy. The guiding star is a distrust of every concentration of power, be it corporate or government.

First, to address the current hot topics of healthcare, energy, and the financial crisis:

Make the HMOs compete

Health insurance companies are seen as evil, in part because they sometimes do evil things. They refuse to cover procedures they should cover. They mislead with fine print. They slow-walk reimbursements.

The Left sees a dysfunctional marketplace and responds with regulation. What's really called for is radical deregulation.

First, dismantle the big-government infrastructure that props up the employer-based healthcare system. End the tax favors for employer-based health insurance, and pair that elimination with an across-the-board tax cut for all taxpayers. Most people would get tax cuts, except for some union members whose votes aren't up for grabs anyway. End the special regulatory protections the 1974 ERISA law set up for employer-based health insurance. Oppose the employer mandates Wal-Mart and Nancy Pelosi are pushing.

"The last thing the health insurance industry wants," Congressman John Shadegg told me, "is to have to compete for every single customer."

When more people buy insurance on the individual market, insurers will feel competitive pressure to keep rates lower and improve customer satisfaction. Even better, open up the insurance market so that individuals can buy across state lines. This will trigger regulatory competition among the states, too. If you want very comprehensive insurance, you may buy yours in New York. If you want cheaper insurance, you may buy it in Idaho.

All of these policies will depress insurers' profits, decrease government control, and improve the general welfare.

Keep the drug makers honest

Pharmaceutical companies make nearly miraculous products, and many of their drugs have saved lives. But that doesn't mean we should protect them from competition.

First, it's time to stop forcing Americans to finance all their R&D. Barack Obama, behind closed doors, promised to retain the laws that ban reimportation of prescription drugs from countries like Canada, where the drug makers sell them cheaper. Republicans should oppose Obama and Big Pharma on this.

Drug companies make a free-market-sounding argument for their protectionism: *don't import price controls.* But the drug makers spend more than any other industry lobbying in Washington, so maybe they can lobby in Canada, too. If you don't like Canadian price controls, kill them.

An outright threat to refuse to sell to Canada might spur Canada to break the drug makers' patents—and the World Trade Organization could take Canada's side. But the drug makers could certainly try to negotiate with the WTO, EU leaders, and Canadian leaders—if they had the incentive.

As of now, Pharma plays the pussy-cat to Canada and Europe and drives a hard bargain here in the United States. Make them stand up to those Canadians and French, however intimidating they might be. Give the drug makers time, though. Propose a bill allowing reimportation beginning in 2012. Then let Pfizer and PhRMA figure out a way to save their own hides. A Cato Institute paper from 2004 put it this way: "The current ban should be lifted, therefore, not to encourage reimportation, but to allow the incentives to surface that will 'force' wider use of market practices and the international trade regimes that reflect such practices."[11]

They could lobby to allow higher prices in Canada. As Cato scholar Roger Pilon suggested, Pharma companies could impose no-resale contracts and then sue companies that violate them, or just refuse to sell to those companies—still a curb on reimportation, but by shifting the enforcement costs from taxpayers to the company, you encourage some downward pressure in U.S. prices as a supplemental way of discouraging reimportation.[12]

And why not pick up the campaign promise Obama dropped: allow Medicare to negotiate with drug companies on the price it pays for drugs. This might make some conservatives wince, but, honestly, once you have Medicare paying for the drugs, free-market arguments are pretty specious. If Republican politicians aren't willing to try to dismantle Medicare Part D, they should at least save taxpayers money and reduce subsidies to Big Pharma with Medicare negotiation.

End energy subsidies

Ethanol proved to be a costly, destructive corporate welfare boondoggle. We're all going to realize this about wind and solar, too. But fossil fuels also get subsidies—especially coal.

Republicans should stand up to Big Oil and Big Coal. Their fuels are the most efficient, cheapest sources of energy we've ever found—petroleum and coal really are miracle fuels. But that doesn't mean we should subsidize them. Quite the opposite: it means these companies can stand on their own.

And there's nothing inherently wrong with wind, solar, and biofuels. But right now they require huge subsidies, and subsidies are destructive. They distort the economy, and—as we learned with ethanol and can begin to suspect with plug-in cars—there are often unforeseen negative consequences from the rapid, widespread adoption of "green" technologies. And who's really benefitting from these alternative energy subsidies? Largely the likes of Goldman Sachs and GE.

Start repealing these subsidies, pointing out along the way just how much the subsidies cost regular Americans and just who is pocketing the profits.

Kill cap-and-trade

Americans generally think global warming is a problem, but most aren't willing to pay much to battle it. If you were to stress that the higher rates from cap-and-trade plans translate into industry profits, the people might get angry.

So Republicans should kill cap-and-trade. And during the debate, here's a tactic for them to employ: if we are going to cap greenhouse gas emissions, why should government give away the credits to industry? Why not auction off every emissions permit? The cap-and-trade scheme will raise consumers' prices, so we should make it up to them: divvy up the proceeds from the emissions auction among every American and send them a check. Democrats get their emissions reductions, and the utilities and energy companies pay the bill.

Democrats would never pass such a proposal, in part because all their corporate backers would withdraw their support. Such a proposal, though, would bring to light the corporate stake in the entire cap-and-trade enterprise.

Undo the Wall Street bailouts

Not all the money from the Troubled Asset Relief Program has been loaned out or spent. Republicans should move immediately to ensure it never is. Propose a bill rescinding the authorization Congress gave the Treasury in late 2008.

And the TARP money that is out there—call it back. Give companies a reasonable time period—six months, nine months, or even a year—but make them pay it all back, quickly. Make sure

Obama can't spend this money, either. Require it all to go to pay down the national debt.

Then shut down the other financial bailouts currently operating through the Federal Reserve, the Federal Deposit Insurance Corporation, and the Treasury. Force President Obama to explicitly defend spending your money, putting your money at risk, or sticking your children with debt in order to save Wall Street fat cats.

Audit and consider abolishing the Federal Reserve

The Federal Reserve—almost a government agency, almost a bank—was the original catalyst and the main driver of 2008's bailout mania. The Fed bent the rules and made a mockery of the law in order to bail out AIG in August before shooting the moon and leading the charge for the Great Wall Street Bailout.

Even the everyday operations of the Fed act as corporate welfare. The Fed creates money out of thin air, which eventually spurs inflation. But because banks and the biggest businesses receive this money first, they get to spend it before the market has reacted to the inflation. The end effect is that Wall Street's dollars are worth more than Main Street's dollars.

The Fed was the key driver behind the housing bubble, which was the key instigator of the 2008 meltdown. But it operates largely in secret. Congressman Ron Paul has proposed a bill to audit the Federal Reserve, and he has also called for killing the Fed. Friends of the free market should have no love for this disruptive, unaccountable entity.

● ● ●

In addition to these items of immediate interest, there are some long-term policies and structural changes an anti-Big Government, pro-regular American agenda should advance.

Ban earmarks

Earmarks are a very small part of the entire federal budget, but they play a role far larger than their price tag. A huge part of what lures businesses into hiring lobbyists is the promise of earmarks, which have been a major driver of congressional corruption in recent years. Abolishing earmarks could have a significant downward effect on spending in the long run if it took away some of the incentive to inflate spending bills.

Publicize the anti-competitive effects of new legislation

Congress must include a cost analysis in every bill it passes. We should also require it to include an analysis of the anti-competitive effects of a bill. We all knew Congress's toy safety regulations would favor Big Business by killing its competitors—any honest assessment would have found the same thing. Congress should be forced to admit what it is doing.

Kill corporate welfare

Dozens of government programs and agencies exist for the purpose of funneling taxpayer money into corporate coffers. Politicians justify these programs as "promoting innovation," "creating jobs," or "saving the planet."

But in the long run, these corporate welfare programs are often detrimental to all those aims. Republicans should propose and rally behind bills to kill corporate welfare programs.

The Export-Import Bank of the United States might be a good place to begin. This is a little-known agency whose express purpose is subsidizing U.S. exporters. Most of their subsidy dollars are spent on Boeing sales. Big companies like Boeing, GE, Bechtel, and Caterpillar make up a vast majority—dollarwise—of all the deals Ex-Im finances.

In recent years, Ex-Im has moved off-budget—it funds its new loans and guarantees with fees charged on loan guarantees and repayments coming in from old (taxpayer-funded) loans. But still, taxpayers will take a bath in the event of default. Risking taxpayer money in order to make Boeing's sales more profitable is more Robin Hood in Reverse. Democrats have consistently voted to preserve this agency. Republicans should take a principled stand in favor of killing Boeing's bank.

Abolishing the Department of Commerce would be a good step, too. Republicans pushed this idea after taking over Congress in 1994. One Republican congressman at the time called the agency "little more than a welfare department for big corporations."[13]

There is no popular constituency for the Department of Commerce. The constituents are big corporations. Cutting spending and getting the rhetorical advantage of battling Washington-entrenched Democrats and Big Business make this a no-brainer.

The Corporate Welfare Reform Commission

Cato Institute scholar Steve Slivinski, along with other scholars and lawmakers on both the Left and Right, has proposed a Corporate Welfare Reform Commission—a non-partisan commission that would identify all the government programs and agencies that amount to wealth transfers to corporations. The commission would have authority to send a bill before Congress to close all these programs and agencies permanently.

No amendments would be allowed. It would be one big take-it-or-leave-it measure. The upside: tens of billions of dollars—if not more than $100 billion—per year in savings. If Congress approved the bill killing the programs, they could then fight over whether to cut taxes, pay down the national debt, simply reduce that current year's deficit, or find other worthy spending items. Anybody opposing such a bill would be arguing that enriching Goldman, GE, and Boeing is the best possible use of the money.

A balanced budget amendment and Pay-as-You-Go rules

The Great Wall Street Bailout of 2008 and the stimulus of 2009 were both passed on borrowed money. Because of the huge deficit in 2009, so were Cash for Clunkers and other late additions to spending. Imagine if Bush had been forced to come up with $700 billion in spending cuts—or if he had to raise taxes—in order to bail out Goldman Sachs and J. P. Morgan. What if Obama needed to take $787 billion from American taxpayers in 2009 in order to finance his stimulus? Can you imagine voters taking kindly to a billion-dollar tax hike for clunkers?

Republicans have supported a balanced budget amendment to the Constitution before. The era of Obamanomics calls for its revival.

A cleaner tax code

Much corporate welfare takes the form not of transfer payments, but of special tax carveouts. The labyrinthine tax code benefits bigger businesses whose accountants can navigate it and whose lobbyists probably wrote it.

Republicans should propose a corporate tax code with almost no distortions and barely any incentives. They should propose an individual tax code that's cleaner and that doesn't pick winners and losers. Republicans have often advocated a simple flat tax with no deductions at all, which would be ideal. But even a *progressive* tax structure, where earners pay higher percentages as their incomes rise, could be a *clean* tax structure.

A clean tax structure would also make it tougher, especially under PAYGO rules, to create new spending programs. Remember, Obama financed his expansion of children's health insurance subsidies by hiking the tobacco tax. Republicans should come up with a way to force any advocate of new spending to raise all taxes. That way people can decide whether it's worth the cost.

An anti-bailout constitutional amendment

We should amend the Constitution to outlaw bailouts. We've amended the Constitution only seventeen times since the Bill of Rights, and so this one is admittedly a stretch—but the effort would draw out the truth about Obama and Obamanomics.

The amendment would state that the government may not buy companies, buy stakes in companies, loan money to businesses, or even guarantee or subsidize loans to business.

Imagine the debate: Obama arguing explicitly on GM's and Goldman Sachs' side, with Republicans arguing to protect taxpayers and Main Street. It would be a good political cudgel, as well as excellent policy.

THE HURDLES

This agenda is only a first draft—and a partial draft, too. Admittedly, it has its problems. Some of the planks may be overly ambitious (constitutional amendments) and some may be too obscure to generate any political wind (abolishing the Export-Import Bank).

But the main difficulty with this agenda is that it works in the opposite manner of most successful legislation. Most "reforms" provide concentrated benefits with diffuse costs. Think of health-care reform: enrich Pharma, the HMOs, and the unions at everyone else's expense. Think of the Export-Import Bank: every $1 billion spent helping Boeing costs the average taxpayer $3.

The agenda presented here provides diffuse benefits and concentrated costs. This makes passing it tough, but it might also present new political problems. For one, it would turn off the traditional donors to the Republican Party. While the Chamber of Commerce may support many of these provisions, you're not going to get Boeing's sign-off on the platform.

But the 2008 election taught us some lessons about political money. One of the most impressive fundraisers of the entire presidential race was Republican congressman Ron Paul. His quixotic campaign showed the power of a coherent, free-market, anti-establishment message. One day in November, for instance, in an event organized by supporters rather than the campaign, Paul took in more than $4 million in donations. A month later, in a second "money bomb," Paul enjoyed a $6 million day.

So, Republicans should reorient their fundraising as they take up the anti-corporate welfare mantle. They still could haul cash from rich people—but from entrepreneurs rather than *Fortune* 500 CEOs.

The agenda above is an entrepreneur's agenda rather than a manager's agenda. It would be good news for everyday Americans rather than the well-connected.

KNOW HOPE

It's time to grab the pitchforks.

Obamanomics is about taking economic power away from the regular guy and giving it to elected officials and lobbyists. The result is protection of the biggest—General Electric, Philip Morris, Pfizer, Mattel, and Goldman Sachs—and pain for small business, consumers, and taxpayers. It's not that Obama hates Mom 'n' Pop—it's that the rules of Obamanomics favor Big Business and K Street over Main Street and the taxpayer.

Big Business is not good in itself. Instead, it is like a machine— good only insofar as it does good things. And, like a machine, it does what its masters program it to do. The fuel of business will always be the pursuit of profit, and so the "programmers" are those with the money. In a free market, the money comes from individuals and other businesses acting freely. Under Obamanomics, the money comes from government.

In a free market, business is guided by investors, and it answers to customers. In Obamanomics, business is guided by politicians, and it answers to bureaucrats. This power shift makes lobbyists more influential—and it makes you more powerless.

But the unholy alliance of Big Government and Big Business is not unbreakable, in part because Obamanomics so clearly leaves the vast majority of the country in the cold.

The results of Obamanomics are so clearly unfair and so damaging to the economy that voters would undoubtedly *demand* action if they knew what was really going on behind closed doors. Candidate Obama vowed to open those doors, but President Obama has taken up a comfortable seat behind them, alongside the lobbyists and corporate titans that are crucial to advancing his agenda.

So above all else, our immediate task is to shine a light on the dark, smoke-filled rooms where the fine print of Obamanomics is hashed out away from public scrutiny. We need to draw attention to these dirty deals, and explain the harm done to the average worker and taxpayer when legislation is crafted to suit the needs of Big Business. Much of the mainstream media buys into the Big Myth that Big Business and Big Government are mortal foes, but enough sunlight can reveal their devious collusion.

Opponents of Obama's proposed healthcare overhaul need to talk about how the insurers are pushing for the individual and employer mandates because millions of new customers will be forced to sign up with them. Opponents of global warming legislation must let people know that power utilities are lobbying furiously for a cap-and-trade scheme because it would allow them to drastically raise your power bills. Opponents of out-of-control government spending should go to townhall meetings and ask their congressmen to end the TARP program and make all its beneficiaries repay the money we taxpayers were forced to give them.

And we need to call out Big Business, too. Just as liberals have been loud in decrying corporate polluters, free-market advocates need to expose and publicly chastise the regulatory robber barons. GE, Goldman, Nike, and Wal-Mart should not get a free pass when they use government for unfair advantage.

Obamanomics has proven beneficial for bureaucrats who seek more power, politicians who seek campaign cash, and for the corporations and lobbyists who increasingly get their money for nothing. These are the most powerful people in the country. But they are a small minority.

And so we can take inspiration, ironically, from Obama himself. Candidate Obama's rhetoric—assailing a government that has become the plaything of the powerful—resonated for a reason. And largely, Obama's rhetoric on this score was correct. We need to show how Obama not only perpetuates, but even strengthens the corrupt system he assailed—and continues to assail.

Once the gap between Obama's rhetoric and his actions is exposed—once he is forced to defend transfers of wealth from taxpayers to Wall Street and K Street—the American people will rise up and repudiate Obamanomics.

Our adversaries are powerful, but they can only succeed when they keep their work hidden. American workers, taxpayers, families, and small businessmen can prevail if we get the truth out.

ACKNOWLEDGMENTS

I did not fully understand why so many authors profusely thank their spouse in their acknowledgments until I wrote my first book while married—with two children. And a third on the way.

And I also never fully appreciated my wife's strength, dedication, and love until she carried this family on her back for a summer while I holed up with my laptop and stacks of research. Thank you, Katie. You are my inspiration.

I also need to thank my parents, who never planned on turning out conservative sons, but who instilled in us a hunger for truth, high standards for ourselves, and the passion for fighting the good fight. All three of my brothers played formative roles in this book, as they do in all my work.

Many friends and colleagues urged me to take another crack at corporate-government collusion in the wake of the Bush bailouts and Obama's election. Specifically, my *Examiner* colleague Bill Myers and my fellow journalist Peter Suderman helped convince me the moment was ripe for my arguments. Harry Crocker at Regnery never wavered in his confidence and encouragement. This book exists today because of you all.

Jack Langer, my ruthless and deft editor, made a homely manuscript presentable. Christian Tappe, Farahn Morgan, and Mary Beth Baker reliably tightened the screws. The incomparable design team at Regnery is the model of professionalism, skill, and diligence—Regnery and all its authors are lucky to have you.

Without the *Washington Examiner* and my editors Mark Tapscott and Stephen Smith, this book never would have been possible. Thank you for the semi-weekly task of digging up dirt, and thank you for the liberty to write this book.

For sending me down—and keeping me on—the path of investigative journalism, I am grateful to the National Journalism Center, the Phillips Foundation, the Competitive Enterprise Institute, and the Intercollegiate Studies Institute.

And for their mentorship and example, I thank my old bosses, Tom Winter, Terry Jeffrey, and of course Bob Novak, to whom I dedicate this book.

NOTES

Chapter 1

1. Rick Pearson, "Obama blasts influence of oil, drug industries," *Chicago Tribune*, July 31, 2007; available online at: http://www.chicagotribune.com/news/politics/obama/chi-obama_tuejul31,0,3036878.story.
2. David D. Kirkpatrick, "Drug Industry to Run Ads Favoring White House Plan," *The New York Times*, August 8, 2009; available online at: http://www.nytimes.com/2009/08/09/health/policy/09lobby.html.
3. For Obama's remarks, see: Lynn Sweet, "Obama, a teen smoker, talks about kicking 'this habit' at tobacco bill signing," *Chicago Sun-Times*, June 22, 2009; available online at: http://blogs.suntimes.com/sweet/2009/06/obama_a_teen_smoker_talks_abou.html; Philip Morris's involvement in drafting the bill was reported by National Public Radio: Greg Allen, "Many Decisions Remain Over Tobacco Regulation," NPR, June 12, 2009; available online at: http://www.npr.org/templates/story/story.php?storyId=105315166.
4. For example, see "Obama's healthcare townhall transcript—remarks, audience questions," *Los Angeles Times*, August 11, 2009; available online at:

http://latimesblogs.latimes.com/washington/2009/08/obama-healthcare-transcript-new-hampshire.html.

5. One of many examples, can be found here: Alex Koppelman, "Strange bedfellows: GOP uses big business to slam Dems," Salon, August 18, 2009; available online at: http://www.salon.com/politics/war_room/2009/08/18/phrma/index.html

6. Keith Epstein, "Endangered Markets? $100 Million Campaign Aims to Free Free Enterprise," *BusinessWeek*, June 10, 2009; available online at: http://www.businessweek.com/blogs/money_politics/archives/2009/06/a_big_campaign.html.

7. "The Democratic Debate," *The New York Times*, December 13, 2007; available online at: http://www.nytimes.com/2007/12/13/us/politics/13text-debate.html?pagewanted=13.

8. Nina Easton, "Democrats' war on corporate greed: Mostly bluster," CNN-Money.com, December 14, 2007; available online at: http://money.cnn.com/2007/12/14/magazines/fortune/easton_democrats.fortune/index.htm.

9. Margaret Talev, "'Cash for clunkers' program headed for big expansion," *McClatchy*, July 31, 2009; available online at: http://www.mcclatchydc.com/economy/story/72873.html.

10 Top Industries Giving to Members of Congress, 2008 Cycle, http://www.opensecrets.org/industries/mems.php?party=A&cycle=2008.

Chapter 2

1. "Text of Barack Obama's speech," *USA Today*, February 11, 2007; available online at: http://www.usatoday.com/news/washington/2007-02-11-obama-text_x.htm.

2. Center for Responsive Politics, OpenSecrets.org.

3. Goldman Sachs: Recipients, 2008 cycle, http://www.opensecrets.org/orgs/toprecips.php?id=D000000085. (Accessed August 24, 2009.)

4. Nancy Benac, "AP Impact: The people in Obama's army of small donors," May 8, 2008; available online at: http://www.sfgate.com/cgi-bin/article.cgi?f=/n/a/2008/05/08/politics/p121225D70.DTL&type=printable#ixzz0Of2KgcRV.

5. Health: Top Recipients, 2008 cycle, http://www.opensecrets.org/industries/recips.php?ind=H&cycle=2008&recipdetail=A&mem=Y&sortorder=U.

6. Data compiled from Health Services/HMOs: Top Recipients, 2008 cycle, http://www.opensecrets.org/industries/recips.php?ind=H03&cycle=2-008&recipdetail=A&mem=Y&sortorder=U.

7. Pharmaceutical Manufacturing: Top Recipients, 2008 cycle, http://www.opensecrets.org/industries/recips.php?ind=H4300&cycle-=2008&recipdetail=A&mem=Y&sortorder=U.

8. Transcript from "Obama Outlines Energy Plans," *Solar Today*, June 24, 2008; available online at: http://ases.org/index.php?option=com_myblog&show=Obama-outlines-energy-plans.html&Itemid=27

9. "Obama attacks 'Big Oil' McCain and gets Gwyneth Paltrow on his side as he strikes back in the great ad war," *The Daily Mail* (UK), August 5, 2008; available online at: http://www.dailymail.co.uk/news/worldnews/article-1041549/Obama-attacks-Big-Oil-McCain-gets-Gwyneth-Paltrow-strikes-great-ad-war.html.

10. "The McCain Plan to Cut Oil Company Taxes by Nearly $4 Billion," Center for American Progress Action Fund; available online at: http://www.american-progressaction.org/issues/2008/pdf/oil_tax.pdf. (Accessed August 24, 2009.)

11. "Big Oil, like all companies, would get tax break," Politifact.com (*St. Petersburg Times*), July 8, 2008; available online at: http://www.politifact.com/truth-o-meter/statements/563/

12. Data compiled from OpenSecrets.org.

13. Data compiled from OpenSecrets.org.

14. "Transcript of first presidential debate," updated October 14, 2008, University of Mississippi; available online at: http://www.cnn.com/2008/POLITICS/09/26/debate.mississippi.transcript/.

15. BarackObama.com, "Debate Reality Check: McCain vs. Renewable Energy," September 26, 2008; available online at: http://factcheck.barackobama.com/factcheck/2008/09/26/debate_reality_check_mccain_vs.php.

16. Editorial, "Green with Hypocrisy," *St. Petersburg Times*, April 25, 2002.

17. Zachary Coile, "Senators rap ethanol mandate; Energy bill provision call 'corporate welfare' for Midwest producers," *San Francisco Chronicle*, April 12, 2002.

18. *Energy Policy Act,* HR 6,109th Cong., 1st Sess., *Congressional Record* (June 15, 2005): pp. S6601–6602.

19. "Barack Obama's Plan to Make America a Global Energy Leader," available at http://web.archive.org/web/20080102204910/http://www.barackobama.com/issues/pdf/EnergyFactSheet.pdf. (Accessed June 25, 2006.)

20. Ron Way, "GOP platform's new opposition to ethanol susbsidies has ag world buzzing," MinnPost.com, September 5, 2008; available at: http://www.minnpost.com/ronway/2008/09/05/3408/gop_platforms_new_opposition_to_ethanol_subsidies_has_ag_world_buzzing.

21. Transcript of the second McCain–Obama presidential debate, Commission on Presidential Debates, October, 7, 2008; available online at: http://www.debates.org/pages/trans2008c.html. (Accessed on August 24, 2009.)

22. Ibid.

23. Kevin Sack, "Business Cool Toward McCain's Health Coverage Plan," *The New York Times*, October 7, 2008; available online at: http://www.nytimes.com/2008/10/07/us/politics/07health.html?pagewanted=print.

24. "Ad Roundup: John McCain and Barack Obama Make Their Final Arguments in Ads," *US News & World Report*, November 3, 2008; available online at: http://www.usnews.com/articles/news/campaign-2008/2008/11/03/ad-roundup-john-mccain-and-barack-obama-make-their-final-arguments-in-ads.html.

25. Mike Dorning, "Rahm Emanuel: From Clinton aide to money maker," *Chicago Tribune*, November 9, 2003.

26. Steve Warmbir et al, "Daley Machine Corruption Helps Emanuel Win First House Race," *Chicago Sun-Times*, May 3, 2005.

27. Stephen Labaton, "The 1992 Campaign: Campaign Finances; Democrats Have Money Machine Up and Running," *The New York Times*, July 27, 1992; available online at: http://www.nytimes.com/1992/07/27/us/the-1992-campaign-campaign-finances-democrats-have-money-machine-up-and-running.html?pagewanted=2.

28. Charles Gasparino, "The Trouble with Consultants," *The Bond Buyer*, November 16, 1993.

29. Charles R. Babcock and David S. Hilzenrath, "Million-Dollar Advisers to The President," *Washington Post*, March 23, 1993.

30. Charles Gasparino, "The Trouble with Consultants."

31. Charles R. Babcock and David S. Hilzenrath, "Million-Dollar Advisers to The President."

32. Charles R. Babcock, "Clinton Campaign Should Refund $4.1 Million, Federal Auditors Say," *Washington Post*, December 13, 1994.

33. Stephen Labaton, "The 1992 Campaign: Campaign Finances; Democrats Have Money Machine Up and Running."

34. Charles R. Babcock, "Clinton Campaign Should Refund $4.1 Million, Federal Auditors Say."

35. Ibid.

36. Ibid.

37. You can see the donor list here: http://web.archive.org/web/20080409033938/http://www.opensecrets.org/clinton/inaugu.htm.

38. Charles R. Babcock and Michael Weisskopf, "Change of Party, Same Game; Fund-Raising Keeps Its Prominence," *Washington Post*, January 15, 1993.

39. Mike Dorning, "Rahm Emanuel: From Clinton aide to money maker," *Chicago Tribune*, November 9, 2003.

40. David Johnston, "Justice Dept. Memo Says Donor Was Cleared," *The New York Times*, June 9, 2000; available online at: http://www.nytimes.com/2000/06/09/us/justice-dept-memo-says-donor-was-cleared.html.

41. "Clinton Defends China Satellite Waiver," CNN, "All Politics"; available online at: http://www.cnn.com/ALLPOLITICS/1998/05/22/china.money/.

42. Finance/Insurance/Real Estate: Top Recipients, 2002 cycle; http://www.opensecrets.org/industries/recips.php?ind=F&cycle=2002&recip detail=H&mem=N&sortorder=U.

43. Securities & Investment: Money to Congress, 2002 cycle; http://www.opensecrets.org/industries/summary.php?ind=F07&cycle=-2002&recipdetail=H&mem=N.

44. Political Parties Overview, 2006 cycle; http://www.opensecrets.org/parties/index.php?cmte=&cycle=2006.

45. "PRESIDENT-ELECT BARACK OBAMA HOLDS A NEWS CONFERENCE," Political Transcript Wire, December 3, 2008.

46. Ibid.

47. TJ Sullivan, "The Curious Case of Cambers and Dunhill," NBCLosAngeles.com, January 6, 2009; available online at: http://www.nbclosangeles.com/news/local-beat/The-Curious-Case-of-Chambers-and-Dunhill.html. (Accessed August 24, 2009.)

48. Martin Z. Braun and William Selway, "Grand Jury Probes Richardson Donor's New Mexico Financing Fee," Bloomberg News, December 15, 2008; available online at: http://www.bloomberg.com/apps/news?pid=20601087&sid=aL0GGUluJeT8.

49. Press release available at http://www.sec.gov/news/press/2007/2007-208.htm. (Accessed August 24, 2009.)

50. Martin Z. Braun, "Blagojevich Fundraiser Represented Firm in New Mexico Probe," Bloomberg News, April 24, 2009; available online at: http://www.bloomberg.com/apps/news?pid=20601109&sid=ayBs1Xt8hsd0.

51. Federal Election Commission, page by page report display, http://images.nictusa.com/cgi-bin/fecimg/?28992664065.

52. Justin Rood, "Funds Tie Obama to Richardson Probe Figure," ABC News, January 6, 2009; available online at: http://abcnews.go.com/Blotter/Politics/story?id=6586275&page=1.

53. John Fritze, "Richardson Abandons Cabinet Bid," USA Today, January 4, 2009; available online at: http://www.usatoday.com/news/politics/2009-01-04-richardson-withdraw_N.htm.

54. Rob Gurwitt, "Deals and Ideals," Governing, November 2007.

55. Bill Richardson, Top Contributors, http://www.opensecrets.org/pres08/contrib.php?cycle=2008&cid=N00024821. (Accessed August 24, 2009.)

56. Barry Massey, "Richardson Signs Legislation Benefitting Donor," Associated Press, April 10, 2007.

57. Data compiled from OpenSecrets.org

58. Thomas J. Cole, "Racino Applicant Has Ties to Governor," Albuquerque Journal, November 26, 2008.

59. Thomas Munro, "Backers of governor's health plan seek early knockout while opponents urge a slower pace," *New Mexico Business Weekly*, November 5, 2007.

60. Bill Richardson, Top Contributors, http://www.opensecrets.org/pres08/contrib. php?cycle=2008&cid=N00024821.

61. Quoted in: Glenn Greenwald, "The Daschles: feeding at the Beltway trough," *Salon*, February 1, 2009; available online at: http://www.salon.com/opinion/greenwald/2009/02/01/daschle/.

62. Ibid.

63. Ceci Connolly et al, "Daschle Delayed Revealing Tax Glitch," *Washington Post*, February 1, 2009; available online at: http://www.washington-post.com/wp-dyn/content/article/2009/01/31/AR2009013102021_pf.html.

Chapter 3

1. Charlie Savage and David D. Kirkpatrick, "Technology's Fingerprints on the Stimulus Package," *The New York Times*, February 10, 2009; available online at: http://www.nytimes.com/2009/02/11/technology/11corporate.html?src=linkedin.

2. Keith Koffler, "Techies Get Friendly White House Reception," *Roll Call*, January 29, 2009; available online at: http://www.rollcall.com/issues/54_80/news/31866-1.html.

3. Rick Pearson, "Obama blasts influence of oil, drug industries," *Chicago Tribune*, July 31, 2007; available online at: http://www.chicagotribune.com/news/politics/obama/chi-obama_tuejul31,0,3036878.story.

4. Charlie Savage and David D. Kirkpatrick, "Technology's Fingerprints on the Stimulus Package."

5. John Harwood, "The Lobbying Web," *The New York Times*, August 1, 2009; available online at: http://www.nytimes.com/2009/08/02/weekinreview/02harwood.html?_r=1&fta=y&pagewanted=all.

6. Ibid.

7. Jeffrey Young and Kevin Bogardus, "Obama Boom for K Street," *The Hill*, January 21, 2009.

8. Olga Pierce, "Stimulus Lobbying Disclosure Promise Still Not Fulfilled," *Pro Publica*, September 1, 2009; available online at: http://www.propublica.org/ion/stimulus/item/stimulus-lobbying-disclosure-promise-still-not-fulfilled-901.

9. Jennifer Kho, "Smart-Grid Companies in 'Feeding Frenzy' over Stimulus," eart2tech, March 16, 2009; available online at: http://earth2tech.com/2009/03/16/smart-grid-companies-in-feeding-frenzy-over-stimulus/.

10. Mr. Edmund Graber, Lobbying Registration form, available online at: http://soprweb.senate.gov/index.cfm?event=getFilingDetails&filingID=a000 87b4-7b84-4029-a8b8-a1835c362b10.

11. Center for Responsive Politics, OpenSecrets.org.

12. Amanda Ruggeri, "Obama's Stimulus Projects Won't Amount to Major Infrastructure Overhaul," *US News & World Report*, May 22, 2009; available online at: http://www.usnews.com/articles/news/stimulus/2009/05/22/obamas-stimulus-projects-wont-amount-to-major-infrastructure-over-haul.html.

13. Recovery.gov, Track the Money, http://www.recovery.gov/?q=content/invest-ments.

14. "Cement Consumption Could Increase with Stimulus Package," PCA News-room, February 3, 2009, http://www.cement.org/newsroom/Infrastruc-ture_WOC2009.asp.

15. Olga Pierce, "Stimulus Lobbying Disclosure Promise Still Not Fulfilled."

16. Veronique de Rugy, "Why the Stimulus Plan Won't Work," reason.com, February 13, 2009; available at: http://www.reason.com/news/show/131661.html.

17. "President Obama Speaks at Townhall Meeting in Elkhart, Ind.," *Washington Post*, February 9, 2009; available online at: http://www.washington-post.com/wp-dyn/content/article/2009/02/09/AR2009020901156_pf.html.

18. HR 1, Page 67.

19. 111th Congress, HR 1.AS, p 74.

20. Amy Schatz, "Judge Refuses to Dismiss Suits Against Cheney Task Force," Cox News Service, May 23, 2002.

21. "Remarks of Senator Barack Obama: Taking our Government back," States News Service, June 22, 2007; available online at: http://www.barack-obama.com/2007/06/22/remarks_of_senator_barack_obam_17.php.

22. Remarks by Senator Barack Obama, Presidential Candidate, at a Town Hall Meeting in Billings, Montana, May 19, 2008.

23. "YouTube Snowman Asks. Candidates Answer," *The Daily Green*, July 24, 2007; http://www.thedailygreen.com/environmental-news/latest/4219.

24. Kurt Erickson, "Coal Gives Illinois an Advantage," *The Pantagraph* (Bloomington, Illinois), July 26, 2006.

25. "Trouble in Store," *Economist*, March 5, 2009.

26. "FutureGen Alliance Selects Mattoon, Illinois as the Final Site for the First-of-a-kind, Near-Zero Emissions Coal-fueled Power Plant," FutureGen Alliance press release December 18, 2007; available online at: http://www.futuregenalliance.org/news/releases/pr_12-18-07.stm.

27. Lobbying Registration, Cassidy & Associates, January 17, 2007.

28. See the Lobbying Registrations for Susan Carver, September 26, 2007, and Gephardt Group, LLC, October 29, 2007, at the Senate Office of Public Records.

29. Lobbying Registration, Bryan Cave LLP, February 27, 2008, Senate Office of Public Records.

30. Lobbying Registration, Alexander J. Beckles, LLC, May 30, 2008, Senate Office of Public Records.
31. Lobbying Registration, The Livingston Group, LLC, November 19, 2008, Senate Office of Public Records.
32. Lobbying Registration, Maddox Strategies, LLC, June 1, 2008, Senate Office of Public Records.
33. "Dr. Coburn Offers Amendments to Stimulus Bill," February 3, 2009; available at: http://coburn.senate.gov/public/index.cfm?FuseAction=LatestNews.PressReleases&ContentRecord_id=3d97fd6d-802a-23ad-4656-8435b17a3a0d
34. Kimberly Kindy, "New Life for 'Clean Coal' Project," *Washington Post*, March 6, 2009; available online at: http://www.washingtonpost.com/wp-dyn/content/article/2009/03/05/AR2009030502138_pf.html.
35. Ibid.
36. Andrew Leonard, "Steven Chu Explains: 'Coal Is My Worst Nightmare,'" *Salon*, January 13, 2009; available online at: http://www.salon.com/tech/htww/2009/01/13/steven_chu_hearing_2/.
37. "Secretary Chu Announces Agreement on FutureGen Project in Mattoon, IL," U.S. Department of Energy, http://www.energy.gov/news2009/7454.htm.
38. Kimberly Kindy, "New Life for 'Clean Coal' Project."
39. Michael Isikoff, "Obama Closes Doors on Openness," *Newsweek*, June 20, 2009; available online at: http://www.newsweek.com/id/202875.
40. Transcript of first presidential debate, October 14, 2008; available online at: http://www.cnn.com/2008/POLITICS/09/26/debate.mississippi.transcript/.
41. Louise Radnofsky, "Big Firms, Little Competition Mark Federal Stimulus Deals," *The Wall Street Journal*, September 12, 2009; available online at: http://online.wsj.com/article/SB125271679727405411.html.
42. Jeffrey R. Immelt, Steven M. Fludder, Letter to Stakeholders, 2009 Ecomagination Report, General Electric; available online at: http://ge.ecomagination.com/annual-reports/letter-to-stakeholders.html.
43. William K. Rashbaum, "Stimulus Funds Go to Company Under Cloud," *The New York Times*, September 3, 2009; available online at: http://www.nytimes.com/2009/09/04/nyregion/04stimulus.html.
44. Michael Pipe, "New Television Ad in Nevada," Community Blog, comment made on December 11, 2007; available at: http://my.barackobama.com/page/community/post/michaelpipe/CBLS.
45. Scott Helman, "PACs and lobbyists aided Obama's rise," *Boston Globe*, August 9, 2007; available online at: http://www.boston.com/news/nation/articles/2007/08/09/pacs_and_lobbyists_aided_obamas_rise/.
46. Federal Election Commission, page by page report display, 216 of 3000, http://images.nictusa.com/cgi-bin/fecimg/?28992656286.

47. Federal Election Commission, page by page report display, 362 of 3000, http://images.nictusa.com/cgi-bin/fecimg/?28932630362

48. Senate Office of Public Records.

49. Federal Election Commission, page by page report display, 7 of 46, http://images.nictusa.com/cgi-bin/fecimg/?28991948647

50. Federal Election Committee, page by page report display, 7 of 28, http://images.nictusa.com/cgi-bin/fecimg/?28933503774

51. Lobbying Registration, Covington & Burling LLP, October 1, 2008, Senate Office of Public Records.

52. Federal Election Committee, page by page report display, 2660 of 2672, http://images.nictusa.com/cgi-bin/fecimg/?27990268660

53. Sutart E. Eizenstat, Partner, Covington & Burling, LLP, http://www.cov.com/seizenstat/.

54. Ibid.

55. Lobbying Registration, Covington & Burling LLP, January 8, 2009, Senate Office of Public Records.

56. Parts of this section are adapted from my article, "Secretary Loophole," *American Spectator*, May 2009; available online at: http://spectator.org/archives/2009/05/15/secretary-loophole.

57. Executive Order—Ethics Commitments by Executive Branch Personnel, http://www.whitehouse.gov/the_press_office/ExecutiveOrder-EthicsCommitments/.

58. Lobbying Report, Dorsey & Whitney, LLP, First Quarter 2008, April 9, 2008.

59. There's a list at Ed Morrissey, "The list of lobbyists in the Obama administration," *Hot Air*, February 3, 2009, http://hotair.com/archives/2009/02/03/the-list-of-lobbyists-in-the-obama-administration/.

60. Mark Murray, "Obama admin gives waiver for Lynn," MSNBC FirstRead, January 23, 2009; available online at: http://firstread.msnbc.msn.com/archive/2009/01/23/1758932.aspx.

61. "Senate Leadership: Bush Works to Preserve Agenda," *The Hotline*, June 6, 2001.

62. Lobbying Registration, Goldman, Sachs & Co., August 29, 2005, Senate Office of Public Records, and Lobbying Report, The Goldman Sachs Group, Second Quarter 2009, July 18, 2009, Senate Office of Public Records.

Chapter 4

1. David M. Herszenhorn and Sheryl Gay Stolberg, "Health Deals Could Harbor Hidden Costs," *The New York Times,* July 7, 2009; available online at: http://www.nytimes.com/2009/07/08/health/policy/08health.html.

2. "Obama has praised single-payer plans in the past," Politifact.com, *St. Petersburg Times*, August 11, 2009; available online at: http://www.politi-fact.com/truth-o-meter/statements/2009/aug/12/barack-obama/obama-has-praised-single-payer-plans-past/. (Accessed August 29, 2009.)

3. "Obama's healthcare townhall transcript—remarks, audience questions," *Los Angeles Times*, August 11, 2009; available online at: http://latimesblogs.latimes.com/washington/2009/08/obama-healthcare-transcript-new-hamp-shire.html

4. Ibid.

5. "Transcript: Obama's News Conference," CBSNEWS.com, July 22, 2009; available at: http://www.cbsnews.com/stories/2009/07/23/politics/main5182101.shtml. (Accessed August 29, 2009.)

6. Richard Cowan, "Pelosi lashes out against insurance companies," Reuters, July 30, 2009; available at: http://www.reuters.com/article/politicsNews/idUSTRE56T4CZ20090730.

7. Michael D. Shear, "Polling Helps Obama Frame Message in Health-Care Debate," *Washington Post*, July 31, 2009; available online at: http://www.washingtonpost.com/wp-dyn/content/article/2009/07/30/AR2009073001547.html.

8. Available at http://www.youtube.com/watch?v=R36YJl8SagU. (Accessed August 29, 2009.)

9. Transcript, "President Obama's Address to a Joint Session of Congress on Health Care," *The Washington Post*, September 9, 2009; available online at: http://www.washingtonpost.com/wp-dyn/content/article/2009/09/09/AR2009090902341.html.

10. Alex Nussbaum, "Pelosi's 'Immoral' Insurers May Gain in Obama Plan," Bloomberg, September 11, 2009; available at: http://www.bloomberg.com/apps/news?pid=20601109&sid=aSG76SFnfJaM.

11. "Health Plans Propose Guaranteed Coverage for Pre-Existing Conditions and Individual Coverage Mandate," November 19, 2008; available at: http://www.ahip.org/content/pressrelease.aspx?docid=25068. (Accessed August 29, 2009.)

12. "Obama's healthcare townhall transcript—remarks, audience questions," *Los Angeles Times*.

13. The facts of Florence Corcoran's case come from http://www.harp.org/corcor.htm.

14. Health Services/HMOs: Top Recipients, 2010, http://www.opensecrets.org/industries/recips.php?ind=H03&cycle=2010&recipdetail=H&mem=N&sortorder=U.

15. Elise Gould, "The Erosion of Employer-Sponsored Health Insurance," EPI Briefing Paper, October 9, 2008. http://epi.3cdn.net/d1b4356d96c21c91d1_ilm6b5dua.pdf. (Accessed August 29, 2009.)

16. Ezra Klein, "Heath Reform for Beginners: The Employer Tax Exclusion," *Washington Post,* May 21, 2009; available online at: http://voices.washingtonpost.com/ezra-klein/2009/05/health_reform_for_beginners_th.html. (Accessed August 29, 2009.)

17. Interview with the author.

18. Ezra Klein, "Heath Reform for Beginners: The Employer Tax Exclusion," *Washington Post.*

19. Ibid.

20. McKinsey Global Institute, "Accounting for the cost of US health care: A new look at why Americans spend more," December 2008; available at: http://www.mckinsey.com/mgi/publications/US_healthcare/pdf/US_health-hcare_Chapter1.pdf.

21. Dennis Cauchon, "Medical miscalculation creates doctor shortage," *USA Today,* March 2, 2005; available online at: http://www.usatoday.com/news/health/2005-03-02-doctor-shortage_x.htm.

22. Shikha Dalmia, "The Evil-Mongering of the American Medical Association," *Forbes,* August 26, 2009; available online at: http://www.forbes.com/2009/08/25/american-medical-association-opinions-columnists-shikha-dalmia.html.

23. Video and transcript available at http://www.msnbc.msn.com/id/32276889/ns/msnbc_tv-countdown_with_keith_olbermann/. (Accessed August 29, 2009.)

24. All campaign finance date from the Center for Responsive Politics

25. "DASHPAC," 2004, http://www.opensecrets.org/pacs/pac2pac.php?cycle=2004&cmte=C00342980.

26. By "more than $18 million," Olbermann apparently meant $19.4 million, because that's the number Olbermann's source, OpenSecrets.org, gives. See http://www.opensecrets.org/industries/recips.php?ind=H&cycle=2008&recipdetail=A&mem=Y&sortorder=U

27. Jeffrey Young, "Wal-Mart backs health benefits mandate," *The Hill,* June 30, 2009; available online at: http://thehill.com/business-a-lobbying/48937-wal-mart-backs-health-benefits-mandate.

28. Matthew Yglesias, "CAP, Wal-Mart, SEIU Join Forces in Support of Employer Mandate," *Yglesias* "Think Progress," June 30, 2009; available at: http://yglesias.thinkprogress.org/archives/2009/06/cap-wal-mart-seiu-join-forces-in-support-of-employer-mandate.php.

29. Matthew Yglesias, "Getting Away With It," TheAtlantic.com, August 1, 2008; available at http://matthewyglesias.theatlantic.com/archives/2008/08/getting_away_with_it.php. (Accessed August 29, 2009.)

30. http://walmartstores.com/CommunityGiving/204.aspx. (Accessed August 29, 2009.)

31. Ylan Q. Mui and Dale Russakoff, "Wal-Mart, Union Join Forces on Health Care," *Washington Post*, February 8, 2007; available online at: http://www.washingtonpost.com/wp-dyn/content/article/2007/02/07/AR2007020700944.html.

32. Michael F. Cannon, "Why Wal-Mart Supports an Employer Mandate," Cato@Liberty, July 1, 2009; available at: http://www.cato-at-liberty.org/2009/07/01/wal-mart-supports-employer-mandate/.

33. FIRST LADY HILLARY RODHAM CLINTON ADDRESSES THE AMERICAN ACADEMY OF PEDIATRICS WASHINGTON CONVENTION CENTER, WASHINGTON DC, November 1, 1993.

34. Peter Kerr, "The Changing Definition of Health Insurers," *The New York Times*, May 10, 1993; available online at: http://www.nytimes.com/1993/05/10/business/the-changing-definition-of-health-insurers.html.

35. Ibid.

36. Lisa Girion, "Private insurance companies push for 'individual mandate,'" *Los Angeles Times*, June 7, 2009; available online at: http://articles.latimes.com/2009/jun/07/business/fi-healthcare7.

37. Subtitle J, HR 2015, 105th Congress, and Elicia J. Herz et al, "State Children's Health Insurance Program (SCHIP): A Brief Overview," Congressional Research Service, RL30473, updated March 12, 2008.

38. HR 3162, 110th Congress.

39. *Hardball with Chris Matthews*, transcript from October 3, 2007, available at http://www.msnbc.msn.com/id/21132598/. (Accessed August 29, 2009.)

40. Jeffrey H. Bimbaum, "A Look Back at the Year's Winners and Losers," *Washington Post*, January 1, 2008; available online at: http://www.washingtonpost.com/wp-dyn/content/article/2007/12/31/AR2007123101787.html.

41. Rep. Nancy Pelosi, "NATION NEEDS HEALTHY DEBATE ON HOW TO LOWER NUMBER OF UNINSURED AMERICANS," press release, November 14, 2006.

42. Press release, "AHIP Briefs Congressional Staff on New Access Proposal; Plan Would Expand Access to Health Insurance Coverage to All Americans," AHIP, November 30, 2006.

43. Press release, "REPS. EMANUEL, RAMSTAD, ROSS, LAHOOD, SCHWARTZ, SHEA-PORTER UNVEIL BIPARTISAN HEALTH CARE PLAN," Rep. Rahm Emanuel, February 16, 2007.

44. Press release, "AHIP Praises Bipartisan Senate Vote on SCHIP," AHIP, August 2, 2007.

45. PhRMA, "Platform for a Healthy America," Executive Summary, p. 2.

46. "The State Children's Health Insurance Program," Congressional Budget Office, May 2007, p. 6, table 2.

47. The State Children's Health Insurance Program," Congressional Budget Office, May 2007, p. 9.

48. David Kirkpatrick, "Daschle has Ear of White House and Industry," *The New York Times,* August 22, 2009; available online at: http://www.nytimes.com/2009/08/23/health/policy/23daschle.html?_r=1&pagewanted=2.

49. Ibid.

50. Ibid.

Chapter 5

1. Rick Pearson, "Obama blasts influence of oil, drug industries," *Chicago Tribune,* July, 31, 2009; available online at: http://www.chicagotribune.com/news/politics/obama/chi-obama_tuejul31,0,3036878.story.

2. You can watch the video and read the transcript at http://www.huffingtonpost.com/2009/08/09/flashback-obama-promises_n_254833.html.

3. Tom Hamburger, "Obama gives powerful drug lobby a seat at healthcare table," *Los Angeles Times*, August 4, 2009; available online at: http://www.latimes.com/features/health/la-na-healthcare-pharma4-2009aug04,0,3660985.story.

4. David D. Kirkpatrick, "Drug Industry to Run Ads Favoring White House Plan," *The New York Times*, August 8, 2009; available online at: http://www.nytimes.com/2009/08/09/health/policy/09lobby.html.

5. Top spenders, 2009, http://www.opensecrets.org/lobby/top.php?showYear=2009&indexType=s. (Accessed August 31, 2009.)

6. Center for Responsive Politics: http://www.opensecrets.org/lobby/clientlbs.php?lname=Pharmaceutical 1 Rsrch 1 %26 1 Mfrs 1 of 1 America &year=2009.

7. The Breaux Lott Leadership Group lobbying report, http://soprweb.senate.gov/index.cfm?event=getFilingDetails&filingID=63f84d7e-f4ad-4601-8d18-d98ea059ac04

8. Mehlman Vogel Castagnetti, Inc. lobbying report, http://soprweb.senate.gov/index.cfm?event=getFilingDetails&filingID=51d355ac-c218-47e0-a237-a47ed81cd73b.

9. Center for Responsive Politics, http://www.opensecrets.org/lobby/clientsum.php?lname=Biotechnology 1 Industry 1 Organization&year=2009.

10. Center for Responsive Politics, http://www.opensecrets.org/lobby/top.php?showYear=2009&indexType=s.

11. Center for Responsive Politics, http://www.opensecrets.org/lobby/top.php?indexType=i. (Accessed August 31, 2009.)

12. News Conference by the President, July 22, 2009; available at: http://www.whitehouse.gov/the_press_office/News-Conference-by-the-President-July-22-2009/.

13. "The Health Care Follies," CBS News, July 9, 2009; available online at: http://www.cbsnews.com/stories/2009/07/09/opinion/main5147635.shtml.

14. Tom Hamburger, "Obama gives powerful drug lobby a seat at healthcare table," *Los Angeles Times*.

15. "Barack Obama's Plan for a Healthy America," BarackObama.com; available at: http://www.barackobama.com/pdf/HealthPlanFull.pdf. (Accessed August 31, 2009.)

16. Data available at: http://biz.yahoo.com/p/sum_qpmd.html.

17. PhRMA Press Release, "House Tri-Committee Bill Would Hurt Patients and Kill Jobs," PhRMA, July 31, 2009; available online at: http://www.phrma.org/news_room/press_releases/house_tri-committee_bill_would_hurt_patients_and_kill_jobs/. (Accessed August 31, 2009.)

18. White House Press Release, "Statement from the President Obama on Agreement to Bring Down Drug Prices for Americans Seniors," June 20, 2009; available online at: http://www.whitehouse.gov/the_press_office/Statement-from-President-Obama-on-Agreement-to-Bring-Down-Drug-Prices-for-Americas-Seniors/. (Accessed August 31, 2009.)

19. Timothy Noah, "Obama's Biggest Health Reform Blunder," *Slate*, August 6, 2009; available online at: http://www.slate.com/id/2224621/.

20. Tom Hamburger, "Obama gives powerful drug lobby a seat at healthcare table," *Los Angeles Times*.

21. NewsHour Interview with Barack Obama, July 20, 2009; available online at: http://www.pbs.org/newshour/extra/video/blog/2009/07/newshour_interview_with_presid.html.

22. "Obama Outlines Expectations for Health Reform Timeline, Economic Recovery," PBS, July 20, 2009; available online at: http://www.pbs.org/newshour/bb/politics/july-dec09/obama_07-20.html.

23. Paul Krugman, "Harry, Louise and Barack," *The New York Times,* May 10, 2009; available online at: http://www.nytimes.com/2009/05/11/opinion/11krugman.html.

24. "Obama's crusade to make US healthcare work efficiently and effectively," PipelineReview.com, February 21, 2009; available online at: http://www.pipelinereview.com/index.php/2009022125302/Expert-View/Obamas-crusade-to-make-US-healthcare-work-efficiently-and-effectively.html.

25. Jeffrey Young, "Big pharma's top lobbyist said what?" *The Atlantic*, March 6, 2009; available online at: http://business.theatlantic.com/2009/03/big_pharmas_top_lobbyist_said_what.php.

26. David Brennan, "Healthcare Reform: Getting It Right," PhRMA, April 3, 2009; available online at: http://www.phrma.org/news_room/speeches/healthcare_reform:_getting_it_right/.

27. Ibid.

28. Federal Election Commission, page by page report display, 1167 of 1194; available at: http://images.nictusa.com/cgi-bin/fecimg/?28932001167.
29. Schering-Plough Legislative Resources, LLC, lobbying report; available at: http://soprweb.senate.gov/index.cfm?event=getFilingDetails&filingID=58ca 2688-1796-4232-a6da-e0e35e688d5b. (Accessed August 31, 2009.)
30. 110th Congress, S. 2347.
31. PL 111-8, Section 221.
32. Editorial, "Progress on Family Planning," *The New York Times,* March 13, 2009; available online at: http://www.nytimes.com/2009/03/14/opinion/14sat4.html.
33. Eric Hoover, "Spending Bill Could Lower Price of Contraceptives at Campus Health Centers," *The Chronicle of Higher Education*, March 12, 2009; available online at: http://chronicle.com/article/New-Law-Could-Lower-Price-of/1579
34. Joseph Curl, "'Snowflake' baby stars opposite Obama," *Washington Times,* March 10, 2009; available online at: http://www.washingtontimes.com/news/2009/mar/10/snowflake-baby-stars-opposite-obama/.
35. Google Finance.
36. "Clergy Statement on Stem Cell Research," Planned Parenthood; available at: http://www.plannedparenthood.org/about-us/boards-initiatives/clergy/stem-cell-13414.htm. (Accessed August 31, 2009.)
37. Rob Stein, "Obama to Loosen Stem-Cell Funding," *Washington Post*, March 7, 2009; available online at: http://www.washingtonpost.com/wp-dyn/content/article/2009/03/06/AR2009030602285.html.
38. "BIO Applauds President Obama's Action to Expand Federal Funding of Embryonic Stem Cell Research," *Bio*, March 9, 2009; available online at: http://www.bio.org/news/pressreleases/newsitem.asp?id=2009_0309_02.
39. Biotechnology Industry Organization, 2008; http://www.opensecrets.org/lobby/clientsum.php?year=2008&lname=Biotechnology 1 Industry 1 Or ganization&id=
40. Senate Office of Public Records.
41. Johnson, Madigan, Peck, Boland & Stewart, lobbying registration, available at: http://soprweb.senate.gov/index.cfm?event=getFilingDetails&filingID=9568 8195-6c61-4d82-97d1-51c1b732f445.
42. Bryan Cave LLP, lobbying registration, available at: http://soprweb.senate.gov/index.cfm?event=getFilingDetails&filingID=6928aca3-3d74-4460-a011-7141467018c1.
43. For example, see Novartis's 2003 year-end Lobbying Report, filed February 6, 2004, with the Senate Office of Public Records.
44. See AstraZeneca's 2007 mid-year Lobbying Report, filed August 14, 2007, with the Senate Office of Public Records.

45. You can watch the video at: http://www.youtube.com/watch?v=8Q1hPanrtGk

46. PhRMA Press Release, "Harry and Louise Return to Health Care Reform Debate with a New Perspective"; available at: http://www.phrma.org/news_room/press_releases/harry_and_louise_return_to_health_care_refo rm_debate_with_a_new_perspective/. (Accessed August 31, 2009.)

47. Transcript available at: http://www.msnbc.msn.com/id/32358445/ns/msnbc_tv-rachel_maddow_show/

48. "The Medicines Company Responds to Incorrect News Reports," The Medicines Company; available at: http://ir.themedicinescompany.com/phoenix.zhtml?c=122204&p=irol-newsArticle&ID=1318945&highlight.

49. David Mark, "Armey leaves firm amid health care flap," *Politico*, August 14, 2009; available online at: http://www.politico.com/news/stories/0809/26128_Page2.html#ixzz0PidmuXoy.

Chapter 6

1. "Text of Obama's speech Tuesday," Breitbart, June 3, 2008; available at: http://www.breitbart.com/article.php?id=D912VD200&show_article=1.

2. Peter Orszag speaking at a March 3, 2009, hearing of the House Budget Committee.

3. Bjørn Lomborg, "The Climate-Industrial Complex," *Wall Street Journal*, May 22, 2009; available online at: http://online.wsj.com/article/SB124286145192740987.html.

4. Waxman-Markey permit data comes from: Kate Sheppard, "Everything you always wanted to know about the Waxman-Markey energy/climate bill—in bullet points," grist.beta, June 3, 2009; available at: http://www.grist.org/article/2009-06-03-waxman-markey-bill-breakdown/.

5. Full text available at: http://www.gao.gov/htext/d09950t.html.

6. Peter Orszag speaking at a March 3, 2009, hearing of the House Budget Committee.

7. White House endorses Waxman-Markey, Senate Majority Leader Whip Durbin says he doesn't have 60 votes for it—House GOP keeps lying," *Climate Progress*, March 31, 2009; available at: http://climateprogress.org/2009/03/31/white-house-endorses-waxman-markey-senate-majority-whip-durbin-says-he-doesnt-have-60-votes-for-it-house-gop-keeps-lying/.

8. "Green Peace Opposes Waxman-Markey," Greenpeace, June 25, 2009; available at: http://www.greenpeace.org/usa/press-center/releases2/green-peace-opposes-waxman-mark.

9. "WEEKLY ADDRESS: President Obama Calls Energy Bill Passage Critical to Stronger American Economy," June 27, 2009; available at: http://www.whitehouse.gov/the_press_office/UPDATED-and-FINAL-

WEEKLY-ADDRESS-President-Obama-Calls-Energy-Bill-Passage-Critical-to-Stronger-American-Economy/.

10. Waxman-Markey permit data comes from: http://www.grist.org/article/2009-06-03-waxman-markey-bill-breakdown/.

11. Data compiled from the Senate Office of Public Records.

12. Edison Electric Institute, 2009, http://www.opensecrets.org/lobby/clientsum.php?lname=Edison+Electric+Institute&year=2009.

13. Senate Office of Public Records.

14. "CLIMATE: 'Fragile compromise' of power plant CEOs in doubt as Senate debate approaches," E&E Publishing, LLC, August 5, 2009; available at: http://www.eenews.net/public/EEDaily/2009/08/05/1.

15. American Electric Power Company, Inc. and Affiliated Corporations, lobbying report, http://soprweb.senate.gov/index.cfm?event=getFilingDetails&filingID=c0b289ea-2574-4943-9fa5-81a4e91e9f0c.

16. Andy Stone and Jonathan Fahey, "Utilities Could Cash In On Climate Bill," Forbes, June 17, 2009; available at: http://www.forbes.com/2009/06/16/aep-global-warming-business-energy-utilities.html.

17. Tom Philpott, "Will Big Ag plow under Waxman-Markey?" grist.beta, June 10, 2009; available at: http://www.grist.org/article/2009-06-10-big-ag-waxman-markey/.

18. Ibid.

19. Lobbying Report, Ogilvy Government Relations on behalf of Monsanto, First Quarter 2009, April 17, 2009.

20. Tom Philpott, "Will Big Ag plow under Waxman-Markey?"

21. Matthew Carr, "Pollution Permits Burn European Customers; E.On Gains (Update 2)," Bloomberg, June 18, 2007; available at: http://www.bloomberg.com/apps/news?pid=20601109&refer=home&sid=aeFSX.0e2ga8.

22. Chicago Climate Exchange, http://www.chicagoclimatex.com/about/pdf/CCX_Overview_Brochure.pdf.

23. http://www.aep.com/about/leadership/profile.aspx?id=Sandor&type=board.

24. "Innovate for a Better World," Nike FY05-06 Corporate Responsibility Report, p 68; available online at: http://www.nikebiz.com/responsibility/documents/Nike_FY05_06_CR_Report_C.pdf.

25. You can read the full email here: Steve Milloy, "GE seeks support for GE-minded politicians," Canada Free Press, August 20, 2009; available at: http://www.canadafreepress.com/index.php/article/13930.

26. Timothy Noah, "Blaming Liberalism for Enron," Slate, January 21, 2002; available online at: http://www.slate.com/id/2061023/.

27. At the Senate Office of Public Records.

28. Simon Tuck, "Goldman Sachs Sees Green in Biofuel Firm," Globe and Mail, May 1, 2006.

29. PL 112-140, Section 202.

30. "Fulcrum BioEnergy Announces Next Generation Ethanol Breakthrough," Reuters, September 1, 2009; available at: http://www.reuters.com/article/pressRelease/idUS203688+01-Sep-2009+PRN20090901.

31. Re: Goldman, see: "Goldman Sachs Makes Significant Investment in Nordic Windpower," Business Wire, October 1, 2007; article available at: http://www.encyclopedia.com/doc/1G1-169300743.html; and re: Duke and GE, see Poornima Gupta, "Duke Energy to Build Wind Farm in Wyoming," Reuters, September 1, 2009; available online at: http://www.reuters.com/article/GCA-GreenBusiness/idUSTRE5802I220090901.

32. The transcript, and account of Obama's visit to the bolt factory comes from Robert Hendin, "Obama Hits Ohio," CBS News Political Hotsheet, January 16, 2009; available online at: http://www.cbsnews.com/blogs/2009/01/16/politics/politicalhotsheet/entry4727659.shtml.

33. "Remarks of President-Elect Barack Obama—As Prepared for Delivery, Cardinal Fastenery & Specialy Co. Inc.," January 16, 2009; available online at: http://i.usatoday.net/news/TheOval/Obama-in-Ohio-1-16-2009.pdf.

34. See Editorial, "The Ambush of Van Jones," *The Nation*, September 9, 2009; available online at: http://www.thenation.com/doc/20090928/editors2; and "Fun Fact: Van Jones Is Not a Communist," http://www.youtube.com/watch?v=tBEki6U0cYQ.

35. Van Jones, *The Green Collar Economy: How One Solution Can Fix Our Two Biggest Problems* (New York: Harper Collins, 2008), 86.

36. Data available at: http://graphics8.nytimes.com/packages/images/nytint/docs/latest-new-york-times-cbs-news-poll/original.pdf.

37. Data available at: http://www.nationalcenter.org/NCPPR_National%20Omnibus_MQ_Cap%20and%20Trade%20Questions_080519.pdf.

38. "Barack Obama and Joe Biden: New Energy for America," www.barackobama.com, http://www.barackobama.com/pdf/factsheet_energy_speech_080308.pdf.

39. "Remarks of President-Elect Barack Obama—as Prepared for Delivery, Cardinal Fastener & Specialty Co. Inc.," January 16, 2009, Cardinal Heights, Ohio; available online at: http://i.usatoday.net/news/TheOval/Obama-in-Ohio-1-16-2009.pdf.

40. "Study of the effects on employment of public aid to renewable energy sources," Universidad Rey Juan Carlos; available online at: http://www.juandemariana.org/pdf/090327-employment-public-aid-renewable.pdf.

41. "Fox News pushing questionable Spanish study on green jobs," *Media Matters*, April 15, 2009; available online at: http://mediamatters.org/research/200904150032.

42. "Study of the effects on employment of public aid to renewable energy sources," Universidad Rey Juan Carlos.

43. The White House, "REMARKS BY THE PRESIDENT ON NATIONAL FUEL EFFICIENCY STANDARDS," May 19, 2009; available online at: http://www.whitehouse.gov/the_press_office/Remarks-by-the-President-on-national-fuel-efficiency-standards/.

44. Administration of Barack H. Obama, "Remarks on Fuel Efficiency Standards," May 19, 2009; available online at: http://www.gpoaccess.gov/presdocs/2009/DCPD-200900377.htm.

45. "A Culture Change on Climate Change," posted by Jesse Lee, The White House blog, May 19, 2009; available at: http://www.whitehouse.gov/blog/A-Culture-Change-on-Climate-Change/.

46. Jackie Calmes, "Former Clinton Aide Will Become Treasury Counselor," *The New York Times*, May 6, 2009; available online at: http://thecaucus.blogs.nytimes.com/2009/05/06/former-clinton-aide-will-become-treasury-counselor/.

47. Federal Election Commission, page by page report display, 801 of 13,200; available at: http://images.nictusa.com/cgi-bin/fecimg/?28992653871.

48. Nigel Wilson, "Alcoa wants carbon trading exemption," *The Australian Business*, April 30, 2008; available online at: http://www.theaustralian.news.com.au/story/0,25197,23619564-5005200,00.html.

49. Chuck Squatriglia, "Feds lend Tesla $465 million to build electric car," CNN.com/technology, June 24, 2009; available at: http://www.cnn.com/2009/TECH/06/23/tesla.electric.cars/.

50. Kendra Marr, "3 Automakers Get Loans to Build More Efficient Cars," *The Washington Post*, June 24, 2009; available online at: http://www.washingtonpost.com/wp-dyn/content/article/2009/06/23/AR2009062301444.html.

51. Geert De Lombaerde, "Nissan gets $1.6B loan for Smyrna plant," NashvillePost.com, June 23, 2009; available at: http://www.nashville-post.com/news/2009/6/23/nissan_gets_government_loan_for_smyrna_plant.

52. Kendra Marr, "3 Automakers Get Loans to Build More Efficient Cars."

53. Kimberly S. Johnson and Ken Thomas, "Ford, Nissan, Tesla's electric plans get $8B jolt," SignOnSanDiego.com, June 23, 2009; available at: http://www3.signonsandiego.com/stories/2009/jun/23/us-ford-energy-062309/.

54. "Obama Administration Awards First Three Auto Loans for Advanced Technologies to Ford Motor Company, Nissan Motors and Tesla Motors," U.S. Department of Energy, June 23, 2009; available online at: http://www.energy.gov/news2009/7544.htm.

55. "Energy Programs, Energy Efficiency and Renewable Energy," Library of Congress, http://icreport.loc.gov/cgi-bin/cpquery/?&dbname=cp111&sid=cp111t64JM&refer=&r_n=hr016.111&item=&sel=TOC_72442&.

56. House Report 111-016, MAKING SUPPLEMENTAL APPROPRIATIONS FOR JOB PRESERVATION AND CREATION, INFRASTRUCTURE INVESTMENT, ENERGY EFFICIENCY AND SCIENCE, ASSISTANCE TO THE UNEMPLOYED, AND STATE AND LOCAL FISCAL STABILIZATION, FOR THE FISCAL YEAR ENDING SEPTEMBER 30, 2009, AND FOR OTHER PURPOSES; available online at: http://ecip.loc.gov/cgi-bin/cpquery/?&sid=cp111KGP4l&refer=&r_n=hr016.111&db_id=111&item=&sel=TOC_112324&.

57. "Barack Obama and Joe Biden: New Energy for America."

58. 111th Congress, HR 1, Sec. 30D.

59. 111th Congress, HR 1, Sec. 1143.

60. Data available at: http://www.eia.doe.gov/emeu/mer/pdf/pages/sec7_5.pdf.

61. Cited in "Federal Energy and Fleet Management," United States Government Accountability Office, June 2009, Table 1.

62. "Bolivia pins hopes on lithium, electric vehicles," MSNBC, March 1, 2009; available online at: http://www.msnbc.msn.com/id/29445248/.

63. "Hazardous Materials; Transportation of Lithium Batteries," Federal Register Environmental Documents, August 9, 2007; available online at: http://www.epa.gov/EPA-IMPACT/2007/August/Day-09/i15213.htm.

64. "Bolivia pins hopes on lithium, electric vehicles," MSNBC.

65. "Corn boom could expand 'dead zone' in Gulf," MSNBC, December 17, 2007; available online at: http://www.msnbc.msn.com/id/22301669/.

66. "BARACK OBAMA'S PLAN TO MAKE AMERICA A GLOBAL ENERGY LEADER," available at http://web.archive.org/web/20080222013139/http://www.barackobama.com/issues/pdf/EnergyFactSheet.pdf.

67. "President Barack Obama's Inaugural Address," The White House, The Briefing Room, January 21, 2009; available online at: http://www.whitehouse.gov/the_press_office/President_Barack_Obamas_Inaugural_Address/.

68. 2007 Year End Lobbying Report, FMC Corp., February 15, 2008.

69. Center for Responsive Politics, OpenSecrets.org.

70. 2009 First Quarter Lobbying Report, Podesta Group on behalf of Altair Nanotechnologies, April 20, 2009.

71. Lobbying Registration, Gephardt Group Government Affairs on behalf of International Battery, April 1, 2009.

72. Senate Office of Public Records.

Chapter 7

1. Center for Responsive Politics.

2. Credit my colleague Michael Barone with this phrase in the context of Chrysler.

3. See GM's quarterly lobbying filings, at the Senate Office of Public Records Lobbying Disclosure Database.
4. Martin Fackler, "Toyota Expects Its First Loss in 70 Years," *The New York Times*, December 22, 2008; available online at: http://www.nytimes.com/2008/12/23/business/worldbusiness/23toyota.html?_r=2.
5. Peter Valdes Dapena, "Honda cleans up in consumer reports picks," CNN.com Autos, March 2, 2006; available at: http://www.cnn.com/2006/AUTOS/carreviews/03/01/cr_top_picks/index.html.
6. HR 6, Section 136.
7. David Shepardson, "Lawmakers fast-track auto loans," *Detroit News*, September 25, 2008.
8. David Shepardson, "UAW chief hopeful Congress will pass loans for automakers," *Detroit News*, September 11, 2008.
9. David Shepardson, "Bush approves $25B auto loan program," *Detroit News*, October 1, 2001.
10. David M. Herszenhorn, "SENATE ABANDONS AUTO BAILOUT BID AFTER G.O.P. BALKS," *The New York Times*, December 12, 2008; available online at: http://query.nytimes.com/gst/fullpage.html?res=9500E7DE1F3EF931A25751C1A96E9C8B63&sec=&spon=&pagewanted=all.
11. Ron Paul, "The Bailout Surge," November 2008; available at The Tenth Amendment Center, http://www.tenthamendmentcenter.com/2008/11/28/the-bailout-surge/.
12. John D. McKinnon and John D. Stoll, "U.S. Throws Lifeline to Detroit," *The Wall Street Journal*, December 20, 2008; available online at: http://online.wsj.com/article/SB122969367595121563.html.
13. David E. Sanger, "The 31-Year-Old in Charge of Dismantling GM," *The New York Times*, May 31, 2009; available online at: http://www.nytimes.com/2009/06/01/business/01deese.html?hpw.
14. Michael Barone, "White House puts UAW ahead of property rights," *The Examiner*, May 6, 2009; available online at: http://www.washingtonexaminer.com/politics/White-House-puts-UAW-ahead-of-property-rights-44415057.html.
15. Federal Election Commission, page by page report display, 645 of 1663; available at: http://images.nictusa.com/cgi-bin/fecimg/?28020350645.
16. "White House Denies Charge by Attorney that Administration Threatened to Destroy Investment Firm's Reputation," ABC News, May 2, 2009; available online at: http://blogs.abcnews.com/politicalpunch/2009/05/bankruptcy-atto.html.
17. Ibid.
18. John Carney, "White House 'Directly Threatened' Perella Weinberg Over Chrysler," *Clusterstock*, May 3, 2009; available online at:

http://www.businessinsider.com/white-house-directly-threatened-perella-weinberg-over-chrysler-2009-5.

19. Center for Responsive Politics and OpenSecrets.org.

20. "Treasury to Chrysler: 'The President Doesn't Negotiate Second Rounds,'" *The Wall Street Journal*; available online at: http://online.wsj.com/public/resources/documents/retro-EXHIBIT0905.html.

21. "White House Denies Charge by Attorney that Administration Threatened to Destroy Investment Firm's Reputation," ABC News.

22. "Obama Administration Auto Restructuring Initiative," Chrysler-Fiat Alliance, April 30, 2009; available at: http://www.financialstability.gov/docs/AIFP/Chrysler-restructuring-factsheet_043009.pdf.

23. "Objection to Chrysler Sale Motion," available at: http://www.scribd.com/doc/14952818/Objection-to-Chrysler-Sale-Motion.

24. Post from "Barack Obama can get the Job Done," by James Waisbrot; available at: http://my.barackobama.com/page/community/post/jameswaisbrot/gGxSd3.

25. All PAC data from Center for Responsive Politics and OpenSecrets.org.

26. Center for Responsive Politics, OpenSecrets.org, and https://www.taxpayerservicecenter.com/RP_Detail.jsp?ssl=0158%20%20%20%200809.

27. UAW's 2001 Form 990.

28. "We Learn Best By Doing," *Solidarity*, March 2002.

29. "Emotion," http://www.gm.com/corporate/about/history/historyPopUp.jsp?2.

30. Senate Office of Public Records Lobbying Disclosure Database, General Motors Second Quarter Lobbying Report, July 17, 2009.

31. Catarina Saraiva, "Mexico's Peso Advances for Fifth Week as U.S. Recession Eases," Bloomberg, August 14, 2009; available at: http://www.bloomberg.com/apps/news?pid=conewsstory&tkr=STD:US&sid=aNnw.sjHS.3g.

32. "GM launches light truck joint venture with China's FAW," Xinhua, August 30, 2009; available online at: http://eng.chinamil.com.cn/news-channels/2009-08/31/content_4030579.htm.

33. See, for example, "More Czars Than the Romanovs," TPM Photo Features; available online at: http://www.talkingpointsmemo.com/photofeatures/2009/06/more-czars-than-the-romanovs.php?img=1.

34. "Dancing with the Czars," Taxpayers for Common Sense, July 2, 2009; available online at: http://www.taxpayer.net/search_by_category.php?action=view&proj_id=2651&category=Wastebasket&type=Project.

35. Center for Responsive Politics and OpenSecrets.org.

36. Maureen White, National Finance Chair, The Democratic Party, http://www.democrats.org/a/party/white.html.

37. Taylor Marsh, "DNC Paging Steve Rattner," *The Huffington Post*, August 17, 2006; available online at: http://www.huffingtonpost.com/taylor-marsh/dnc-paging-steve-rattner_b_27484.html.

38. "Obama bundlers contributing to the transition," Becoming 44: Tracking Obama's Transition Team and Appointees; available at: http://www.becoming44.org/content/obama-bundlers-contributing-transition.

39. Ibid.

40. "Quadrangle's Connections," *BusinessWeek*, November 1, 2004; available online at: http://www.businessweek.com/magazine/content/04_44/b3906102_mz020.htm.

41. Senate Office of Public Records Lobbying Disclosure Database, Navigant Lobbying Registration, August 18, 2005.

42. "Quadrangle's Connections," *BusinessWeek*.

43. Brody Mullins and Kara Scannell, "Hedge funds use lobbyists for tips in Washington," post-gazette.com, December 8, 2006; available at: http://www.post-gazette.com/pg/06342/744652-28.stm#ixzz0NUi97kUN.

44. Kenneth Lovett, "Low-rent film 'Chooch' tied to Albany pension fund scandal," *Daily News*, March 25, 2009; available online at: http://www.nydailynews.com/news/2009/03/25/2009-03-25_lowrent_film_chooch_tied_to_albany_pensi.html#ixzz0NVMiFpTH.

45. Peter Lattman and Craig Karmin, "Rattner Involved in Inquiry on Fees," *The Wall Street Journal*, April 17, 2009; available online at: http://online.wsj.com/article/SB123992516941227309.html.

46. "Rattner leaves autos force, probe intensifies," Reuters, July 14, 2009; available at: http://www.reuters.com/article/politicsNews/idUSTRE56C5UU20090714.

47. Kirsten Danis, "Mayor Bloomberg's moneyman is Hillary Clinton's top fundraiser," *Daily News*, January 16, 2008; available online at: http://www.nydailynews.com/news/politics/2008/01/16/2008-01-16_mayor_bloombergs_moneyman_is_hillary_cli.html.

48. "Cash for clunkers should be scrapped: James Pethokoukis," Reuters, August 3, 2009; available at: http://www.reuters.com/article/reutersComService4/idUSTRE57243O20090803.

49. US Auto Sales Suffer Sept Rollercoaster As Incentives Fade," *The Wall Street Journal*, October 1, 2009; available at: http://online.wsj.com/article/BT-CO-20091001-715180.html.

50. Frederic Bastiat, "That Which Is Seen and That Which Is not Seen," 1850.

51. Henry Hazlitt, *Economics in One Lesson*, Chapter 2.

52. Senate Office of Public Records Lobbying Disclosure Database, Wiley Rein, LLP, Second Quarter Lobbying Report, July 20, 2009.

53. Capital Project Summary, "New York State Environmental Investment Program," Nucor Steele Auburn, Inc.; available at: http://www.empire.state.ny.us/pdf/polution_prevention_recycle/1104002CNucorSteelAuburnInc.pdf.

54. "Key Senators Endorse Extension of 'Cash for Clunkers,'" FoxNews.com, August 3, 2009; available at: http://www.foxnews.com/politics/2009/08/03/key-senators-endorse-extension-cash-clunkers/.

55. Michael Barone, "How much cash for a clunker? Congress had no clue," *The Washington Examiner*, August 4, 2009; available online at: http://www.washingtonexaminer.com/opinion/blogs/beltway-confidential/How-much-cash-for-a-clunker-Congress-had-no-clue-52438437.html.

56. "'Clunkers' rebates look likely for another month," *Charleston Daily Mail*, August 5, 2009; available online at: http://www.dailymail.com/Business/200908050163.

57. "Barack Obama on the Economy," *Fortune*, July 1, 2008; available online at: http://money.cnn.com/2008/06/29/news/economy/obama_transcript.fortune/.

58. John Carey, "Cash for Clunkers: How Green Is It?" *BusinessWeek*, August 15, 2009; available online at: http://www.businessweek.com/bwdaily/dnflash/content/aug2009/db2009085_823256.htm?chan=rss_topStories_ssi_5.

59. U.S. Chamber of Commerce Sends 'Cash for Clunkers' Extension Letter to Senate, July 31, 2009; available at: http://www.theautochannel.com/news/2009/07/31/472516.html.

60. "Rep. Chu Votes to Boost 'Cash for Clunkers' Program," Congresswoman Judy Chu, July 31, 2009; available at: http://chu.house.gov/2009/07/rep-chu-votes-to-boost-cash-for-clunkers-program.shtml.

Chapter 8

1. "Bush says sacrificed free-market principles to save economy," December 16, 2008; available at: http://www.breitbart.com/article.php?id=081216215816.8g97981o&show_article=.

2. Editorial Staff, "Geithner on Reducing Systemic Risk," Securities Industry News, June 23, 2008.

3. "Obama: crisis is time of 'great opportunity,'" MSNBC, March 7, 2009; available online at: http://www.msnbc.msn.com/id/29567427/.

4. Transcript of Barack Obama's Inagural Address, January 20, 2009; available online at: http://www.nytimes.com/2009/01/20/us/politics/20text-obama.html.

5. This section is adapted from my article, "Secretary Loophole," *American Spectator*, May 15, 2009.

6. "Report Pursuant to Section 129 of the Emergency Economic Stabilization Act of 2008: Bridge Loan to the Bear Stearns Companies Inc. Through

JPMorgan Chase Bank, N.A."; available at: http://www.federalreserve.gov/monetarypolicy/files/129bearstearnsbridgeloan.pdf.

7. 12 USC 3 § 248 (R)(2)(a).

8. Josh Marshall, "More lowdown on AIG," Talking Points Memo, March 5, 2009; available at: http://www.talkingpointsmemo.com/archives/2009/03/lowdown_on_aig.ph.

9. Josh Ydstie, "AIG Bonus Mess Adds to Geithner's Rough Stretch," *Morning Edition,* NPR, March 20, 2009; available online at: http://www.npr.org/templates/story/story.php?storyId=102150228.

10. Data available at: http://www.senate.gov/legislative/LIS/roll_call_lists/roll_call_vote_cfm.cfm?congress=110&session=2&vote=00213.

11. Michael Cooper and Elisabeth Bumiller, "Candidates Clash on Economy and Iraq," *The New York Times,* September 26, 2008; available online at: http://www.nytimes.com/2008/09/27/us/politics/27debatecnd.html.

12. Nick Kimball, "Barack's government reform town hall in Cedar Rapids," Community Blog, comment made on July 30, 2007; available at: http://my.barackobama.com/page/community/post/nickkimball/CpZq.

13. Mike Glover, "In rural NW Iowa, Obama touts farm, wind plans, raps lobbyists," Associated Press, December 17, 2007.

14. David Corn, "Obama for the Heart, Edwards for the Head?" *The Nation,* July 19, 2007; available online at: http://www.thenation.com/blogs/capitalgames/206543.

15. "Treasury Department Releases Details on Public Private Partnership Investment Program," March 23, 2009; available at: http://www.treas.gov/press/releases/tg65.htm.

16. Marie Cocco, "Convict Bush, McCain and the GOP for the Economy," *Real ClearPolitics*, September 30, 2008; available at: http://www.realclearpolitics.com/articles/2008/09/convict_bush_mccain_and_the_go.html.

17. "Obama on Bernanke: 'Bold Action and Outside-the-Box Thinking,'" *The Washington Wire*, comment made on August 5, 2009; available at: http://blogs.wsj.com/washwire/2009/08/25/obama-on-bernanke-bold-action-and-outside-the-box-thinking/.

18. Olivier Armantier and Sandra Krieger and James McAndews, "The Federal Reserve's Term Auction Facility," July 2008; available online at: http://www.newyorkfed.org/research/current_issues/ci14-5/ci14-5.html.

19. Data available at: http://www.federalreserve.gov/newsevents/press/monetary/20080311a.htm.

20. Scott Lanman, "Fed to Lend $200 Billion, Accept Mortgage Securities," Bloomberg, March 11, 2008; available at: http://www.bloomberg.com/apps/news?pid=20601087&sid=aMxbCGWcY5J0.

21. Data available at: http://www.federalreserve.gov/newsevents/press/other-/20080907a.htm.

22. Data available at: http://www2.goldmansachs.com/our-firm/investors/financials/archived/10k/docs/2007-form-10-k-file.pdf.

23. Binyamin Appelbaum, "Goldman Sachs Earnings Easily Surpass Expectations," *Washington Post,* July 15, 2009; available online at: http://www.washingtonpost.com/wp-dyn/content/article/2009/07/14/AR2009071400818.html.

24. Joe Hagan, "Tenacious G," *New York Magazine*, July 26, 2009.

25. Ibid.

26. Justin Fox, "Why the AIG bailout just keeps getting bigger," *Time,* March 2, 2009; available online at: http://curiouscapitalist.blogs.time.com/2009/03/02/why-the-aig-bailout-just-keeps-getting-bigger/.

27. Center for Responsive Politics, http://www.opensecrets.org/orgs/toprecips.php?id=D000000085&type=P&sort=A&cycle=2008.

28. Charles Piller, "Billionaire Buffett benefits from bailout he promoted," *The Sacramento Bee,* April 5, 2009; available online at: http://www.sacbee.com/341/story/1756261.html.

29. Michael Lind, "How I learned to stop worrying and live with the bomb," *Salon*, March 2, 2009; available at: http://www.salon.com/politics/war_room/2009/03/02/aig/.

30. Mark DeCambre, "BUFFETT'S GOLDMAN GAMBLE WINS," *New York Post,* July 24, 2009; available online at: http://www.nypost.com/seven/07242009/business/buffetts_goldman_gamble_wins_180934.htm.

31. Nick Kimball, "Barack's government reform town hall in Cedar Rapids," Community Blog, comment made on July 30, 2007; available at: http://my.barackobama.com/page/community/post/nickkimball/CpZq.

32. Charles Gasparino, "The Trouble With Consultants," *The Bond Buyer*, November 16, 1993.

33. John D. McKinnon and T. W. Farnam, "Hedge Fund Paid Summers $5.2 Million in Past Year," *Wall Street Journal,* April 5, 2009; available online at: http://online.wsj.com/article/SB123879462053487927.html.

34. James Sheehan, "How Nafta Caused the Mexican Bailout," *The Free Market,* July 1995; available online at: http://mises.org/freemarket_detail.aspx?control=237.

35. John D. McKinnon and T.W. Farnam, "Hedge Fund Paid Summers $5.2 Million in Past Year," *Wall Street Journal,* April 5, 2009; available online at: http://online.wsj.com/article/SB123879462053487927.html.

36. Center for Responsive Politics, http://www.opensecrets.org/pres08/indus.php?cycle=2008&cid=N00009638.

37. Center for Responsive Politics, Hedge Funds, top recipients 2008, http://www.opensecrets.org/industries/recips.php?ind=F2700&cycle=2008&recipdetail=A&mem=Y&sortorder=U.

38. Center for Responsive Politics, Commercial Banks, top recipients 2008, http://www.opensecrets.org/industries/recips.php?ind=F03&cycle=2008&re cipdetail=A&mem=Y&sortorder=U.

39. Center for Responsive Politics, Securities & Investment: Top Contributers to Federal Candidates and Parties 2008, http://www.opensecrets. org/industries/contrib.php?ind=F07&cycle=2008.

40. Center for Responsive Politics, Morgan Stanley: Recipients 2008, http://www.opensecrets.org/orgs/toprecips.php?id=D000000106&type=P& sort=A&cycle=2008.

41. "Washington Outlook, Capital Wrapup," *Businessweek,* May 24, 1993; available online at: http://www.businessweek.com/archives/1993/b332036. arc.htm.

42. "Tom Nides, Chief Administrative Officer and Secretary Morgan Stanley," available at: http://www.prfirms.org/index.cfm?fuseaction=Page.View-Page&PageID=706.

43. Data available at: FEC.gov.

44. "WEEKLY ADDRESS: President Obama Highlights Tough New Consumer Protections," June 20, 2009; available at: http://www.whitehouse. gov/the_press_office/WEEKLY-ADDRESS-President-Obama-Highlights-Tough-New-Consumer-Protections/.

45. See, for example, Easton Bank president Michael Menzie's testimony to Congress, http://www.house.gov/apps/list/hearing/financialsvcs_dem/men-zies.pdf.

46. Ibid.

47. Megan Murphy, "BarCap pay offer questioned," *Financial Times,* August 17, 2009; available online at: http://www.ft.com/cms/s/e9d4423e-8ac4-11de-ad08-00144feabdc0,Authorised=false.html?_i_location=http%3A%2F%2Fwww. ft.com%2Fcms%2Fs%2F0%2Fe9d4423e-8ac4-11de-ad08-00144feabdc0.html&_i_referer=.

48. Aaron Kirchfield and Jann Bettinga, "Goldman's Blankfein Calls for Pay Rules to Stem Risk," Bloomberg, September 9, 2009; available at: http://www.bloomberg.com/apps/news?pid=20601103&sid=aeob.WGdm6_o.

49. Kevin Drawbaugh, "Wall St group backs Obama broker standard pro-posal," Reuters, July 17, 2009; available at: http://www. reuters.com/article/domesticNews/idUSTRE56G7HG20090717?pageN-umber=1&virtualBrandChannel=0.

50. Michael McKee, "Volcker Criticizes Obama Plan to Expand Fed's Role," Bloomberg, September 18, 2009; available at: http://www. bloomberg.com/apps/news?pid=20601103&sid=aXfl8ebTBO0c.

51. Mike Dorning, "Volcker Criticizes Obama Plan on 'Systematically Important' Firms," Bloomberg, September 24, 2009; available at: http://www.bloomberg.com/apps/news?pid=20601070&sid=aKPBxT0cjj5E.

Chapter 9

1. Lynn Sweet, "Obama, a teen smoker, talks about kicking 'this habit' at tobacco bill signing," *Chicago Sun-Times*, June 22, 2009; available online at: http://blogs.suntimes.com/sweet/2009/06/obama_a_teen_smoker_talks _abou.html.
2. Public Law No: 111–31.
3. Kelly Wallace, "Katie Couric's Notebook: Smoking," CBS News blogs, June 22, 2009; available at: http://www.cbsnews.com/blogs/2009/06/23/couri-candco/entry5106499.shtml.
4. Cancer Action Network, "Thank Washington for kicking Big Tobacco's butts," http://action.acscan.org/site/PageServer?pagename=fda_thank_you _card.
5. Lyndsey Layton, "Senate Passes Bill to Let FDA Regulate Tobacco," *Washington Post*, June 12, 2009; available online at: http://www.washington-post.com/wp-dyn/content/article/2009/06/11/AR2009061100323.html.
6. "Harkin Hails Passage of Landmark Legislation to Allow FDA to Regulate Tobacco," Tom Harkin, Iowa's Senator web page, June 11, 2009; http://www.radioiowa.com/gestalt/go.cfm?objectid=1849924F-5056-B82A-3773CACA321BEAF8.
7. "Federal Regulation of Tobacco," Philip Morris USA, Legislative Issues; available online at: http://philipmorrisusa.com/en/cms/Responsibility/Government_Relations/Legislative_Issues/FDA_and_Tobacco.aspx.
8. Letter, Michael E. Szymanczyk to The President of the United States, June 12, 2009. http://www.altria.com/download/pdf/MES_Letter_061209.pdf.
9. Greg Allen, "Many Decisions Remain Over Tobacco Regulation," NPR, June 12, 2009; available online at: http://www.npr.org/templates/story/story.php?storyId=105315166.
10. Brody Mullins, "How Philip Morris, Tobacco Foes Tied the Knot," *Roll Call*, October 5, 2004; available online at: http://www.roll-call.com/issues/50_39/news/7035-1.html?type=printer_friendly.
11. Samuel Loewenberg, "Smoke Screen," *Slate*, July 25, 2002; available online at: http://www.slate.com/id/2068476/.
12. Altria Group, Inc., 2004 Annual Report, p. 26.
13. Peter Hardin, "No FDA Control a Setback for Altria," *Richmond Times-Dispatch*, October 11, 2004.
14. Center for Responsive Politics.
15. Lobbying Reports from the Senate Office of Public Records.

16. 2004 Year-End Lobbying Report, R.B. Murphy & Associates, January 26, 2005.

17. Dan Morgan and Helen Dewar, "House Blocks FDA Oversight of Tobacco," *Washington Post*, October 12, 2004; available at: http://www.washingtonpost.com/ac2/wp-dyn/A24429-2004Oct11?language=printer.

18. From PhilipMorrisUSA.com, which cites the IRI/Capstone Total Retail Panel for its figures.

19. Financial Review, Altria Group, Inc. 2007 Annual Report, http://www.altria.com/annualreport/ar2007/2007ar_08_0209.aspx.

20. For a more thorough explanation of this effect, see W. Kip Viscusi, *Smoke-Filled Rooms* (Chicago: University of Chicago Press, 2002), 38.

21. Altria Group 2007 Annual Report, p. 26.

22. David Ress, "Tobacco regulation could lead to more competition," *Richmond Times-Dispatch*, June 23, 2009; available online at: http://www2.timesdispatch.com/rtd/business/local/article/TOBA23_200906 22-221604/275537/.

23. Paula Smalera, "Cool, Refreshing Legislation for Philip Morris," *The Big Money*, June 8, 2009; available online at: http://www.thebigmoney. com/articles/judgments/2009/06/08/cool-refreshing-legislation-philip-morris.

24. Altria Group 2007 Annual Report, p. 29.

25. Data compiled from the Center for Responsive Politics, OpenSecrets.org.

26. Senate Office of Public Records.

27. Lynn Sweet, "Obama, a teen smoker, talks about kicking 'this habit' at tobacco bill signing," *Chicago Sun-Times*.

28. Michael Falcone, "Obama: Stop Chinese Toy Imports," *The New York Times*, December 19, 2007; available online at: http://thecaucus.blogs. nytimes.com/2007/12/19/obama-stop-chinese-toy-imports/.

29. Herb Weisbaum, "How to buy toys without a lot of worry," MSNBC, November 28, 2007; available online at: http://www.msnbc.msn. com/id/22008766/ns/business-consumer_news/.

30. Press Release, "Obama-Cardin Amendment Set to Become Law as Senate Passes CPSC Modernization," July 31, 2008.

31. Hearing of the Senate Commerce, Science, and Transportation Committee, June 16, 2009.

32. "Mattel chief lays out plan for toy testing," MSNBC, October 24, 2007; available online at: http://www.msnbc.msn.com/id/21462674/.

33. Data retrieved from http://www.opensecrets.org/lobby/clientsum.php? lname=Mattel+Inc.

34. Mattel Inc, 2008, http://www.opensecrets.org/lobby/clientsum.php?year=2008&lname=Mattel+Inc&id=.

35. Lobbying Registration, August 24, 2007.

36. "CNN Student News Transcript: February 10, 2009," CNN.com/living, February 10, 2009; available at: http://www.cnn.com/2009/LIVING/studentnews/02/09/transcript.tue/index.html.

37. Press Release, "CPSC Clarifies Requirements of New Children's Product Safety Laws Taking Effect in February *Guidance Intended for Resellers of Children's Products, Thrift and Consignment Stores*, News from CPSC, January 8, 2009; available at: http://cpsc.gov/cpscpub/prerel/prhtml09/09086.html.

38. Consumer Product Safety Improvement Act: Guidance for Small Manufacturers, Importers, and Crafters of Children's Products; available at: http://www.cpsc.gov/ABOUT/Cpsia/smbus/manufacturers.html.

39. "Children's Products Containing Lead; Determinations Regarding Lead Content Limits on Certain Materials or Products; Final Rule," U.S. Consumer Product Safety Commission, August 6, 2009; available online at: http://www.cpsc.gov/library/foia/ballot/ballot09/leaddetermine.pdf.

40. Vote Sheet, Consumer Product Safety Commission, http://www.cpsc.gov/library/foia/foia09/brief/sevenlabs.pdf; see also: "Third-party safety tests not required for Mattel," MSNBC, August 27, 2009; available online at: http://www.msnbc.msn.com/id/32582238/ns/business-retail/.

41. CPSC.gov

42. James Rosen, "Seller, beware: Feds cracking down on garage sales," *McClatchy Newspapers*, August 20, 2009; available online at: http://www.mcclatchydc.com/economy/story/74102.html.

43. Cammie Croft, "Weekly Address: Reversing a Troubling Trend in Food Safety," The White House Blog, March 14, 2009; available at: http://www.whitehouse.gov/blog/09/03/14/Food-Safety/.

44. Michael Taylor, JD, faculty biography; available at: http://www.gwumc.edu/sphhs/faculty/taylor_michael.cfm.

45. Michael Taylor, JD, Statement before the Committee on Agriculture, United States House of Representatives, July 16, 2009; available online at: http://www.hhs.gov/asl/testify/2009/07/t20090716a.html;
see also: Patty LaNoue Stearns, "What's Cooking" *Detroit Free Press,* December 28, 1994.

46. Michael Ollinger, "The Direct and Indirect Costs of Food Safety Regulation," U.S. Census Bureau, Center for Economic Studies, September, 2008, Table 1.

47. Michael Ollinger, "The Direct and Indirect Costs of Food Safety Regulation," U.S. Census Bureau, Center for Economic Studies, September, 2008, abstract.

48. Jesse Lee, "Update on Lobbyist Contacts Regarding the Recovery Act," The White House Blog, April 27, 2009; available at: http://www.white-

house.gov/blog/09/04/26/Update-on-Lobbyist-Contacts-Regarding-the-Recovery-Act/.

49. Food and Drug Administration Proposed Rule, *Federal Register* vol. 66. No. 12 (January 18, 2001).

50. Ibid., 4729.

51. FDA Docket # 00N-1396, vol. 261, c 6895.

52. Michael Taylor, JD, Statement before the Committee on Agriculture.

53. Mike Nizza, "The Salmonella Outbreak Hits 1,000 Cases With a New Culprit," *The New York Times*, July 9, 2008; available online at: http://thelede.blogs.nytimes.com/2008/07/09/the-salmonella-outbreak-hits-1000-cases-with-a-new-culprit/.

54. Investigation Update: Outbreak of Salmonella Typhimurium Infections, 2008–2009, Centers for Disease Control and Prevention; available at: http://www.cdc.gov/salmonella/typhimurium/update.html.

55. Cammie Croft, "Weekly Address: Reversing a Troubling Trend in Food Safety."

56. *Food Safety Enhancement Act of 2009*, HR 2749, 111th Cong., 1st sess., July 29, 2009; available at: http://www.gop.gov/bill/111/1/hr2749.

57. Timothy P. Carney, "Obama food policy may mean end of farmers markets, family farms," *The Washington Examiner*, March 20, 2009; available online at: http://www.washingtonexaminer.com/opinion/columns/Timothy-Carney/Obama-food-policy-may-mean-end-of-farmers-markets-family-farms-41555407.html.

58. *Congressional Record*, House of Representatives, July 29 2009, p. H9013.

59. Drew McDonald, prepared statement before the U.S. House of Representatives Agriculture Committee, July 16, 2009; available online at: http://www.house.gov/agriculture/testimony/111/h071609/McDonald.pdf.

60. Carolyn Lochhead, "Crops, ponds destroyed in quest for food safety," *San Francisco Chronicle*, July 13, 2009; available online at: http://www.sfgate.com/cgi-bin/article.cgi?file=/c/a/2009/07/13/MN0218DVJ8.DTL.

61. Ibid.

62. Ibid.

63. "CDC's Role During a Multi-State Foodborne Outbreak Investigation," Centers for Disease Control and Prevention, January 23, 2009; available online at: http://www.cdc.gov/salmonella/typhimurium/cdc_role_outbreak.html.

Chapter 10

1. GE 2008 Annual Report; available at: http://www.ge.com/ar2008/pdf/ge_ar_2008_letter.pdf.

2. Top Spenders, 1998–2009, http://www.opensecrets.org/lobby/top.php? indexType=s.
3. Jane Sasseen with others "Obama: What Business Thinks," *Business Week*, August 10, 2009.
4. Congressional Record, March 28, 2006, S2435.
5. Data compiled from the Center for Responsive Politics and OpenSecrets.org.
6. Lobbying Registration, LHD & Associates, Inc., http://soprweb.senate.gov/index.cfm?event=getFilingDetails&filingID=313e2a38-accb-4f5d-8eed-76ffe726feb0.
7. See the transcript and watch the video at: Brad Wilmouth, "Matthews: Obama Speech Caused 'Thrill Going Up My Leg,'" http://newsbusters.org/blogs/brad-wilmouth/2008/02/13/matthews-obama-speech-caused-thrill-going-my-leg.
8. You can watch the video here: "Matthews: 'I Want to Do Everything I Can to Make This... New Presidency Work,'" *TVNEWSER*, November 6, 2008, http://www.mediabistro.com/tvnewser/msnbc/matthews_i_want_to_do_everything_i_can_to_make_thisnew_presidency_work_99843.asp.
9. You can read the full email here: http://media.sfexaminer.com/documents/rice-email.doc.
10. Ibid.
11. All campaign finance data from Center for Responsive Politics.
12. General Electric: Recipients, 2008; http://www.opensecrets.org/orgs/toprecips.php?id=D000000125&type=P&sort=A&cycle=2008.
13. Data compiled from the Federal Election Commission, FEC.gov.
14. See FEC records: Federal Election Commission, page by page report display, 1807 of 3340, http://images.nictusa.com/cgi-bin/fecimg/?28933135751 and http://images.nictusa.com/cgi-bin/fecimg/?28992936924.
15. Federal Election Commission, page by page report display, 211 of 30,430, http://images.nictusa.com/cgi-bin/fecimg/?28930534061.
16. Federal Election Commission, page by page report display, 573 of 3000, http://images.nictusa.com/cgi-bin/fecimg/?28930926573.
17. Federal Election Commission, page by page report display, 1598 of 3000, http://images.nictusa.com/cgi-bin/fecimg/?28930927598.
18. Federal Election Commission, page by page report display, 2123 of 3000, http://images.nictusa.com/cgi-bin/fecimg/?28993868123.
19. Data compiled from OpenSecrets.org.
20. 2008 PAC to PAC data, General Electric, http://www.opensecrets.org/pacs/pac2pac.php?cycle=2008&cmte=C00024869.
21. General Electric Contributions to Federal Candidates, 2008 cycle, http://www.opensecrets.org/pacs/pacgot.php?cycle=2008&cmte=C00024869.

22. "Illinois Sen. Barack Obama's Announcement Speech," *Washington Post*, February 10, 2007; available online at: http://www.washingtonpost. com/wp-dyn/content/article/2007/02/10/AR2007021000879.html.

23. Top Spenders, 1998–2009, http://www.opensecrets.org/lobby/top.php? indexType=s.

24. Top Spenders, 2009, http://www.opensecrets.org/lobby/top.php?showYear= 2009&indexType=s.

25. Data compiled from the Senate Office of Public Records.

26. General Electric, Firm Profile: Lobbyists 2009, http://www.opense- crets.org/lobby/firmlbs.php?lname=General 1 Electric&year=2009.

27. Lobbying Registration, Breaux Lott Leadership Group, http://soprweb.sen- ate.gov/index.cfm?event=getFilingDetails&filingID=47e67e5e-0074-44f7- 8a29-125f0f50240c.

28. Lobbying Report, Gephardt Group Government Affairs, http:// soprweb.senate.gov/index.cfm?event=getFilingDetails&filingID=475ff146- b917-44be-b267-9f4dbd5282b8.

29. Ibid.

30. Lobbying Registration, LHD & Associates, http://soprweb.senate. gov/index.cfm?event=getFilingDetails&filingID=313e2a38-accb-4f5d-8eed- 76ffe726feb0.

31. Rick Pearson, "Obama blasts influence of oil, drug industries," *Chicago Tribune*, July 31, 2007; available online at: http://www.chicagotribune. com/news/politics/obama/chi-obama_tuejul31,0,3036878.story.

32. "General Electric at Goldman Sachs Fourth Annual Alternative Energy," *Fair Disclosure Wire*, May 21, 2009.

33. "Ecomagination is GE," 2008 ecomagination Annual Report; available online at: http://ge.ecomagination.com/_files/downloads/reports/ge_2008_ ecomagination_report.pdf. (Accessed August 27, 2009.)

34. Amanda Griscom Little, "Just my 'ecomagination,' " *Salon*, May 12, 2005; available online at: http://dir.salon.com/story/opinion/feature/2005/05/12/ muckraker/index.html.

35. You can read the full text of the letter at Steve Milloy's "Green Hell Blog": "GE seeks support for GE-minded politicians," Green Hell Blog, August 19, 2009; available at: http://greenhellblog.com/2009/08/19/gepac-advises-ge- employees-to-support-waxman-markey-because-of/.

36. www.US-CAP.org.

37. From GE's Lobbying Disclosure Act filings from 2008 and 2009.

38. Greenhouse Gas Services, a GE AES venture, "Our Projects," http://www.ghgs.com/ghgs/index?page=our_projects_overview&currentpicn um=2&&view=GHGS_VIEW&locale=en. (Accessed August 27, 2009.)

39. Jos Lelieveld, "Climate change: A nasty surprise in the greenhouse," *Nature*, September 28, 2006; available online at: http://www.nature.com/nature/journal/v443/n7110/full/443405a.html.

40. Press Release, "Greenhouse Gas Services," September 17, 2008; available online at: http://www.aes.com/pub-sites/sites/GHGS/content/live/020139b 86944011c9713f45b007ce7/1033/GHGS%20a%20GE%20AES%20Venture%20to%20Create%20GHG%20Credits%20in%20NC.pdf. (Accessed August 27, 2009.)

41. Greenhouse Gas Services, a GE AES venture, Contact Us, http://www.ghgs.com/ghgs/index?page=contact_us&currentpicnum=5&&view=GHGS_VIEW&locale=en.

42. Rolfe Winkler, "GE seeks nuclear, appliance incentives in CO_2 bill," Reuters, July 23, 2009; available online at: http://www.reuters.com/article/GCA-GreenBusiness/idUSTRE56N0HY20090724?sp=true.

43. Barack Obama and Joe Biden: New Energy for America, http://www.barackobama.com/pdf/factsheet_energy_speech_080308.pdf.

44. You can watch the video at: Jay Yarow, "Miami's Massive Smart-Grid Project a Gift to Cisco And GE (GE, CSCO, FPL)," Green Sheet, *The Business Insider*, April 20, 2009; available online at: http://www.businessinsider.com/miami-hooks-up-with-ge-cisco-silver-spings-florida-power—light-for-smart-grid-2009-4.

45. "Obama's speech on the economy," *The New York Times*, January 8, 2009; available online at: http://www.nytimes.com/2009/01/08/us/politics/08text-obama.html?ref=politics&pagewanted=all.

46. Jay Yarow, "Miami's Massive Smart-Grid Project a Gift to Cisco And GE (GE, CSCO, FPL)," Green Sheet, *The Business Insider*.

47. "Ecomagination is GE," 2008 ecomagination Annual Report.

48. Ibid.

49. Brigette Fanning, "GE requests stimulus for advanced batteries—and green collar jobs," *Blue Planet Green Living*, July 9, 2009; available online at: http://www.organicgreenandnatural.com/2009/07/09/ge-requests-stimulus-funds-for-advanced-batteries-and-green-collar-jobs/. (Accessed August 27, 2009.)

50. Ibid.

51. Ibid.

52. "Obama unveils high-speed passenger rail plan," CNN.com, April 16, 2009; available online at: http://www.cnn.com/2009/POLITICS/04/16/obama.rail/. (Accessed August 27, 2009.)

53. Lobbying Registration, LHD & Associates, June 11, 2009, http://soprweb.senate.gov/index.cfm?event=getFilingDetails&filingID=313e 2a38-accb-4f5d-8eed-76ffe726feb0.

54. "General Electric at Goldman Sachs Fourth Annual Alternative Energy," *Fair Disclosure Wire*, May 21, 2009.

55. Michael Lind, "How I learned to stop worrying and live with the bomb," *Salon*.

56. Policy, Transmission & Regulation, production tax credit, American Wind Energy Association, http://www.awea.org/policy/ptc.html.

57. Ibid.

58. Ibid.

59. Abhay Singh and Rakteem Katakey, "GE Revives Indian Wind Business as Subsidies Improve," Bloomberg, September 29, 2009; available at: http://www.bloomberg.com/apps/news?pid=20601091&sid=a_ruj0b4EyLg.

60. "General Electric at Goldman Sachs Fourth Annual Alternative Energy," *Fair Disclosure Wire*, May 21, 2009.

61. Frank Bentayou, "GE looks to close Niles glass factory and end production of incandescent bulbs," Cleveland.com, July 24, 2009; available at: http://www.cleveland.com/business/index.ssf/2009/07/ge_looks_to_close_nil es_glass.html.

62. General Electric press release, "GE Consumer & Industrial announces intent to close Winchester Lamp Plant," July 23, 2009.

63. "Obama to Announce New Plan to Make America A Global Energy Leader," Obama News and Speeches, Organizing for America; available at: http://www.barackobama.com/2007/10/08/obama_to_announce_new_plan _to.php.

64. John Fialka, "Homes would need new bulbs to meet efficiency rules," Associated Press, May 7, 2007.

65. Energy Savers: When to Turn Off Your Lights, U.S. Department of Energy, http://www.energysavers.gov/your_home/lighting_daylighting/index.cfm/my topic=12280.

66. Kathryn Kranhold, "Cornering market on energy-saving bulbs," *Seattle Times*, December 28, 2007.

67. "CE Lighting Bags 5-M Fluorescent Bulbs SupplyDeal," Philippines News Agency, July 10, 2009.

68. Michael Sheridan, "'Green' lightbulbs poison workers," *Times* (UK), May 3, 2009; available online at: http://www.timesonline.co.uk/tol/news/ world/asia/article6211261.ece.

69. "GE Announces Advancement in Incandescent Technology; New High-Efficiency Lamps Targeted for Market by 2010," Imagination at Work, February 23, 2007; available online at: http://www.businesswire.com/portal/ site/ge/index.jsp?ndmViewId=news_view&newsId=20070223005120. (Accessed August 27, 2009.)

70. "A Vision for High Speed Rail," The White House Blog, April 16, 2009; available at: http://www.whitehouse.gov/blog/09/04/16/a-vision-for-high-speed-rail/. (Accessed August 27, 2009.)

71. Ibid.

72. Jim Martin, "GE offers look at future," *Erie Times-News,* May 19, 2009; available online at: http://www.goerie.com/apps/pbcs.dll/article?AID=/20090519/NEWS02/305189932/-1/NEIGHBORS.

73. Executive Order, "Removing Barriers to Responsible Scientific Research Involving Human Stem Cells," The White House Briefing Room, March 9, 2009; available online at: http://www.whitehouse.gov/the_press_office/Removing-Barriers-to-Responsible-Scientific-Research-Involving-Human-Stem-cells/.

74. Geron News Release, "GE Healthcare and Geron Announce Exclusive Global Agreement to Commercialize Stem Cell Drug Discovery Technologies," June 30, 2009; available online at: http://www.geron.com/media/pressview.aspx?id=1181.

75. Ibid.

76. Peter Apps, "ANALYSIS—US firms, others may gain from shield pullback," Reuters, September 17, 2009; available online at: http://www.reuters.com/article/asiaCrisis/idUSB688381.

77. See the transcript at: Geoffrey Dickens, "Matthews on Obama Victory: 'Rebuke' for Bush?" NewsBusters, January 4, 2008; available online at: http://newsbusters.org/blogs/geoffrey-dickens/2008/01/04/chris-matthews-psyched-about-obama.

78. Richard Harris, "The Mystery of Global Warming's Missing Heat," NPR, March 19, 2008; available online at: http://www.npr.org/templates/story/story.php?storyId=88520025.

79. You can watch the video here: Mark Finkelstein, "Scare-Mongering on Steroids: NBC Warns Oceans Could Rise 200 Feet!" NewsBusters, November 17, 2008; available online at: http://newsbusters.org/blogs/mark-finkelstein/2008/11/17/scare-mongering-steroids-nbc-warns-oceans-could-rise-200-feet.

80. You can read the transcript here: Tim Graham, "Tom Brokaw's Nostalgia for '70s Liberalism in Earth Day Lecture," NewsBusters, April 22, 2008; available online at: http://newsbusters.org/blogs/tim-graham/2008/04/22/tom-brokaws-nostalgia-70s-liberalism-earth-day-lecture.

81. Brian Stelter, "Voices from above silence a cable TV feud," *The New York Times,* July 31, 2009; available online at: http://www.nytimes.com/2009/08/01/business/media/01feud.html?_r=2&src=twt&twt=nytimes.

82. Glenn Greenwald, "GE's silencing of Olbermann and MSNBC's sleazy use of Richard Wolffe," *Salon,* August 1, 2009; available online at: http://www.salon.com/opinion/greenwald/2009/08/01/ge/.

83. Howard Kurtz, "The Prez, The Press, The Pressure," *Washington Post,* August 3, 2009; available online at: http://www.washingtonpost.com/wp-dyn/content/article/2009/08/02/AR2009080202045.html.

84. Glenn Greenwald, "The Scope—and dangers—of GE's control of NBC and MSNBC," *Salon,* August 3, 2009; available online at: http://www.salon.com/opinion/greenwald/2009/08/03/general_electric/index.html.

85. Steve Lohr, "In Strategy shift, G.E. plans lower-cost health products," *The New York Times,* May 7, 2009; available online at: http://www.nytimes.com/2009/05/08/business/08health.html?_r=1.

Chapter 11

1. Mike Wereschagin, "RNC Chairman Steele blasts Dems' health care vision as weak," *Pittsburgh Tribune-Review*, July 24, 2009; available online at: http://www.pittsburghlive.com/x/pittsburghtrib/news/pittsburgh/s_635106.html.

2. "Bill Would Prevent Rationing," The Heartland Institute, August 2009; available at: http://www.heartland.org/full/25694/Bill_Would_Prevent_Rationing.html.

3. Jonathan Chait, "Thought Rationing," *The New Republic*, July 15, 2009; available at: http://www.tnr.com/article/politics/thought-rationing.

4. See Jonathan Chait, "Mad About You," *The New Republic*, September 29, 2003, which began, "I hate President George W. Bush"; available at: http://www.tnr.com/article/mad-about-you.

5. Jonathan Chait, "Thought Rationing," *The New Republic*.

6. *Congressional Record*, 111th Congress, First Session, June 26, 2009, p. H7654.

7. *Congressional Record*, 111th Congress, First Session, June 26, 2009, p. H7658.

8. *Congressional Record*, 111th Congress, First Session, June 26, 2009, p. H7625.

9. *Congressional Record*, 111th Congress, First Session, June 26, 2009, p. H7670.

10. Michael Brendan Dougherty, "Social Adjustment: Washington's young conservatives ponder life in the minority," *Washington Monthly*; available at: http://www.washingtonmonthly.com/features/2006/0612.dougherty.html.

11. Cato Daily Dispatch, December 22, 2004; available at: http://www.cato.org/dispatch/12-22-04d.html.

12. Ibid.

13. Timothy P. Carney, "Judd Gregg's Wisdom: Abolish Commerce Department," *The Washington Examiner*, February 5, 2009; available online at: http://www.washingtonexaminer.com/opinion/columns/TimothyCarney/Judd-Greggs-wisdom-Abolish-Commerce-Department39169732.html.

INDEX